Ellington at the White House 1969

Edward Allan Faine

Happy Jazz!

IM PRESS

Takoma Park, MD

PO Box 5346
Takoma Park, MD 20913-5346
301-587-1202
efaine@yahoo.com

ISBN: 978-0-9857952-0-7

First printing 2013
Manufactured in the United States of America

Front and back cover photographs courtesy of the
National Archives, College Park, Maryland, and
the Nixon Library, Yorba Linda, California.

Book design by Sandra Jonas

Visit www.ellington1969.com

To my mother

Numerous times throughout my adult life, my mother would approach me at family gatherings, ease me over to a quiet corner of the room, and whisper so no one else could hear, "Are you a success?"

Why I had a tough time answering that question I'll never know, but I would mumble something like "Yeah, I guess," and then tell her what I had been doing of late. I never said yes directly. My mother would then slink away. She wanted that yes so badly.

Because of the grief I caused her during my teenage years, she had written me off early, certain I'd end up a no-goodnik, a wastrel. But I did a turnaround in my twenties, went to college, got engineering degrees, got a job, got married, all to her surprise. That's why she kept asking that question. She needed reassurance that my turn to normalcy wasn't a mirage. She wanted proof from my lips that she had been wrong about me.

Yes, Mother, with this book, I'm a success. Rest in peace.

Contents

 ✳

Acknowledgments

I am indebted to:

Duke Ellington, for his music and his insightful memoir; and also to his son, Mercer, for his music and memoir.

The jazz scribes, biographers, and critics Whitney Balliett, Harvey G. Cohen, Stanley Dance, Leonard Feather, Phyl Garland, Gary Giddins, John Edward Hasse, Robert E. Johnson Jr., Dan Morgenstern, Doug Ramsey, and Hollie I. West. Without them, a book like this could not exist. Indeed, likewise, to the newspaper, magazine, and wire service columnists, reporters, journalists, and photographers.

The memoirists and biographers, and the chroniclers of the Nixon administration. Their surprisingly candid memoirs and biographies helped immensely.

Others whose tips led to valuable information: Melinda Schwenk-Burrell, Nicholas Cull, Bruce Herschensohn, and Patricia Woodward.

The friendly and efficient staff at the National Archives in Washington, DC, and College Park, Maryland; the Library of Congress; and the Kennedy, Johnson, and Nixon presidential libraries. Measured solely by the people who staff these institutions, the country is in good shape going forward.

Vera Ekechukwu, Fulbright Research Associate at the University of Arkansas Libraries, who in addition to providing material on the Jazz

Ambassador program, searched in vain for possible Ellington-specific material in their special collections.

Sidney J. Stiber, producer of the USIA documentary *Duke Ellington at the White House*, who shared valuable information on the now historic film he wrote, directed, and produced.

The unheralded photo processors, who took raw archival film and turned it into the telling photographs shown herein: Joe McCary of Photo Response, Gaithersburg, Maryland, and Dave Smith of U-Photo, Beltsville, Maryland.

The graphic experts and printers at Rockville Printing & Graphics, Rockville, Maryland.

Sandra Jonas of Your Book Partners, Boulder, Colorado, whose straightforward, incisive editing of the draft manuscript enhanced the readability of the text a hundredfold. Also to her invaluable work in securing permissions for the various quotes used throughout the book, and indeed to the rights holders for granting such (see text permissions). Further, many thanks for her book design and typesetting expertise.

Lastly, Bill Randall and Bill Gordon, two pop music radio DJs in 1950s Cleveland, Ohio. Closet jazz fans both, they occasionally played tracks by jazz singers Ella Fitzgerald and Sarah Vaughan in their pop music playlists, while overplaying the Four Freshmen, who often managed to sneak a jazz trombone solo into their pop hit offerings. It didn't take long for a teenage boy after he heard these sounds to find the jazz LP section in downtown Cleveland record shops, with their convenient private listening booths at the back (and sympathetic shop owners up front), where he spent wondrous hours discovering a secret music that he—and only he—knew about.

Ellington at the
White House 1969

The Year Everything Changed for Jazz

IN HIS BOOK *1969: The Year Everything Changed*, author Rob Kirkpatrick summed up the year musically:

It was a year of firsts. The Stooges [with Iggy Pop] and MC5 released the first punk records, while Led Zeppelin's first two albums and U.S. tour launched heavy metal in America. Miles Davis propelled jazz into a new age with the seminal rock-fusion classic *Bitches Brew*, while King Crimson set the mold for progressive rock with *In the Court of the Crimson King*. The Grateful Dead's *Aoxomoxoa* and the Allman Brothers' debut release gave us the initial offerings of jam band music and Southern rock. The Who debuted the rock opera *Tommy*, and Crosby, Stills and Nash and Blind Faith appeared on the scene as rock's first supergroups. The Rolling Stones reached their creative peak, and, with their 1969 U.S. tour, assumed the mantle of Greatest Rock 'n' Roll Band in the World.[1]

It was also a year of lasts. The year that Elvis Presley recorded his swan hit songs, "In the Ghetto" and "Suspicious Minds," and the Beatles recorded their final master album, *Abbey Road*.

Another often-overlooked milestone occurred in 1969, when President Nixon presented America's highest civilian award, the Medal of Freedom, to America's premier composer, Duke Ellington. The ceremonial concert, held at the White House on the maestro's seventieth birthday, may not have meant much to the general public, but it changed everything for the jazz art community: that loose coalition of musicians, fans, critics, enlightened academics, radio DJs, record producers, nightclub owners, festival organizers, and magazine publishers.

By honoring Duke—the most prolific composer and respected person in jazz for over four decades—Nixon was honoring jazz itself, the first time a U.S. president had done so.[2] In America, the closest the country comes to bestowing knighthood is a Presidential Medal and an East Room ceremony. Duke was knighted and so was jazz. And, dear reader, if you are struggling with assimilating the import of all of this, please realize that jazz had not been performed in the White House until 1962,[3] and its antecedents, authentically rendered Dixieland and ragtime, did not have their unveiling there until 1969 and 1974, respectively.[4]

Thus, 1969 was the year that jazz received its long-overdue respect from the highest level of government. The year that jazz *officially* became *art*. This development was as important to jazz as the birth of a new stylistic change or the discovery of a wunderkind artist. Jazz today is recognized as serious art by the government and academia, as well as by private institutions and foundations—and we can safely assume, by the majority of Americans. It wasn't always so.

Following Duke's coronation, Nixon initiated funding for jazz under the auspices of the National Endowment for the Arts (NEA), an institution established by his predecessor, Lyndon B. Johnson. The first jazz grant of $5,500 went to composer George Russell. Annual funding followed: rising from $20,000 in 1970 to $272,000 in 1972, to $1.5 million in 1980, and to more than $2.8 million in 2005.[5]

Nixon turned the money spigot on for jazz—and kept it on—but his immediate predecessors had their hands on the handle, too. President Eisenhower initiated federal support for the art form through the State Department's Jazz Ambassador program that launched Dizzy, Louis, Duke, Benny, and other jazz greats around the world to spread the word of jazz and democracy. Begun in 1956, the program continued through the late 1980s. Eisenhower also launched the Voice of America (VOA), with its daily jazz broadcasts beyond America's shores by Willis Conover, and the United States Information Agency (USIA), which produced the occasional magazine article, documentary film, or newsreel segment on jazz for overseas distribution.

For his part, President Kennedy chartered an Arts Council in 1963 ("a great nation deserves great art") that led to the establishment of the NEA by President Johnson in 1965, which in turn begat the NEA Jazz Panel in 1968 that recommended the first $5,500 grant to jazz awarded in 1969.[6]

This NEA money (coupled with foundation monies) has supported a wide range of activities, including jazz festivals, Billy Taylor's Jazzmobile in New York City, Thelonius Monk Institute's Jazz Sports program, educational jazz programming on National Public Radio (NPR), Artists in Schools, and research. Since 1982, the NEA has awarded annual Jazz Masters Fellowships to recognize outstanding musicians for their lifelong achievements. Each fellowship has included a monetary award of $25,000. In addition, since 1982, the NEA has tracked participation in the arts by its creators and by the public, monitoring attendance at jazz events as well as at theater, opera, ballet, and classical music performances.[7]

Through the better part of the twentieth century, the Smithsonian Institution (SI) followed jazz developments as part of its folkloric programs. Beginning in the late 1960s, with an increase in funding, the SI ramped up its efforts to preserve and perpetuate the historical legacy of jazz. In 1972 the SI initiated the Jazz Oral History Project, which—with fits and starts—continues today. A year later, the SI issued its definitive *Collection of Classic Jazz*, a six-LP set curated by critic Martin Williams (available since 1983 in a ten-CD box set). Only recently, in 2011, the SI released a revised and updated six-CD edition: *Jazz: The Smithsonian Anthology*.[8]

In 1990, the Smithsonian Jazz Masterworks Orchestra (SJMO) was formed to sustain jazz by re-creating the greatest performances of all time. Its first concert in 1991 featured the music of Duke Ellington. Since then the SJMO has given over fifty concerts, performing in twenty-six states and nine countries. In 1999, the orchestra crisscrossed the United States to perform in celebration of the hundredth anniversary of Duke Ellington's birth. The 1990s and 2000s witnessed additional SI activities: touring exhibitions, sponsored performances, educational programs, special events, and the transcribing of classic recordings to create scores for jazz ensembles.

In 1987 Congress passed a joint resolution declaring jazz to be a "unique art form" and a "rare and valuable national American national treasure to which we should devote our attention, support and resources to make certain it is preserved, understood and promulgated." (See http://www.hr57.org for the full resolution.)

Jazz projects are also funded by state and local governments—in fact, significantly so. They have been appropriating more money for the arts than the federal government since 1985 (see the illustration on page 11) and, it is believed, although difficult to quantify, more money for jazz as well.

While government recognition of jazz proceeded at a tortoise's pace, academics and educators—once engaged—bounded ahead like the proverbial hare. As noted by *DownBeat* publisher Charles Suber in 1963:

> The 1950s marked the turning point in attitudes of educators towards jazz. For the first time educators began speaking in large numbers, and without apology, of jazz as an art form and began implementing their talk with courses in jazz history, officially sanctioned stage bands, and lectures and seminars ... Throughout the 1950s, articles favoring jazz began to appear in [prominent music education] magazines.[9]

Paul Lopes (*The Rise of the Jazz Art World*) further elaborated:

Besides special concerts and workshops, music conservatories for jazz were established in the 1950s including Berklee . . . in Boston, Westlake . . . in Los Angeles, and . . . Contemporary Music in Toronto . . . The college band movement, however, was the most successful foray into music education during the 1950s. The first national college [jazz] festival was held in 1956 . . . In 1958, two annual college festivals were inaugurated . . . at Notre Dame University and at the University of Kansas. In 1960, the first annual Intercollegiate Jazz Festival was inaugurated at Villanova University . . . The growth of high school and college stage bands led to the establishment of the successful National Stage Band camps in 1959. [10]

Charles Suber once again took stock of the growth of jazz education in 1976:

In 1960, while 5,000 high schools had stage/jazz bands, only forty colleges had jazz courses and only half gave academic credits. By 1975, around 20,000 junior and senior high schools had stage/jazz bands and around 400 colleges were offering for credit at least one jazz performance group or jazz course. Postgraduate programs in jazz were offered at Indiana University, North Texas State University, Wesleyan University, [University of Northern Colorado], as well as the Eastman School of Music and the New England Conservatory of Music. In 1969, there were 75 college jazz festivals and 170 secondary and elementary school jazz festivals. The presence of jazz education in American educational institutions had unquestionably established itself in the 1960s, culminating with the [1968] formation of the National Association of Jazz Educators [the forerunner of the International Association of Jazz Educators (IAJE) established in the 1980s]. [11]

Nowadays, jazz is accepted at virtually every institution of higher learning. Over a hundred accredited colleges and universities offer a baccalaureate degree in jazz; fifty-seven offer a master's degree. Moreover, the big news as of late is the degree of jazz penetration into the nation's high schools.

While academic acceptance and curricula implementation of jazz had been underway for over a decade in 1969, the same could hardly be said for financial support of the art form by the nation's foundations.

Early on, America's own music did not appear on the radar screens of many grant-making foundations, and would remain that way through the 1970s, despite continuing federal government support for jazz that began in 1969. A relatively slow economy and a tax law revision enacted in 1969 are often given as reasons for the lackluster foundation performance during the seventies. The 1980s saw the beginnings of a turnaround. The number of grant-making foundations increased dramatically from 25,000 in 1985 to 75,000 in 2007, an expansion fueled by economic growth boomlets in the middle 1980s, 1990s, and 2000s.

Foundation giving likewise soared, increasing its total outlay from $6 billion in 1985 to $47 billion in 2007. Jazz benefited as well. Annual outlays that totaled less than $100,000 in the 1970s, grew to $500,000 in the 1980s, then to $1.5 million in the 1990s, and finally to $10 million and more in the 2000s. But it took more than foundation growth to vault jazz to its current $15 million funding plateau. It took the advent of the super jazz grant.[12]

For years, the typical jazz grant to music projects was in the $10,000–$25,000 range. Starting in the 1990s, huge multiyear grants materialized. It began in 1990 with a combined grant of $4 million from the Lila Wallace–Reader's Digest Fund to establish a National Jazz Network, a consortium of arts presenters and organizations to increase touring opportunities for jazz musicians. The Digest Fund renewed support for the network with an additional four-year $5 million grant in 1994. Taken together, these grants exceeded the total monies given to jazz by foundations up to that time.

Also in 1990, the Penn Foundation allocated $2.5 million for the construction of the first jazz art institution: the Philadelphia Clef Club of Jazz and Performing Arts. Not resting on its largesse, the Digest Fund in 1992 awarded two more super grants: over $2 million in 1991 to NPR to increase jazz awareness via its airwaves and a $7 million (ten-year) grant to the Smithsonian Institution to preserve and promote America's own music.

Toward the decade's end, additional super grants materialized to cover the costs of constructing jazz art institutions in Kansas City and New York City. In 1999 the Jazz District Redevelopment Corporation of Missouri gave over $1 million for the American Jazz Museum (and a concomitant upgrade of the surrounding Eighteenth and Vine neighborhood), and in the same year, the Diamond and Goldsmith Foundations gave $1 million and $1.5 million, respectively, for a permanent home in Manhattan for Jazz at Lincoln Center.

If foundation philanthropy in the 1990s was relatively generous, then what happened in the first decade of the twenty-first century was even more so. The number of annual jazz grants leaped into the hundreds by 2003, reaching a peak of 450 by 2007. Most years saw grant totals in excess of $10 million, with 2005 and 2007 peaking around $15 million. One recipient, Jazz at Lincoln Center, whose new performance temple—the Frederick P. Rose Hall—commanded a lion's share of the donations: approximately a third of all grants and about half (around $8 million) of the total monies most years.

Based on the number of foundations granting, and the dollars awarded, the building of a permanent home for jazz in the heart of Manhattan was obviously deemed a worthy national project. Grants came in all sizes from nearly every state of the union: from $127,000 to $150,000 on up to $1.5 million.

More than thirty years ago, in August 1978, *Ebony* magazine interviewed George Wein, the Newport Jazz Festival impresario, on the occasion of President Carter's first White House Jazz Festival, and captured him ruminating about the impact that event might have on the music:

Hopefully, [the White House festival] will mean more money for
jazz from the NEA and the state arts councils and more financial
support from the corporations. Maybe more support will be given
in the academic world for research and teaching of the subject.
You know, the culture in this country has always been supported
by the rich people, and they are the ones who have set up the
foundations. Customarily, they support art museums, ballet, opera,
symphony orchestras and a few other artistic endeavors, but they
don't even know what it is to have an agenda for jazz. An Avery
Fisher gave seven million to redo the acoustics and change the
name of Philharmonic Hall to New York's Lincoln Center. Until
someone gives money to build a jazz theater and then funds it so
that money will be available for performance, jazz can never attain the status it really should have. If someone gave ten million
to jazz, he'd go down in history, because no one's ever done that.[13]

Someone came close, George, and the jazz theater in Manhattan
bears his name: Frederick P. Rose. His foundation gave in excess of $6
million.

Other worthy musical endeavors received super grants throughout
the 2000s. The Doris Duke Charitable Trust allocated $1 million to
Chamber Music America in 2000, upping the ante by another half million in 2007 to support various small group experimental efforts. Also
in 2007, the Digest Fund gave a half million to the San Francisco Jazz
Organization, and the Ford Foundation gave another half million to
Columbia University.

Government funding at the federal, state, and local levels, together
with academic acceptance, foundation grants, and corporate donations,
has solidified jazz's stature in its home country. Permanent performance
spaces and numerous year-round festivals across the land are testimony
to its broad acceptance. This deserved respect, though late in coming,
had its beginnings in 1969, when a most unlikely suitor slipped the glass
slipper on jazz's waiting foot.

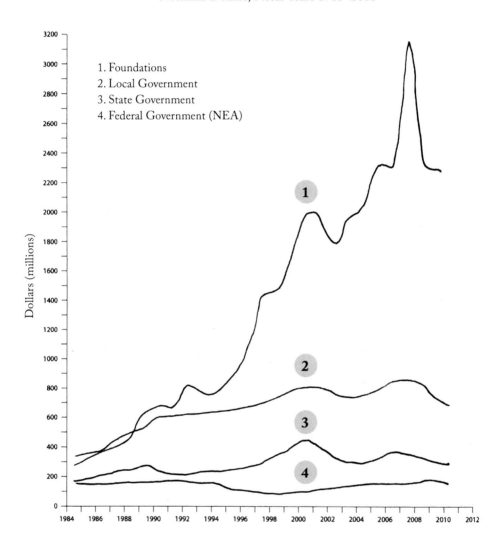

Foundation Giving and Government Appropriations to the Arts
Nominal Dollars, Fiscal Years 1985–2011

1. Foundations
2. Local Government
3. State Government
4. Federal Government (NEA)

Sources: Foundation data gathered by the author from research of resources available at the Foundation Center, Washington, DC. This data is based on all grants of $10,000 or more awarded by a national sample of 1,263 larger United States foundations, including 800 of the 1,000 largest ranked by total giving.

Data on the federal, state, and local government appropriations and expenditures on the arts obtained from Angela Han's "Public Funding for the Arts: 2009 Update" and Kelly Barsdate's "Public Funding for the Arts: 2011 Update," in Grantmakers in the Arts *Reader*, vols. 20 and 22, respectively. Both sources provided by Ryan Stubbs, Research Director, National Assembly of State Arts Agencies (NASAA), Washington, DC.

On Sunday, December 26, 1965, Duke Ellington and his orchestra, backed by three choirs, presented a Concert of Sacred Music (8 p.m. and midnight) at the Fifth Avenue Presbyterian Church in New York City. The CBS-TV network filmed the concert for later broadcast. Duke Ellington and Billy Strayhorn (*p*); Herbie Jones, Cootie Williams, Cat Anderson, and Mercer Ellington (*tps*); Lawrence Brown, Buster Cooper, and Chuck Connors (*tbs*); Harry Carney, Johnny Hodges, Russell Procope, Jimmy Hamilton, and Paul Gonsalves (*saxes*); John Lamb (*b*); Louis Bellson (*dms*); and Lena Horne (*v*) in the Herman McCoy choir.

CHAPTER I

America's Premier Composer

ON APRIL 29, 1969, ONLY three months after his inauguration, President Nixon bestowed the Medal of Freedom, the nation's highest civilian honor, to Edward Kennedy "Duke" Ellington on the occasion of his seventieth birthday. This marked the first time in American history that anyone in jazz had been so honored.[1] The accompanying declaration read:

> Edward Kennedy Ellington, pianist, composer, and orchestra leader, has long enhanced American music with his unique style, intelligence, and impeccable taste. For more than forty years, he has helped to expand the frontiers of jazz, while at the same time retaining in his music the individuality and freedom of expression that are the soul of jazz. In the royalty of American music, no man swings more or stands higher than the Duke.

By honoring Ellington—the most articulate spokesman, prolific composer, and honored personage in jazz for over four decades—Nixon was honoring jazz itself. And it was about time. According to jazz commentator Gary Giddins,

No one experimented as constantly and variously over so long
a period of time as Ellington did with his orchestra or dared as
substantial a body of through-composed work . . . Ellington was,
in fact, his orchestra's composer, arranger, conductor, pianist, talent
scout, entertainer, agent, nursemaid, and advocate . . . His legacy
is immense: some fifteen hundred copyrighted pieces . . . He was
not a composer who borrowed from jazz, as Gershwin and others
did, but a jazz composer.[2]

While Ellington did not invent the jazz orchestra—sections of similar instruments playing off one another over a jazz rhythm—he perfected
it. And he did so by creating unusual sounds with unusual combinations
of instruments, and by focusing on the individual player and not the
individual instrument. As Ellington himself said,

I regard my entire orchestra as one large instrument, and I try to
play on that instrument to the fullest of its capabilities. My aim
is and always has been to mold the music around the man . . . I
study each man in the orchestra and find out what he can do best,
and what he would like to do.[3]

Billy Strayhorn, Duke's composing and arranging partner, dubbed
the maestro's approach the "Ellington effect":

Each member of the band is to him a distinctive tone color and
set of emotions, which mixes with others equally distinctive to
produce a third thing, which I like to call the Ellington effect.
Sometimes this mixing happens on paper and frequently right
on the bandstand.[4]

New Yorker magazine jazz critic Whitney Balliett weighed in on this
special style as well:

Most of the big bands that surrounded Ellington in the 1930s and 1940s came in two distinct parts—their leaders (Tommy Dorsey, Glenn Miller, Artie Shaw) and the dispensable hired help. But Ellington and his musicians were indivisible. He wrote specifically for his musicians, and they played what he had written specifically for him. They often amended or enlarged on his melodies at rehearsals or in the recording studio, and then he amended or enlarged on their changes.[5]

In addition to his orchestral advances, Duke, along with Harold Arlen, Irving Berlin, George Gershwin, Jerome Kern, Cole Porter, Richard Rodgers, and others, wrote the Great American Songbook for the first half of the twentieth century. Where Duke ranks among these elite songwriters is debatable of course, but critics would certainly place him in the top ten, some in the top five. Without dispute, he is the most widely performed of all jazz composers.

Taking into account Ellington's total compositional oeuvre, his songs, and his longer pieces (suites, concertos, theatrical and film scores, and all the rest), his most fervent admirers contend that he is the greatest American composer. Critic Whitney Balliett has noted,

This suggests that [Duke] surpassed [Americans] Charles Ives, Virgil Thomson, Aaron Copland, Elliot Carter, Samuel Barber, and the rest, to say nothing of such resident imports as Varese, Bartok, Schoenberg, Stravinsky, and Hindemith. But all of them were European apples, and Ellington was an American orange. The Coplands and Thomsons used traditional European compositional methods and the usual "classical" instruments.[6]

So let's not compare apples to oranges. How does Ellington stack up against the other American oranges: Berlin, Gershwin, Kern, Porter, and Rodgers? Only Berlin, Gershwin, and Rodgers composed long works but not to the extent that Ellington did. And how do those long pieces fare next to his? Answer that, and you'll know who stands out as the greatest. Hint: his nickname is Duke.

And he did all this as a commercial enterprise without financial help from foundations or the government, save for his overseas trips for the State Department's Jazz Ambassador program.

The pioneering accomplishments of Ellington and his orchestra are too numerous to list in total, but here in sum are a few:[7]

First black band respectfully portrayed in film: *Black and Tan* (1929)

Most hit singles by a black artist of the 1930s

First black band selected by Zeigfield for a Broadway show (1930)

First among jazz and popular artists to use multisided ten-inch 78 rpm recordings to present extended original works, such as the nine-minute "Creole Rhapsody" (1931)

First to play the Publix (movie) Theatre circuit in 1931

First to demonstrate that jazz (and popular music) artists could play concerts on a regular basis (Carnegie Hall 1943–1948), in addition to nightclubs, dance halls, and the like

The only black band to strongly perform and promote on behalf of World War II

First black band to garner a lavish spread in the national pictorial magazine *Look* (1943)

First major popular black music figure to create his own publishing company: Tempo Music (1943)

First black band to cultivate a cross-racial audience in the 1940s

First black musical attraction to appear at venues such as the Paramount Theater in New York City (1931), Academy Awards (1934),

Avalon Club in St. Louis (1936), Chez Maurice in Dallas (1936), Orpheum in Memphis (1937), Colgate University (1940), Hurricane Club in New York City (1943), Ciro's in Hollywood (1945), and Texas Southern University (1948)

First to stage a Broadway musical with complete indifference to the actors' color: *Beggar's Holiday* in 1946

First band to musically document emotions and history of blacks: for example, the songs "Black and Tan Fantasy" (1927), "Creole Love Call" (1927), and "Black Beauty" (1928), as well as the musicals *Jump for Joy* (1941), *Black, Brown and Beige* (1943), and *My People* (1963)

First to release an instrumental concept album—grouping of songs meant to evoke a certain mood: *Mood Ellington in 1948*

First black to score a *major* Hollywood motion picture: *Anatomy of a Murder* (1959)

Only band to survive the demise of the Swing Era without interruption; said another way: the only musical unit of its sort not disbanded in more than forty-two years (at the time of the Nixon tribute)

Most foreign goodwill tours on behalf of the State Department

All of the above aside, Ellington's singular lasting contribution to American life is the role he played in helping breakdown the long-standing prejudice against jazz—and by extension, American culture—being viewed as serious art. Seen first from abroad and then eventually at home, as the British critic Spike Hughes said it best in 1931, Duke was the first essentially American composer, the first composer to produce music that was *really* American in its idiom.[8]

Given Ellington's accomplishments and stature, one might have guessed that he would have had numerous presidential suitors hanging around his stage door long before President Nixon came knocking in 1969. Nope, wasn't so. As we shall see, it was the other way around.

Duke Ellington's first appearance inside the White House, in the East Room, occurred on March 27, 1968. The maestro provided the after-dinner entertainment for President and Mrs. Tubman of Liberia, fronting an octet drawn from his orchestra: Duke Ellington (*p*), Jeff Castleman (*b*), Rufus Jones (*dms*), Paul Gonsalves (*ts*), Johnny Hodges (*as*), Harry Carney (*bs*), Cat Anderson (*tp*), and Lawrence Brown (*tb*).

CHAPTER 2

A Long Road
to the White House

BORN AT THE TURN OF the twentieth century in the city of New Orleans and its environs, jazz spread slowly at first but caught like wildfire in the 1920s as it swept through major cites like Chicago, Kansas City, New York City, and even Washington, DC.[1]

But there was a little spot in the nation's capital that remained an impenetrable fortress to this new music—the White House—until, and this is hard to believe, but true, the 1960s. Of course, a few historic anomalies exist. Ragtime, America's first popular music and one of the ingredients in the jazz gumbo, was first heard at the Theodore Roosevelt White House in 1905, played by the Marine Band and occasionally thereafter by them but never by an outside authentic, commercial band until 1974. The Navy Yard Band of Washington, DC, formed a "jazz" ensemble that played for President Warren Harding dances in the 1920s. The only authentic, commercial jazz band to perform at the White House prior to the 1960s occurred at a campaign rally on the South Lawn for President Calvin Coolidge in 1924 (see appendix 1). And that's it.[2]

The White House (which opened its doors in 1801) has never lacked for musical entertainment. Depending on the occupants and the mood of the country, the executive mansion served—in its first century and a half—mostly as a recital hall for famed classical pianists and opera singers. Other music found its way past the front doors from time to time—folk, novelty, choral, cowboy, and even gospel—but no jazz.

Numerous reasons can explain the lack of America's own music at its most famous showplace:

1. The musical tastes of the White House occupants, their appointed impresarios, and their invited guests

2. The times: the twentieth century saw a devastating economic depression, two world wars, numerous regional wars, and a consuming cold war

3. The collective American perception of art in general, which had to be a European import

4. The specific perception that jazz was not art but rather speakeasy, dance hall, or nightclub music, and worse, the "devil's music," inappropriate for the academy or concert hall, and certainly not for the presidential palace

5. The tensions that played across America's racial fault line—jazz after all was largely associated with African Americans

Yet the racial aspect provides only a partial answer. African American opera singers, choral groups, and classical pianists appeared occasionally, if not regularly, at the White House as far back as the nineteenth century. Given that jazz was a proven commodity by the 1940s—it even had a modicum of academic respectability—and given the common-folk sensibilities of President Franklin and First Lady Eleanor Roosevelt, who invited African American singers and choral groups of all genres to perform, jazz could and should have made its debut at the White House during their thirteen-year reign.[3] It just didn't, but came very close. Mrs. Roosevelt arranged for Louis Armstrong and his orchestra to play the President's Ball at the Lincoln Colonnade on U Street (only fifteen blocks from the White House) on January 30, 1942. The First Lady even attended the charity gala and spoke to the predominantly African American audience. And that was that.[4]

The 1930s saw Duke Ellington taking his own steps to bring jazz to the presidential mansion. Among his many talents, even as a youngster, he was a keen observer and practitioner of Jazz Age public relations. His business manager and partner, Irving Mills, joined him in this endeavor. Together, they brought the new corporate advertising aesthetics of the 1920s developed by Albert Lasker (advertising) and Edward L. Bernays (public relations) to bear on popular music, focusing on the image (Ellington the composer) and not the product (the song).[5] Duke noticed how movie stars and theatrical folk (Al Jolson in particular) were beginning to hobnob with presidential candidates to their obvious mutual benefit. Seeking similar validation for himself, Duke arranged through an intermediary an audience with President Hoover in 1931. Despite being publicized in the newspapers, the planned meeting never took place. Undeterred, Ellington posed for photographs on the White House grounds without anyone from the presidential staff present—a trick not possible today, of course.[6]

Three years later, after his orchestra participated in a January 1934 radio broadcast for the benefit of President Roosevelt's Warm Springs Foundation for crippled children, Duke tried again. Also knowing that society dance bands like those of Eddie Duchin, Joe Moses, Meyer Davis, and Eddie Peabody were being invited to the nation's showplace for the first time, Ellington, while performing at Washington's Howard Theater in February 1934, sent a letter to the White House offering to play for First Lady Eleanor Roosevelt.[7] Duke was politely rebuffed. Evidently, Mrs. Roosevelt was away and the president was busy and not planning any entertainment that week. In time, the matter became moot: dances were effectively canceled at the White House after the Pearl Harbor attack in 1941.

In a way, Duke got his chance to play for FDR. On April 15, 1945, while the presidential funeral train was traveling from Hot Springs to

Hyde Park, the Blue Network radio (the predecessor to ABC) broadcast Duke Ellington music for hours from the Radio City Hall studios, playing a long program of his own compositions—the only American music heard on the air that sorrowful day.[8]

Harry Truman—a competent piano player in his own right—inherited the top job after FDR's demise, and Ellington's chances appeared to improve. Invited to a White House musicale as a guest on September 29, 1950, Duke was summoned to the president's quarters, and as he remembered,

> [Truman] dismissed his bodyguard, closed the door of his private study, and invited me to sit down and talk as one piano player to another! He said he was honored to be presented with the original score of *Harlem* [a suite commissioned by the NBC Symphony Orchestra to be premiered in January 1951 at the Metropolitan Opera House by conductor Arturo Toscanini]. After that, you might have thought we were a couple of cats in a billiard parlor, so informal was our conversation. He sort of confessed he was not the piano player I was, but we acted as though he were Doc Perry or Louis Brown [two of Duke's early piano mentors]. I was very happy.[9]

Jazz fans can only wonder what might have happened had Truman resided in the actual White House (which was under major renovation) for a full term instead of at Blair House across the street. Harry and First Lady Bess would have had the opportunity to plan two more seasons of social dinners, and Truman could have been the first to break the jazz sound barrier at the mansion. Sadly, this milestone was still a whole decade off.

With another change of administration, Duke kept trying for the official acknowledgment of his art that only a White House performance would confer, as the following vignette reveals:

When I went to see and play for President Eisenhower at the White House Correspondents' Dinner [held in Washington, DC, on March 5, 1955], I was given a sumptuous suite of rooms in the Mayflower Hotel. As I got off the elevator in the lobby, the president was just entering it. He gave me a big hello, and then, as I was walking away, he called out loudly, "Say, Duke, don't forget to play 'Mood Indigo.'" I thought that was pretty good coming from the victorious general of World War II, and I got a lift from it. During our performance that night, we played "Mood Indigo" four times![10]

The very next day, Duke dashed off a letter to the White House extending "ticket number one" to the president to attend the Second Annual Newport Jazz Festival to be held that summer. In a letter dated March 12, Ike responded by saying, "I would truly like to attend—but a look at my schedule tells me it is practically impossible." Ike's schedule would remain "impossible" through the remainder of his term.[11]

President Eisenhower deserves some credit, however. He initiated federal government support for the art form through the State Department's Jazz Ambassador program that launched Dizzy, Louis, Duke, Benny, and other jazz greats around the world to spread the word of jazz and democracy. Begun in 1956, the program continued through the late 1980s. First Lady Mamie Eisenhower did her part, too. She lent her name as patron and attended the Second Jazz Jubilee benefit concert (featuring the Count Basie Orchestra, pianist Willie "the Lion" Smith, and guitarist Charlie Byrd) held at the Presidential Arms Hotel in Washington, DC, on March 21, 1960. The future First Lady Pat Nixon, wife of the then vice president, joined Mamie in this endeavor.

A new president, a new administration, and things began to brighten. At long last, jazz at the White House! Jazz in the East Room! And it took President John F. Kennedy, whose interest in music was almost nonexistent, and First Lady Jacqueline, whose musical tastes were even more Eurocentric than her predecessors', to make it happen. For the first time in White House history, on November 19, 1962, a jazz concert was held in the East Room.[12] And it matters not that the first to play was the Paul Winter Sextet, a relatively unknown group of twenty-year-olds just back from their cultural exchange tour of Central and South America.

The jazz ice was broken. America's musical poor sister was finally recognized. Yet once again, no cigar for Duke, although he had come close.

Six months before, in May 1962, on the occasion of the First International Jazz Festival in the nation's capital, Ellington had served as the master of ceremonies and main musical attraction. The four-day festival benefited the People to People committee, of which President Kennedy was honorary chairman and former President Eisenhower was executive chairman. On the first day of the festival, Ellington was awarded the keys to his hometown and driven slowly down Pennsylvania Avenue behind an elderly brass band. The group stopped in front of the White House expecting a brief presidential appearance (an invitation had been made to Kennedy to meet with Duke and the brass band parade). But, as before, Duke was left standing at the gate.[13]

Following the first White House jazz concert, JFK's press secretary, Pierre Salinger, set the wheels in motion for Louis Armstrong and Benny Goodman to perform there in 1963. Unfortunately, the intended audience canceled, and that was that—no jazz beyond the Winter Sextet.[14] The Kennedy administration finally recognized Duke, however, in the fall of 1963, sending him and his orchestra on their first State Department–sponsored overseas trip, a three-month goodwill tour of South Asia and the Middle East. The administration also had the United States Information Agency (USIA) film the orchestra in concert at their stopover in Bombay, India, with copies subsequently distributed to USIA posts (termed United States Information Service [USIS] posts) around the world. The film, *Duke Ellington Selections*, is now available for viewing at the National Archives in College Park, Maryland.[15] Unfortunately, the assassination of President Kennedy brought the tour to an abrupt end on November 22.

It was up to the successor president, Lyndon B. Johnson, to act on the jazz precedent set by JFK. And did he ever!

As if to make up for the long oversight, the Johnson administration hosted sixteen jazz events during its sixty-two-month run (see appendix 2). LBJ invited such notable jazz luminaries as Duke Ellington, Stan Getz, Sarah Vaughan, George Shearing, Charlie Byrd, and Dave Brubeck. Jazz had finally received its just due by a president and first lady whose musical tastes would not be described as refined but who believed it their duty to showcase the widest possible range of artistic expression at the nation's showroom.

Unwittingly or not, LBJ made up for the decades of official neglect of America's premier jazz composer by inviting Ellington and his orchestra to give the final performance at the White House Festival of the Arts on June 14, 1965.[16] On an erected stage on the South Lawn, Duke presented sections of what would become his *Far East Suite*, followed by selections from his tone statement on the African American plight in America—*Black, Brown and Beige* (1943), featuring the lovely hymn "Come Sunday." He closed out the concert with an Ellington twelve-hit-song medley that included "Solitude," "Sophisticated Lady," "I'm Beginning to See the Light," and "Caravan" (see appendix 3).

Of interest, LBJ heard Ellington play the year before on May 22, 1964, at the annual White House Correspondents Association (WHCA) dinner at the Sheraton Park Hotel in Washington, DC. Duke was among the guests invited to celebrate the fiftieth anniversary of the American Society of Composers, Authors, and Publishers (ASCAP). The WHCA was celebrating its fiftieth anniversary as well. Duke followed fellow ASCAP songwriters Harold Arlen, Jule Styne, Jerry Herman, and Richard Adler to play a selection of his compositions for the president.[17]

At age sixty-six, Ellington had indeed traveled a long road to his first performance at the White House. At last, he had arrived—after having his offer to play at the mansion rebuffed by Hoover and Roosevelt; after gifting Truman precious original scores and sharing a long private discussion with him in the upstairs quarters; after honoring Ike's request

for "Mood Indigo" four times at the Correspondents' Dinner at the Mayflower Hotel, and then facing Ike's refusal to join him at the Newport
Jazz Festival; and after being overlooked by JFK. He had arrived at the
LBJ White House, not to play a dance, but to render a concert of his
extended compositional works at the Festival of the Arts. At last, he had
achieved a certain deference and respect that might not have occurred
earlier, as indicated by a White House staff member's outburst during
the planning for the arts festival:

> Duke Ellington should *not* play background music during din-
> ner . . . a great composer and international figure does not play
> background music at the White House.[18]

Indeed. Ten months after the White House Festival of the Arts,
Ellington and his orchestra flew off to the First World Festival of Negro Arts in Dakar, Senegal, on behalf of the State Department and the
White House. First Lady Johnson chaired the committee overseeing
the American participation to emphasize the president's identification
with African and African American aspirations. The controversies surrounding the festival, which was mostly termed a success, did not touch
Duke and his band. "Its smash performances clearly established the U.S.
as the festival favorite," so said the *New York Times*. The USIA produced
a documentary film of the Dakar Festival, including a short segment on
Ellington and the orchestra that was subsequently viewed by countless
millions around the world (now also available for viewing at the National
Archives, College Park, Maryland).

A year or so after Dakar, on June 27, 1967, Duke received another
invite from LBJ, this time as a "guest" at a state dinner for the king of
Thailand. The Stan Getz Quintet and the North Texas State University
Lab Band provided the entertainment. Duke and tenor sax great Getz
sat in with the Lab Band for a splendid rendition of Duke's "Take the 'A'
Train"—to the absolute delight of the jazz clarinet-playing monarch.[19]
On March 27 the following year, the maestro made his first East Room

appearance with an octet drawn from his band to entertain the president of Liberia.[20] A jam session with the Marine Band dance group followed. After the concert, Duke on piano joined tenor player Paul Gonsalves, bassist Jeff Castleman, and drummer Rufus Jones in the foyer beneath the grand steps to the upstairs family quarters, and performed for the president and Lady Bird as they danced in their stocking feet until one in the morning.[21] Then, on November 21, eight weeks prior to the close of LBJ's term, Duke, as a member of the newly launched National Council of the Arts (to which he had been appointed by LBJ), attended a celebratory dinner at the White House. He treated an East Room audience to a solo piano rendition of his latter-day hit "Satin Doll."[22]

Clearly, the maestro was held in high esteem by the Johnson administration. Ellington was even overheard telling associates in a Harlem spot that the president had written him a personal letter. Duke, it was said, was both flattered and pleased.[23]

The Washington Navy Yard Jazz Band was the first "jazz" band to play the White House at a garden party for President and Mrs. Harding on May 18, 1921. The Marine Band played concert music on the South Lawn while the Navy Yard Band played for dancing in the East Room. Little is known about the music the band played beyond waltzes. No "earwitness" accounts are known to exist. The above picture is assumed representative, not likely taken in 1921, but perhaps several years later. (See appendix 1.)

The Ray Miller Orchestra accompanied Al Jolson on the South Lawn of the White House on October 17, 1924. President and Mrs. Coolidge stood next to Jolson; Miller had his back to the camera. (See appendix 1.)

Duke Ellington posed on the White House steps on October 1, 1931, after his meeting with President Hoover was canceled.

Duke Ellington and President Truman compared musical notes at the White House on September 29, 1950. Duke gifted the president with the original score for *Portrait of New York Suite*, which he wrote under a commission from symphonic orchestra conductor Arturo Toscanini.

Duke Ellington photographed during an off-stage jam session while at work at Columbia Studios in Hollywood, California, where he conducted his film background score for *Anatomy of a Murder*. For his efforts and for those of Billy Strayhorn (his composing and arranging partner), Duke received three Grammys in November 1959: Best Musical Composition of the Year, Best Performance by a Dance Band, and Best Motion Picture Soundtrack of the Year. Admiring Duke and piano player Billy Strayhorn is director Otto Preminger who would attend the seventieth-birthday celebration for Ellington at the White House. Strayhorn, sadly, would not. He passed on May 31, 1967.

President and Mrs. Kennedy were the first to invite a jazz group to perform inside the White House. The Paul Winter Sextet played a Young People's Concert in the East Room on November 19, 1962. Paul Winter (*as*), Dick Whitsell (*tp*), Les Root (*bs*), Richard Evans (*b*), Warren Bernhardt (*p*), and Harold Jones (*dms*).

The Kennedy administration did not invite Ellington to perform at the White House but did send him and his orchestra on their first overseas trip, a three-month tour of South Asia and the Middle East sponsored by the State Department. Pictured above is Duke's arrival at the Beirut, Lebanon, airport on November 11, 1963. News of the president's assassination ended the tour ten days later.

After traveling a very long road, Duke Ellington finally arrived at his White House destination to give the closing performance at President Johnson's Festival of the Arts on June 14, 1965. On an erected stage on the South Lawn, Duke and his orchestra presented sections of his *Far East Suite*, followed by selections from his tone statement on the African American plight in America, *Black, Brown and Beige*, featuring the lovely hymn "Come Sunday." He closed out the concert with an Ellington twelve-hit-song medley. Members of the orchestra: Duke Ellington (*p*), Rufus Jones (*dms*), John Lamb (*b*), Cat Anderson (*tp*), Ray Nance (*tp*), Cootie Williams (*tp*), Lawrence Brown (*tb*), Buster Cooper (*tb*), Chuck Connors (*tb*), Paul Gonsalves (*ts*), Jimmy Hamilton (*cl*), Johnny Hodges (*as*), Russell Procope (*as*), and Harry Carney (*bs*).

Lady Bird Johnson thanked Ellington and his orchestra at the close of their formal set following the day-long celebratory Festival of the Arts on June 14, 1965. After the First Lady departed, Duke addressed the crowd remaining on the South Lawn: "We have a request for several of the things we have written and we'd like to play some of them for you." With that, Duke and the band offered a medley of Ellington song hits.

Duke at his first East Room appearance on March 27, 1968, gestured to the front-row dignitaries as if to say, "How about these apples, Mr. President?" Apples, *left to right, back row*: Jeff Castleman (*b, not seen*), Rufus Jones (*dms*), Lawrence Brown (*tb*), Cat Anderson (*tp*); *front row*: Duke Ellington (*p*) Paul Gonsalves (*ts*), Johnny Hodges (*as*), and Harry Carney (*bs, behind Hodges*).

All four instigators, Willis Conover, Leonard Garment, Charles McWhorter, and Joe Morgen, attended the Ellington White House event. Shown above are two: Willis Conover (*wearing glasses, top left*) and Leonard Garment (*center on stage*), both staring at trumpeter Clark Terry at the microphone. Shown also is pianist Billy Taylor (*wearing glasses, bottom left*) dancing with his wife, Theodora. Mr. Taylor performed three solo numbers during the concert.

CHAPTER 3

Prelude to a Tribute

W HEN THE LYNDON JOHNSON PRESIDENCY ended, and that of Richard Nixon began on January 20, 1969, expectations were not high for jazz. The popular perception of Nixon's musical tastes, as Frank Getlein stated in his 1971 *New York Times Magazine* article, were that of a "middle American and therefore more interested in football than fugues, baseball than ballet, pinochle than play-going." In short, "The Nixon taste is, in a word, deplorable. Or, in a couple of words, there isn't any."[1]

But Nixon's tastes were far from deplorable, and jazz was fairly represented during the five and a half years he was in office, almost matching that presented by the preceding Johnson administration, both quantitatively and qualitatively.

The Nixons' Aesthetic Tastes

The Nixons rarely watched television and read few newspapers and magazines, although the president thoroughly read his prepared news summary each day.[2] Both were serious book readers, Pat more so than her husband. He enjoyed histories and political biographies; she, biographies and historical novels.[3] As for theater, both were fans (in their youth, they acted in theatrical productions) and went to the theatre or opera weekly during the 1960s while based in New York City.[4] More often than not, they attended musicals.[5] A married couple could not be closer in this respect. Film, however, was an altogether different matter.

While Nixon *loved* movies, wife Pat was indifferent; she would occasionally watch an old favorite or a musical, and that was it. The president had over five hundred films screened for him during his sixty-seven months in office, seven or eight a month in the first term and (not surprisingly) ten a month in the scandal-ridden second term.[6] Most of the movies came from the late 1940s, 1950s, and early 1960s, and few were au courant or foreign. He loved Westerns, John Wayne, and director John Ford. Musicals occupied second place (*South Pacific* his favorite).

By his own admission, and attested to by others, Nixon was a classical music devotee.[7] While president, he had classical music played all the time—so loud said his wife, "You can hear every note. It practically shakes the walls down, but he loves it."[8]

No doubt influenced by his early training on violin and piano,[9] his ardor extended to light or semiclassical (Mantovani, Boston Pops, and 101 Strings) and musical soundtracks (*Gone with the Wind*, *My Fair Lady*, *Carousel*, *Oklahoma*, and *King and I*).[10] Wife Pat shared his passion for musical soundtracks, as did daughters Julie and Tricia to some degree, who cited "Edelweiss" (*Sound of Music*) and the theme from *Doctor Zhivago* as their favorite songs, respectively.[11] Nixon told Washington National Symphony conductor Antal Dorati that his favorite composition was the background music by Richard Rodgers for the motion picture *Victory at Sea*.[12] As one would have guessed, the president held a very dim view of modern art and modern jazz, something—as he confided to top aide H. R. Haldeman—not generally representative of American taste and culture.[13]

Long-term Nixon political operative Charles McWhorter told the *Washington Post* that the president could not be considered a jazz devotee, but he appreciated "the elegance and greatness of Duke Ellington's music." The *Post* added, "The president admittedly is more interested in classical music than in jazz."[14]

While not a fan of the music, Nixon was nonetheless highly cognizant and supportive of the important role jazz musicians had in spreading American freedom and democracy overseas via the State Department's Jazz Ambassador program, supplemented by the daily jazz broadcasts by the Voice of America (VOA) and the occasional USIA documentary film or newsreel screened at commercial theaters, USIS posts, and mobile film units around the globe—efforts all begun during the Eisenhower administration when Nixon was vice president. African American jazz musicians were highly prized in this regard as a means to counter Soviet propaganda over the treatment of minority blacks in America.

Nixon Entertainment Policy

Nixon entered his presidency with fully baked ideas on all aspects of governance at the highest level: notions he had accumulated during his eight years as vice president under Eisenhower, his unsuccessful run against Kennedy for the president in 1960, and his subsequent eight years out of office plotting the takeover of 1600 Pennsylvania Avenue. When it came to entertainment policy, he knew what he wanted to do, and he hit the ground running.

While walking down a corridor on his second evening in the White House as president, Nixon turned to usher J. B. West and said, "You know, we are going to have church services in the East Room."[15] Dutifully, the next day West ordered chairs and brought the altar rigged for Lynda Byrd Johnson's wedding into the East Room. Nixon decided against the altar. "No, the services are going to be interdominational," he pointed out. "I don't want an altar, just a podium." West set up the room with Bess Truman's bentwood chairs, risers for a choir, and an electric organ. At 10 a.m. on Sunday, January 26, 1969, the Reverend

Billy Graham, friend of the previous three presidents, preached the first East Room sermon, and his longtime soloist, George Beverly Shea, sang "How Great Thou Art."

Nixon's purpose here was to reward ordinary people—those who might not qualify for a state dinner—for their past and (hopefully) future support. At the conclusion of his term in office, forty-six such services had been held for an estimated twelve thousand congregants (see appendices 4 and 5). Of interest to jazz fans, Ethel Waters sang at the service on January 24, 1972. Ms. Waters is a vital link in the early blues singer chain and one of the first pioneers of American jazz singing, along with Louis Armstrong and Billie Holiday.[16]

Nixon placed great importance on the dinners he hosted at the White House. The following, written before he was inaugurated, expressed a concern with the dress for social functions and established a standard for his administration:

> With regard to protocol at White House dinners, I have decided that any dinner in the evening will be black tie, even when it is stag. Where women are present, the dinners will always be white tie. Business suit will be appropriate only for luncheons or afternoon receptions.

In another memorandum around the same time, he made clear his dislike for the time he would have to spend at these affairs, seeking to limit both their number and their duration. Nixon would comply with foreign visitors' expectations of a White House dinner, but would nix the return dinner or luncheon at the visitors' embassy. Further eliminated would be separate dinners for Supreme Court or cabinet members, congressmen, or senators. Instead, these officials would be invited as guests at state dinners. Lastly, he wrote:

> As far as formal dinners are concerned, I want them to start around 8:30 rather than 8:00. This will reduce the amount of time I

will have to be there . . . [Also], I want the number of courses to be an absolute minimum. Make the meals very good, but very short.[17]

In his memoir, Nixon aide Charles Stuart said it best: "The President did not like socializing, but if he had to have parties, he wanted to maximize their political benefit." A telling remark, as the pages ahead will illuminate.

Four weeks after his inauguration, President Nixon laid down the rules his administration would follow when it came to entertainers:

> We need as a basic research document the names of all artists and orchestra leaders, etc., who supported us in the campaign. They should come before others who did not, assuming of course, that their quality is high enough. Under no circumstances can we have in the White House, no matter how good a supporter, an artistic group that is sub par because this would reflect on both the group and the White House.[18]

About the time of this injunction to his staff for a "basic research document," the president reached outside the mansion to NBC President Robert Sarnoff to become his "silent" impresario, requesting him to put together a list of suitable entertainers.

Nixon no doubt saw Sarnoff as a fellow traveler—politically and culturally. When he was vice president, Nixon corresponded frequently with Robert's father, David Sarnoff, about effective anticommunist strategy.[19] Son Robert Sarnoff earned his Cold War patriot credibility as vice president of NBC's film unit that oversaw development of the well-lauded *Victory at Sea* TV documentary series, the background music of which was a Nixon favorite. Once elevated to the top corporate rungs at NBC in 1958, Robert Sarnoff practiced a policy of programming to mainstream tastes.[20] Nonetheless, when Sarnoff submitted his list to the president in May 1969 (appendix 6), it had a well-rounded clutch of classical artists (ten were booked). He was very much aware of Nixon's "high brow" tastes. The rest of the list represented a cross-section of mainstream, popular artists one could have seen on the NBC network (and the ABC and CBS networks) on any given week during the mid to late 1960s (seventeen were booked).

This talent list had scant rock and roll (only 5th Dimension), Motown, soul (only Aretha Franklin), folk, popular country, and contemporary classical (Lukas Foss, Phillip Glass)—only pop and classical artists that Sarnoff thought would appeal to Nixon. But the president had his own internal list of personal favorites, and many of them, especially in the classical field, received the call to perform.

Eight jazz artists made the Sarnoff list: singers Ella Fitzgerald, Nina Simone, and Nancy Wilson; instrumentalists Louis Armstrong, Errol Garner, Al Hirt, and Andre Previn; and orchestra leaders Count Basie and Duke Ellington. All popular, all seen sporadically on TV and at concerts with decent record sales for jazz. Only Duke and Al Hirt got the gig.

The presidential directive on entertainer policy issued by Nixon only four weeks after his inauguration signaled (1) the importance the new president placed on social affairs at the mansion, and (2) his intention to ride herd on all aspects of their planning, as appointment secretary Chapin would publicly reveal later in the year:

> You wouldn't believe the detail he gets into on social stuff—the wines, where the reception line will be, the entertainment, what musical numbers will be played. He loves to know all that.[21]

This obsessive attention to detail was not unique to social-event planning. As aide Alexander Butterfield later stressed, Nixon wanted to know the smallest details of just about everything that went on in the

White House, saying publicly in 1994, "Nothing happened that Richard Nixon didn't okay. Nothing."[22]

Chapin's and Butterfield's public remarks are backed up by internal White House memoranda:

> In the future I [President Nixon] would like to see the musical selections for the state dinners submitted to me.[23]

Another example:

> Regarding White House dinners, [the president] prefers not to have receiving lines for the after-dinner guests—he prefers to use this time [between the dinner and the entertainment] to mix with VIPs (perhaps 10 or so) who attend the actual dinner. Once again, he stressed the need to see that VIPs are brought up to him [in the family quarters] so that no guest of importance departs without having been greeted by the President . . . and introduced to the Guest of Honor of the evening (i.e., the visiting Head of State or special celebrity).[24]

Guests who attended the mansion soirees were very important to the president as well. Like the entertainers, supporters were to have first priority. Chief of Staff H. R. Haldeman made certain of that:

> The president is concerned that we've been conned into inviting too many people who basically don't support us to White House events. Obviously every time we do this we're simply rewarding those people who are against us and encouraging their viewpoint . . . Control on the [guest list] has got to be held here [in the West Wing] rather than at the [East Wing] Social Secretary's Office because they of course have no basis for evaluating individuals by this [support/non-support] criterion.[25]

In a memo to the president, aide Patrick Buchanan expressed this position in starker terms:

> The [White House] dinner would provide the president with a host of opportunities to reward his friends with invitations to these great occasions, and to identify and punish his enemies by relegating them to the perpetual darkness outside the manor.[26] [In which cheek did Buchanan plant his tongue when he wrote this?]

Once the guest list was finalized, someone had to oversee seating arrangements at the dinner. Who better than the president: "I want to see the list of people for my table and for Mrs. RN's table for the dinner. I will personally select the people who are to sit at each table."

The media did not escape the watchdogful eye of the president either. He instructed Chief of Staff Haldeman to put Press Secretary Herbert Klein on the right track:

> The President wants to be sure that we are getting a good balance and spread of publishers, editors, top reporters, columnists, broadcasters, and the like, to our White House social functions, particularly to the dinners ... What he wants here is to be sure that we get the people that we want to reward and encourage, rather than covering the whole lot. He wants you to give some special attention to looking for good editors and publishers from smaller papers in the South [consistent with Nixon's famed southern strategy]. He also wants to be sure the *Chicago Sun Times*, and papers of that sort, are well represented ... We have done pretty well also in including these kinds of people in the church services and should continue to do so. This is especially a place where we can reward people who might not be quite on the level to invite to a State Dinner, and he wants to be sure we take advantage of this.[27]

It was the entertainers—and their political loyalties—that were intently scrutinized under the Nixon microscope. The entertainers, after all, by virtue of their celebrity had the potential to influence large segments of the population in support of the president's policies. National Security Advisor Henry Kissinger lent his considerable weight to this particular view:

> I perceive no objection from a foreign policy standpoint to the proposal that the president host an affair for the U.S. entertainers who have donated their time and talent to our troops in Vietnam. I think the idea is a good one and would serve to emphasize the positive side of our policy in Vietnam. Some of our entertainers, for example, Bob Hope, are outspoken in support of our Vietnam policy, and this fact might come through widely in view of the wide popularity that they possess.[28]

This Nixon/Kissinger view on the political usefulness of performers was endemic within the mansion walls. Connie Stuart, the public face for White House social events and the officially designated White House impresario, wrote in May 1970 after a joint West/East Wing meeting,

> We should concentrate on "big" name stars—performers who will "come out" for the President, and thereby influence a number of others to do the same.[29]

Social Secretary Lucy Winchester, who was responsible for implementing social functions, was—like everybody else in the White House—free to make suggestions regarding specific events, but she, too, came under the president's spell. In her February 1972 memo to West Wing aides:

> I propose that the president and Mrs. Nixon give a "Homecoming" party to honor the performers who have given their service as entertainers at the White House . . . I would suggest that the

event be before the [Republican Presidential] Convention so we can use the stars at that time as well as during the campaign.[30]

At the bottom of the memo, a handwritten note, by one of the addressees:

We have had a most impressive array of very talented stars from all facets of the entertainment world. This event would bring to public attention the range and quality of performers who have supported the President, from [violinist] Isaac Stern and [pianist] Rudolph Serkin and [soprano] Beverly Sills to [singers] Pearl Bailey and Johnny Cash and [comedian] Red Skelton. Wow!

Note the assumed quid pro quo: In exchange for their East Room appearance, entertainers owed the president political support. It is doubtful that this was actually said up front, and for many performers it was probably unnecessary—they were already in the Nixon camp. Still, the "with/against us" worldview led to excessive hand-wringing about an entertainer's political leanings, starting with the president himself:

A pianist is what [the prime minister of Great Britain] likes . . . the president suggested [pianist] Roger Williams or [pianist] Henry Mancini if he was with us during the campaign.[31]

Assistant to Connie Stewart:

[After Roger William's performance], Mrs. Nixon was thrilled—told the pianist her husband was really going to be mad if he didn't get to hear him [at Pat's Senate Ladies luncheon]. Roger rang doorbells campaigning for the president—big supporter![32]

Staffer from the Social Secretary's Office:

[Country singer] Loretta Lynn made several comments . . . that led us to believe she was a friend. We don't think she is a registered Republican but have been advised she has never been politically active. [Lynn never got the call.][33]

Dwight Chapin again:

There's a new singing group called the Mike Curb Congregation . . . Out in Indiana the other day, I heard Mike Curb himself doing a recruiting advertisement for the Air Force. Perhaps we should check into him.[34] [Curb's group sang for King Hussein of Jordan on February 6, 1973.]

Sometimes the political history detective work was stretched to absurd lengths. A West Wing aide:

I do not know where Irving Berlin stands politically (Republican or Democrat) but he has written some remarkable music, the sentiment of which is "Nixonian" . . . I see no conflict with a member of the Jewish faith (I assume he is a practicing Jew) featured at Christmas time, particularly since he wrote "White Christmas."[35] [Berlin sang and played his "God Bless America" at the dinner for the returning Vietnam POWs on May 24, 1973.]

It would not take long for administration watchers to pull back the curtain and see what was going on, as one society columnist noted in May 1970:

Certainly the [Nixon] White House has entertained more people and put on more good shows than ever before. But why are they doing it? It's not to have a good time. It's not to project a lifestyle. It's to pay back old campaign debts. Instead of presenting leading people. Instead of spotlighting the most interesting people America has to offer, the [entertainment] guests are the same, dull, dreadful people who financed the campaign. The President is using the White House as a political tool—and he is doing it beautifully.[36]

The above aside, there were times when President Nixon eschewed politics and sought out quality performers, among them classical conductor, composer, and pianist Leonard Bernstein, Mexican comedian Cantiflas, singer Robert Goulet, Mark Twain impersonator Hal Holbrooke, and classical pianist Andre Watts. All of them Democrats and all had played for President Lyndon Johnson. Nixon was able to snare three: Bernstein, Goulet, and Watts.

Through his first term in office and into the start of the second (before Watergate began to take its toll), Nixon captained entertainment planning from a West Wing deck. It was political with him. As Ronald Kessler wrote in *Inside the White House*:

Of all the perks, dinner at the White House is one of the most stellar. For many, it is the achievement of a lifetime. Just to be able to say, "I had dinner at the White House the other night" carries a cachet impossible to surpass.[37]

The entertainment was an integral part of the event. It had to be impressive and memorable. Recall what President Nixon wrote in his initial directive: "Under no circumstances can we have in the White House, no matter how good a supporter, an artistic group that is subpar because this would reflect on both the group and the White House." The purpose of an evening went beyond the honored figures—they were but props in an elaborate show staged for the invited guests to convince them that divinity was looking at them with favor. This was their reward for past political support of the president. This was their encouragement for such in the future.

But at the time of the Ellington tribute, which occurred only three months after Nixon's inauguration, and this cannot be overemphasized, particulars of entertainment policy had not yet coalesced.

As we shall see anon for the Ellington gala, Nixon did not pick the entertainers, their songs, or most of the guests, nor did he decide where they all sat at dinner. And contrary to his preference, there was even a second receiving line! However, for all anyone knows, Nixon might have picked the wines.

An Ellington Gala

As to who initially conceived the idea of a White House party for Duke on his seventieth birthday on April 29, 1969, all available evidence points to the maestro's public relations man, Joe Morgen, who had been Duke's representative for more than twenty years. Morgen was keenly aware of (indeed, intimately involved in) the many tributes being organized for Ellington throughout his seventieth birthday year. And as any media-meister worth his salt would know, nothing could possibly top a celebratory affair in Duke's honor at the nation's mansion. Surprisingly, as son Mercer recounted in his memoir, his father was initially cool to the plan:

> The fact that the White House party took place was almost entirely due to the persistence of his public relations man, Joe Morgen . . . After he hatched up the brilliant idea of the birthday celebration, and had laid the groundwork with his Washington contacts, he was dismayed to find that Ellington himself was cool about the whole project and reluctant to go through with it because it might ally him too much with one political party. Joe insisted and insisted until ultimately [sister] Ruth indicated that she wanted the party to take place. Then Pop agreed to it.[38]

Ellington reluctant to accept another White House gig? After chasing the White House for forty years, after finally landing four invites to play for President Johnson, and after performing at the Nixon inaugural? As far as favoring one political party over the other, Duke already belonged to the Democrats, or so they thought. Duke had accepted LBJ's appointment to the newly formed Arts Council and accepted five of LBJ's eight White House invitations (he performed at four). Moreover, during the Johnson administration, the Ellington Orchestra made their second State Department–sponsored foreign tour, a ten-day stint to Senegal, Africa.

For his part, Duke was careful not to side with either party in public, telling the *Washington Post* jazz critic Hollie I. West when asked if he had campaigned for Nixon, "No. I didn't campaign for *anyone*."[39] And to syndicated columnist Earl Wilson, "I'm not in politics. I'm in the realm of art. I'm welcome in the White House, no matter who's living there." Yet conventional politics could have been on the maestro's mind. Not so much because Nixon was a Republican per se, but because of the nature of his recently concluded presidential campaign where Nixon openly courted whites at the expense of blacks, especially in the South, threatening the gains the latter community had achieved under the Johnson administration.

Then again something other than politics could have been at work here. Duke might have viewed the White House celebration, unlike his other planned birthday tributes, as an attempt to sum up his career while he was still alive and creating—a Lifetime Achievement Award kind of thing—a notion, as biographer Harvey G. Cohen has said, Duke loathed more than anything.[40] Coupled with this loathing was another, as Cohen also noted:

> People close to Ellington claimed that he avoided and disliked visiting Washington in his last years. His sister Ruth felt that the main reason for this rested in a local cemetery's disinterring of their parents in the early 1960s, after the land was sold. The Ellington family was told they that they had to dig up Daisy and James's

bodies or lose them. After that, her brother "had a completely different feeling about Washington. It was as if Washington had disinherited him."

Whatever the reasons for his reluctance, the maestro wisely accepted the advice of publicist Morgen and sister Ruth.

But it took a troika of White House contacts—Charles McWhorter, Leonard Garment, and Willis Conover—and a well-coordinated plan to make the party happen. Charles McWhorter, a lifelong jazz fan, amateur pianist, lawyer, and loyal Nixon campaign strategist and operative, was probably the first contacted by Morgen, most likely during the run up to the Ellington Orchestra's appearance at Nixon's inaugural festivities.[41]

McWhorter brought on board friend Len Garment, a one-time professional musician (he played jazz saxophone and clarinet with Woody Herman's band in the 1940s) and, importantly, a lawyer, a partner in Nixon's New York law firm, and an "outside" advisor parked at the time in Washington a half block from the White House even before he joined the nascent Nixon administration in June 1969. As trusted confidants, both worked the inner machinery of the fledgling bureaucracy to perfection but knew they needed a competent someone with connections, organizational skills, and stewardship to organize a concert for someone as worthy as Ellington in two short months. Enter Willis Conover.

For the previous fourteen and a half years, as a consultant to the State Department, Conover had broadcast music twice daily, six days a week, worldwide, via the Voice of America. He was well known to President Nixon—indeed, literally, to the world—as the voice of American music, the voice of jazz. Appropriately, in 1967, Conover was selected to chair the jazz panel for the newly created National Endowment for the Arts. He had also produced musical events for radio and TV, and concerts at established venues and festivals; at the time of the Duke tribute, he was producing the New Orleans Jazz Festival.[42]

All the pieces were in place; it was time to launch the plan.

Thursday, February 13. In a memo to Chief of Staff H. R. Haldeman, McWhorter wrote,

> On April 29, Duke Ellington will celebrate his [seventieth] birthday. I think it would be a good idea if the president would have some kind of social affair at the White House in Duke's honor . . . I don't have to spell out the advantages that might come from such an event. I already mentioned this to Garment, but I thought you might want to give some thought to the suggestion and, if it makes sense to you, start the ball rolling.[43]

Saturday, February 15. McWhorter wisely copied Appointment Secretary Dwight Chapin on the Haldeman memo. In turn, Chapin sent a memo to his boss, Domestic Advisor John Ehrlichman, seeking his thoughts on the matter and adding a few of his own:

> As you may recall, Ellington has been a Nixon supporter in the past and was during the 1968 campaign. [And the Democrats thought he was in their camp!] Perhaps a White House dinner is in order for one of the kings of American music . . . [Social Secretary] Lucy [Winchester] feels it has a lot going for it also.[44]

Ehrlichman responded with an enthusiastic "Yes!"

Several days after the plan was set in motion, four key players had been briefed and brought on board. Would a presidential seal of approval soon follow?

Thursday, February 20. In a lengthy letter to Lucy Winchester outlining his case to become a part-time White House impresario, Willis Conover gave prominent mention to the Ellington birthday tribute. The letter closed with "I'd appreciate you discussing these ideas with Leonard Garment and Charles McWhorter."[45]

Monday, February 24. Sometime during the previous week, possibly Friday according to Haldeman's diary, the president signed off on the April 29 function.[46] He also approved of Conover, whom he had known in his capacity as vice president in the Eisenhower administration, and authorized him to line up and present the talent for the evening's entertainment. A better choice could not have been made. A close friend of Duke's for several decades, Conover had organized Ellington's first concert in Washington, DC, in 1946 and had interviewed him numerous times on the VOA.

And you can bet your top *and* bottom dollars that once the Ellington proposal reached the president, he gave it an immediate and enthusiastic thumbs-up. He was ready. He had prepared for such an offer. For over a decade, he had given serious thought to what the social policy of his administration would be once in office.

As vice president for eight years, he had witnessed a parade of mainstream entertainers brought to the mansion by President Eisenhower and First Lady Mamie. Out of office, he watched the media fawn over the grand doings at Camelot presided over by President John F. Kennedy and First Lady Jacqueline. Even the subsequent Johnson administration, against expectation, staged a raft of social events at the White House that drew critical praise. The social events bar had been set high, Nixon knew it, and he was determined to scale the bar. He would personally oversee all aspects of White House entertainment, pay attention to the details, limit the courses, pick the wine, select the entertainers and the numbers they would perform, and oversee the guest list. It was political. An unforgettable well-staged White House event was a means to reward his supporters, encourage their future support, and occasionally turn fence sitters into supporters.

In his first month in office, he established the unprecedented Sunday worship service, laid down the rules to staff on how entertainers should be selected, and tapped (unknown to staff at the time) a trusted outsider, Robert Sarnoff, to prepare a list of suitable entertainers.

Turn down a seventieth-birthday celebration for Duke Ellington? Absolutely not! What better way to trump the grandiosity of the JFK Camelot years than with a celebratory affair for a true American original, and the second most widely admired living African American musician (second only to Louis Armstrong). Honoring the Duke would be seen in the media in the same light as JFK's centerpiece: cellist Pablo Casals's triumphant return to the White House in 1961. And the honorarium: It would not be a fancy scroll or university degree as Willis Conover would suggest, but the Presidential Medal of Freedom. Hadn't JFK awarded the first modern-era Medal of Freedom to Pablo Casals? Hadn't LBJ awarded the first to a composer, Aaron Copland?

McWhorter did not have to point out the possible benefits of such a celebration to the ultimate political utilitarian. He knew what impact it would have on the media and the African American community. Other factors figured into the president's flash acceptance. He would prevail upon Ellington to make additional overseas tours on behalf of the State Department. The band had toured South Asia and the Middle East for JFK in 1963 and performed at a festival in Senegal for LBJ in 1966. Both trips had received excellent reviews. ("Duke Ellington conquered," reported the *New York Times*. "His smash performances clearly established the United States as the [Senegal] festival favorite.") The USIA had even produced documentary films of both tours for distribution overseas. The country could use a popular cultural ambassador like Duke, the president must have thought, to show the vitality of American democracy through a successful, highly creative African American, and to counter Soviet propaganda and U.S. commercial media news that focused on U.S. civil rights abuses of its minority citizens.

To double down on this bet, the USIA could make a documentary film of Ellington's big night at the White House and distribute it overseas to be seen by millions of people. What better way to add balance to the commercial news media perspective seen by overseas audiences? What better way for the president to enhance his image overseas?

On the domestic side of politics, Nixon had to view the Ellington event as more than just one-upping JFK and LBJ on the social event scale. He also likely saw it as an opportunity to cultivate Ellington, lure him out of the Democrats' camp. LBJ had invited Duke to eight White House functions (he attended five, performed at four). Nixon knew this, maybe not about all eight events, but a number of them. Moreover, LBJ had appointed Duke to the National Council of the Arts. Maneuvering Ellington into the Republican fold would be quite a coup. Lionel Hampton and Pearl Bailey, two other prominent African American jazz musicians, had already joined the Republican side. Why not the Duke? It must have been a tempting thought.

"I don't have to spell out the advantages that might come from such an event," political operative Charles McWhorter stated in his kickoff memorandum to Chief of Staff H. R. Haldeman. Perhaps the most important of these would be the opportunity to improve the president's image among African Americans—an image that had been tarnished in the run up to the election the previous year. Awarding the nation's highest honor to one of most revered figures in the African American community, Nixon hoped, would be seen as his administration's reaching out to black America, or in White House "zigzag" policy parlance—a racial justice "zig" to accompany a southern strategy "zag."

At this juncture, with the executive decision made, no one knew exactly what was going to take place. But if it was up to the president, as chief aide Haldeman noted in his diary: *P planning dinner for Duke Ellington's birthday, wants to have "all the jazz greats, like Guy Lombardo—oh well!"*[46]

Lucy Winchester telephoned Conover at his Manhattan residence and requested his attendance at a kickoff meeting in her office with McWhorter and others on Wednesday, February 26. In advance of the meeting, Conover jotted down his thoughts in a letter to Lucy on a range of issues, including which guests should and should not be invited, and the honorarium Duke should receive: a presidential medal of some sort, a university degree, or a fancy scroll. On the after-dinner entertainment, he had a suggestion:

The Modern Jazz Quartet [MJQ] playing Ellington standards for a seated audience in the East Room, followed by Ella Fitzgerald and her trio doing Ellington songs, probably with Ellington joining her at the piano when urged by the president and first lady.[47]

This would not come to pass, although the MJQ would get their White House gig later in the year, on October 21.

Tuesday, March 26. One month after the kickoff meeting, producer Conover updated the principals on his progress: "The program [that] I plan: about [forty-five] minutes, divided more or less equally between instrumental and vocal music, all composed by Ellington."

He put forth a list of nine musicians; only five of them would perform on April 29. Of interest to music fans, Lena Horne is penciled in as vocalist (she didn't make it). Bold as ever, Conover waded into guest-list waters:

Mr. Ellington submitted a hefty guest list for the White House approval. [Nixon's secretary] Rose [Woods] has the list. Question: Can President and Mrs. Nixon's own guest list, on this occasion, be a bit shorter than usual in order to accommodate as many as possible of Mr. Ellington's close friends, family, and professional peers?[48]

Mr. Ellington had indeed submitted a hefty guest list to the White House, numbering ninety-nine guests for the dinner and another thirty-five for the after-dinner party (as shown in appendices 7 and 8). And wouldn't you know it, in one of the few instances on record, the leader of the free world acquiesced to the demands of his guest of honor and impresario. The guests attending the festivities on the night of April 29 were overwhelmingly Ellington picks, especially for the dinner, where three-quarters of the guests (or sixty of the eighty-two) owed their seat in the State Dining Room to Duke. At the after-dinner party, the attendees were more or less evenly split between the honoree and the president. The administration was still young, and the president and his West Wing staff had not yet gained full control of the invitation process. Advantage Duke.

Saturday, April 19. Some three weeks after Conover's last update, the jazz all-stars had been lined up. In a memo to his fourteen performing musicians (copies to Garment, McWhorter, and Winchester), he summarized the situation:

1. Rehearsal, Wednesday, April 23, at a Manhattan studio

2. White House dress: tails and white tie (floor-length dress for women)

3. Book your own flight to DC on board American Airlines, 12:30 p.m., Tuesday, April 29

4. No money for anything except hotel accommodations (and transportation from the airport to the hotel)

Conover then put the event into perspective:

This whole affair is a well-deserved tribute to Duke Ellington. Whether or not any political mileage is gained is unimportant: whatever your political leanings the office of the presidency is both important and prestigious, and it is being focused favorably on an American musician. That musician is very happy about it. I am, too, and I believe you are. Your participation will cost you time and some money. I hope you feel it's worth it now; I believe you'll feel it was worth it afterwards.

The program will not be a jazz concert per se, because Ellington is being saluted, not as a jazz musician, but as a composer and a major figure. Hence the program is of Ellington's songs, played for him by other respected musicians who happen to be jazz musicians, too. This doesn't mean nobody will blow; it just means the emphasis in this case should be more toward illuminating and interpreting the material, rather than using the material as a point of departure for the kind of advanced musical exploration that a different audience (a jazz festival audience, for example) would expect.

To put it differently, please don't feel you're under any wraps. Solo as you wish, but please proceed from a basic understanding of what the program is intended to be: a recognizable tribute to the composer. After the program ends, then follow any musical aims you wish.[49]

Conover's memo (from the penultimate paragraph above at "Ellington") found its way into the African American *Chicago Daily Defender* two days after the event, described thus: "Conover's memo to the performers was a classic in setting the purpose of the occasion."[50] The memo could have been given to the *Defender* by anyone, no need to speculate.

Two months after the president authorized his designated impresario to organize the birthday tribute, Conover had locked down the particulars and forwarded them to the White House, where they were approved on behalf of the president. All was in order. Another chapter in jazz history was about to be written.

Cellist Pablo Casals stands before President and Mrs. Kennedy in the East Room of the White House at the conclusion of a concert for Governor and Mrs. Luis Munoz Marin of Puerto Rico on November 13, 1961. The executive mansion had never seen such a gathering of prominent musicians: composers Samuel Barber, Elliot Carter, Aaron Copland, Gian Carlo Menotti, along with world-renown orchestral conductors Leopold Stokowski, Eugene Ormandy, and Leonard Bernstein. Soon after this well-lauded event, the concert was broadcast to the nation over several radio networks (a White House first). Several months later, the concert was available to the general public on a Columbia Records LP (another White House first).

President Nixon set out to match (or trump) this signature Kennedy social event with his seventieth-birthday tribute to Duke Ellington. Most agreed he succeeded.

The all-stars gathered around President Nixon at the close of the concert. Back riser, *left to right*: Dave Brubeck (*p*), Hank Jones (*p*), Jim Hall (*g*), Paul Desmond (*as*), and Gerry Mulligan (*bs*). Front riser, *left to right*: Tom Whaley (*c*), Earl Hines (*p*), Billy Taylor (*p*), Mary Mayo (*v*), Milt Hinton (*b, behind Mayo*), Willis Conover (*tribute programmer, behind Nixon*), Duke Ellington (*p*), Clark Terry (*tp, behind Duke*), Joe Williams (*v*), Urbie Green (*tb*), J. J. Johnson (*tb*), and Bill Berry (*tp*). Louis Bellson not pictured.

CHAPTER 4

The Jazz All-Stars

I N SHORT ORDER, WILLIS CONOVER assembled an outstanding group of jazz musicians from a limited pool of available talent within the immediate environs of New York City. The all-star band for the White House tribute to Duke Ellington consisted of a four-piece rhythm section and a six-horn frontline, complemented by two singers, three guest pianists, and a conductor.

A Stellar Rhythm Section

Conover selected Hank Jones (piano), Jim Hall (guitar), Milt Hinton (bass), and Louis Bellson (drums) to provide the band's rhythm underpinnings. Although not exactly household names at that particular time, all four players were well known and highly regarded in the jazz community. Their public profiles have risen considerably since then, each subsequently acknowledged as a National Endowment for the Arts (NEA) Jazz Master—the nation's third highest honor for jazz, the second being a National Medal of Arts and the first a Presidential Medal of Freedom.

HANK JONES

A member of the famous jazz family that includes brothers Thad (cornet) and Elvin (drums), Hank Jones grew up listening to virtuoso pianists Earl "Fatha" Hines, Fats Waller, and Art Tatum before he embraced the bebop style in the 1940s. He became a Jazz at the Philharmonic mainstay (1940s), an accompanist for singers like Ella Fitzgerald (1950s), a CBS staff musician in New York City (1960s–1970s), and the pianist on a thousand and one record dates. From the 1970s on, Jones became widely regarded as the dean of jazz pianists through his recordings in the trio and duo format, and by his career-topping National Medal of Arts bestowed by President George W. Bush in 2008, followed by a Grammy Lifetime Achievement Award in 2009.[1]

JIM HALL

Jazz guitarist Jim Hall's technique has been called subtle, his sound mellow, and his compositions understated. His name would appear on any top-ten jazz guitar list that could possibly be assembled. He came to the fore in two of the fabled West Coast chamber groups of the 1950s: the Chico Hamilton Quintet and the Jimmy Giuffre 3. He next appeared on *The Bridge* (RCA Victor, 1962), where his classic guitar runs perfectly meshed with Sonny Rollins's fiery tenor saxophone solos. In the 1960s, Hall collaborated with trumpeter Art Farmer and alto saxophonist Paul Desmond before he eventually formed his own trio in 1965, which became a mainstay of his performing and recording career. His influence on the current crop of jazz guitarists—Bill Frisell and Pat Metheny, for example—is said to be immense.[2]

MILT HINTON

Bassist Milt Hinton's career spanned the early swing days of the 1930s with Cab Calloway through the end of the twentieth century with the new guard of jazz, such as reedman Branford Marsalis and bassist Christian McBride. In the early 1950s, Hinton became a staff musician for CBS, one of the first African American musicians welcomed in the TV studios. Adept at different styles of playing, from pop to jazz, he would amass the largest catalog in recorded history. In 2001, he was inducted into the *DownBeat* Jazz Hall of Fame, only the third bassist to be so honored. Hinton was invited back to the White House two more times during Nixon's term in the company of singer Pearl Bailey.[3]

Louis Bellson

Referred to by Duke Ellington as "not only the world's greatest drummer . . . [but also] the world's greatest musician," Louis Bellson has performed on more than two hundred albums, working with Ellington (twice: 1952–53 and 1965–66), Count Basie, Benny Goodman, Louis Armstrong, and Lionel Hampton. Bellson also worked with many vocalists, including Ella Fitzgerald, Sarah Vaughan, Tony Bennett, and wife Pearl Bailey. He accompanied Pearl at her second Nixon White House appearance in 1974.[4]

The Preeminent Frontline

Willis Conover assembled an all-star frontline of two saxophones (altoist Paul Desmond and baritonist Gerry Mulligan), two trombone players (Urbie Green and J. J. Johnson), and two trumpeters, both Ellington alumni (Bill Berry and Clark Terry). Four of the six have been inducted into the *DownBeat* Hall of Fame (all but Berry and Green), and two of the six (Johnson and Terry) are NEA Jazz Masters.

Paul Desmond

The yin to pianist Dave Brubeck's yang in the long-running classic Brubeck Quartet, alto saxophonist Paul Desmond became one of the world's best-known jazz musicians, as much for his lyrical playing as for his famous composition "Take Five." During the quartet's whirlwind days (1951–67), Desmond found time to record with drummer Connie Kay and fellow all-stars guitarist Jim Hall and baritone saxophonist Gerry Mulligan—*Two of a Mind* (Bluebird, 2003) was perhaps the best. After the 1967 breakup of the quartet, Desmond made few appearances and recordings, but then picked up the pace in the mid-1970s, recording for the CTI label and forming his own group before rejoining Brubeck for a twenty-fifth anniversary tour of the classic Brubeck Quartet, his last major gig before his death the following year. In jazz lore, he will be remembered as one of the great stylists on alto saxophone.[5]

GERRY MULLIGAN

Paired with Desmond on the all-star frontline was another esteemed saxophonist of modern jazz: baritone master Gerry "Jeru" Mulligan, a key figure in the catalytic Miles Davis *Birth of the Cool* sessions. Throughout the 1950s and into the 1960s, he led a piano-less quartet (first with Chet Baker on trumpet, then others) that made him famous, dividing the rest of his time between performing solo at countless festivals and concerts and forming and playing with large and small groups. From 1968 to the mid-1970s, he toured occasionally with Brubeck as an "extra added attraction."

For the next two decades, Mulligan organized bands large, medium, and small while also touring and recording. Though an accomplished composer, arranger, and bandleader, Mulligan is mostly remembered for his exploits on the baritone saxophone. His style on the instrument, seemingly fully formed by age twenty, was light in tone but could plumb bottom notes at will.[6]

URBIE GREEN

Largely self-taught, trombonist Urbie Green began his professional career in the late 1940s at age twenty. He took over Bill Harris's trombone chair in Woody Herman's Third Herd in 1948, and by 1954, a year after arriving in New York City, he had established himself as one of the top trombonists in the Big Apple, working on and off with Benny Goodman (1955–57) and Count Basie (1963) before fronting the Tommy Dorsey "nostalgia" band (1966–67). In the 1970s, he led his own big band on the road and in the studio, while during the 1980s and beyond, he remained active but recorded less. Green's trombone sounds smooth, warm, and mellow, and adapts to almost any musical situation, which accounts for his appearance on more than 275 recordings (making him, it is said, the most recorded trombonist of all time).[7]

J. J. JOHNSON

Often referred to as the "Charlie Parker of the trombone" due to his uncanny musical diversity and fluency, J. J. Johnson dominated his instrument for over forty years. He was a perennial jazz magazine poll winner for his peerless playing even during years when he made no records or club or festival dates. Early on, he gigged with Count Basie (1945–46), worked briefly with beboppers Dizzy Gillespie and bassist Oscar Pettiford, then formed the seminal two-trombone group with Kai Winding: the Jay and Kai Quintet (1954–56). In the late 1950s, he began to gain recognition as a composer, receiving commissions for extended works from the Monterey Jazz Festival and Dizzy Gillespie while still gigging with the likes of Miles Davis and Clark Terry. In 1970, J. J. moved to California and immersed himself in lucrative film and television scoring, returning seventeen years later to playing, touring, and recording.[8]

BILL BERRY

After a ten-year apprenticeship, trumpeter-cornetist Bill "Beez" Berry graduated to Woody Herman's thundering herd in 1957. Endless touring followed before Berry secured a position with the New York–based Maynard Ferguson band. In 1961 he landed a coveted spot in the Duke Ellington Orchestra, becoming the "modern" trumpet soloist in Duke's band and the second white man the maestro hired, Louis Bellson being the first. Beez left the Ellington organization in 1964 and joined the Merv Griffin TV show band in New York (his day job), moonlighting with the Thad Jones/Mel Lewis band (1966–68). When *The Merv Griffin Show* (and Berry) moved to California, he formed the L.A. Big Band with a raft of star soloists that proceeded to blow up a West Coast storm for years.[9]

CLARK TERRY

Starting in 1945, Clark "CT" Terry played with a variety of big bands before joining Count Basie's big band (1948–51). For the next nine years, he performed in Duke Ellington's band, soloing on trumpet *and* flugelhorn, effectively introducing the latter instrument to modern jazz. After working with Quincy Jones (1959–60), CT became a member of the Johnny Carson *Tonight Show* orchestra—one of the first African American musicians in a TV house band. He came to prominence through his popular "Mumbles" persona, his unique way of mumbling a scat vocal solo. Through the 1960s, he and valve trombonist Bob Brookmeyer co-led a quintet, and then beginning in 1972, Terry fronted his own Big Bad Band. Terry has established a singular, immediately identifiable sound. "Two bars and you know it's CT," Gary Giddins enthused. One of the earliest practitioners to take time off from the road to enter the classroom, conducting numerous clinics and jazz camps, CT received a Grammy Lifetime Achievement Award in 2010.[10]

Three Acclaimed Pianists

Conover included three "guest" pianists for both content and scheduling reasons—that is, to cover as much Ellington material as possible and to give the all-star band a break.

DAVE BRUBECK

Dave Brubeck is known for his experiments with odd time signatures, improvised counterpoint, and a distinctive harmonic approach. In 1951 pianist Brubeck formed a quartet with saxophonist Paul Desmond and began touring the college circuit. Popularity and a *Time* magazine cover followed in 1954—the first jazz musician to be so honored. In 1959 the classic Brubeck Quartet, with Desmond, Eugene Wright (bass), and Joe Morello (drums), recorded an experiment in time signatures: *Time Out*. Two tunes from that million seller—"Blue Rondo à la Turk" and "Take Five"—appeared on jukeboxes throughout the world and can be heard to this very day on a variety of music players. After the classic quartet disbanded in 1967, Brubeck explored integrating jazz and classical music, occasionally returning to the quartet setting with a variety of musicians, including his three sons. He received a Grammy Lifetime Achievement Award in 1996, a National Medal of Arts in 1999, and a Kennedy Center Honoree tribute in 2009.[11]

EARL HINES

The stars *and* planets had to be aligned on the night of the Ellington tribute. In town for a gig at Blues Alley—a prominent jazz spot in nearby Georgetown—was none other than the father of modern jazz piano, Earl "Fatha" Hines. Conover wisely put him on the bill. Hines announced himself to the world at the same time Louis Armstrong did: on the seminal Hot Five and Hot Seven records of 1928. While Satch packed his horn and figuratively circumnavigated the globe spreading the new jazz gospel, Fatha stayed at home leading a first-rate band at Chicago's Grand Terrace for two decades (1928–48). Fatha rejoined Louis for three years, 1948–51, before falling into relative obscurity that lasted for over a decade until critically acclaimed concerts at the Little Theater in New York City revived his career. Repudiating F. Scott Fitzgerald's axiom that there are no second chances in American lives, Hines commenced a nonstop whirlwind of record dates, concerts, and club appearances for the next fifteen years, all to near-universal praise.[12]

BILLY TAYLOR

Although Billy "BT" Taylor is well known for his tireless promotion of jazz as an educator and broadcaster, along with being highly respected for his tasteful, nonintrusive accompaniment as a sideman, he *is* an exceptional pianist in his own right. Obviously beholden to the 1930s piano giants Fats Waller and Art Tatum, but filtered through the prism of bebop pianist innovator Bud Powell, Taylor fashioned a two-handed orchestral style that has "a solid sense of continuity, a commitment to swing for the fences, and a true jazz ear for harmony." He was invited back to the White House two more times during the Nixon presidential years: as musical director for the David Frost Christmas Show and with his own trio to entertain a visiting head of state. Curiously but deservedly, BT received a *DownBeat* Lifetime Achievement Award in 1984. Curious because Taylor's advocacy on behalf of jazz had only begun—it would continue for another three decades and include a seventeen-year stint as artistic director for jazz at the Kennedy Center in Washington, DC.[13]

A Pair of Gifted Singers

MARY MAYO

Though unfamiliar to the public, vocalist Mary Mayo was well known within the New York recording scene as a top-notch session singer. Gifted with a four-octave range, she sang with the post–World War II version of the Glenn Miller Orchestra. After moving to the Big Apple, she ghosted on "original cast" albums of numerous Broadway musicals and sang in a short-lived jazz vocal combo. Mayo gained some notoriety with the 1963 novelty album *Moon Gas* with jazz pianist Dick Hyman, which featured her ethereal, wordless vocals. Her one truly noteworthy credited appearance, which she herself considered the high point of her musical career, would in fact be the Ellington seventieth-birthday gala.[14]

JOE WILLIAMS

His versatile baritone voice made Joe Williams one of the signature male vocalists in jazz annals, responsible for some of the Count Basie band's main hits in the 1950s: "Alright, Okay, You Win," "The Comeback," and what would become one of his most requested tunes, "Every Day." The classic *Count Basie Swings, Joe Williams Sings* (Verve, 1956) album from that period was ranked seventeenth all-time favorite jazz vocal album by jazz singers in a *DownBeat* magazine June 2004 poll. Starting in the 1960s, Williams was a vocal soloist fronting various piano trios. He continued to expand his range, becoming a superior crooner and exhibiting a real depth of feeling on ballads. Recognition of this growth came in

1974 when Joe won *DownBeat's* Critics Poll as best male vocalist—winning nearly every year thereafter for more than a decade. His stature as a polished and complete singer came in 1993 when he received the NEA Jazz Master Award.[15]

The First-Rate Conductor

Tom Whaley

And to conduct the band and singers, Conover made a sterling choice in Tom Whaley, the one living person (other than Ellington) closest to the maestro's music. In 1941, Duke hired Whaley, a Boston-bred pianist and conductor to serve as the band's main copyist. Except for a short absence in 1950, he would remain with Ellington until the maestro's death.[16]

Afternoon Press Conference

As for the band's arrangements, Conover told the press at the afternoon briefing prior to the event that they were the work of all-stars Mulligan, Bellson, and Whaley, with help from Dick Cary, Jack Hayes, Marty Paich, and Al Ham (Mary Mayo's husband). No one knows, though, who did what in each instance.

Ellington, who had come to the White House to practice on the eleven-foot grand piano in the East Room, stopped by the afternoon press conference and perfunctorily ran down some of his past achievements: pioneering the movie house circuit for big bands (not just black ones but all bands) and breaking the color barrier at the Hurricane Club in the 1930s; regularizing the concert stage for jazz with his 1940s Carnegie Hall concerts; and championing civil rights long before it was popular with his theatrical forays, *Jump for Joy* in the 1950s and *My People* in the 1960s.[17] He answered a few questions as well. How did the maestro come by his royal moniker? "I had a pal here in Washington and he was a pretty fancy kid, and he felt for me to have his constant companionship, I should have a title. I became the Duke." When did he first sit down at the piano? "Twelve, I think," Duke answered. "I took piano lessons like all kids do. But most of the time when my mother wanted me to practice, I was out in the street playing baseball, stickball, throwing bricks at cops.

"Painting was my first interest. I even had a sign shop when I got started in music. If someone came in to get a sign for a dance, I'd say, 'Who's doing your music.' If they came in to ask me to play, I'd say, 'Who's doing your signs?' I was pretty smart. Before I left [Washington], I was sending out four or five bands and I had a house and a car."

How does being seventy affect your composing? Playing? "What's age got to do with music? I don't believe in the generation gap. I believe in regeneration gaps. Each day you regenerate, or else you're not living." And how does he maintain the grueling performance schedule? Clean living? Jogging? "Hey, that's good," Duke said, laughing. "The only thing I do outdoors is concerts."

Before leaving the White House, Duke sat for one more interview with Harold Boxer of the VOA, patiently answering questions the master composer had answered many, many times before on jazz, improvisation, and composition. (See appendix 10 for Duke's views on these matters on the day of his seventieth birthday.) Afternoon business complete, Duke headed back to the hotel to prepare for the evening's festivities.

Lastly, the stars, planets, *and* galaxies were aligned the night of the event. The entire concert was not only recorded but made available to the American public, albeit belatedly, in 2002 on Blue Note Records: *1969 All-Star White House Tribute to Duke Ellington*. While some may not be surprised that the concert was recorded—Nixon, after all, famously taped nearly all his Oval Office conversations—it is the only Nixon-era White House performance offered commercially.

Moreover, and even more significant, the event was filmed for television news broadcasts by the networks, and for an overseas documentary by the USIA, both of which can now be viewed by the public. The three-minute next-day TV broadcasts can be seen at select libraries across the United States (Library of Congress in Washington, DC, for example) that carry the Vanderbilt Television Archive Service. The seventeen-minute USIA documentary *Ellington at the White House* can be seen at the Nixon Library in Yorba Linda, California; the National Archives in College Park, Maryland; and at the Library of Congress.

Several days before the festivities, the social secretary's office briefed selected media outlets around the country about the event to come (one way to ensure coverage the day after). A great lead appeared atop the Newsmakers column in the *Los Angeles Times* on April 28:

It's not just every night that pianist-conductor Duke Ellington comes to your home for dinner. And the squire of 1600 Pennsylvania Ave., Washington, DC, said he was "looking forward" to the event, scheduled for Tuesday night. After all, he's a pianist himself. But President Nixon admitted he had no plans to "sit in" on the after-dinner jam session in the State Dining Room. He conceded he is more of a classical music fan than a jazz bug; he doesn't understand anything too offbeat. But "Ellington—I dig him. He's my generation."[18]

The twenty-four-piece Marine Band under the direction of Colonel Albert F. Schoepper (who also served as a White House music consultant) greeted arriving dinner guests in the Cross Hall with appropriate selections from the Ellington songbook.

CHAPTER 5

The Banquet

THE BIG NIGHT ARRIVED.[1] PHOTOGRAPHERS and film crews gathered at the ground-level diplomatic entrance to record the arrival of the invitees. The guest of honor and his sister, both elegantly attired with Ruth sporting a long, flowing blonde wig, perfunctorily stopped for the cameras, smiled, waved, and moved on.

Duke had made a most appropriate choice for his female companion for the evening—a family intimate and a close business associate as well.[2] Ruth still ran Tempo Music, as she had since Ellington established the publishing company in 1940 for his music (and his composing partner Billy Strayhorn's music as well). Increasingly in the 1960s, however, she had also become involved in Duke Ellington Inc.—the management company originally established with Irving Mills in 1927 to handle the bands bookings, promotion, salaries, and travel arrangements. Neither Duke's wife (and mother of Mercer), separated from Duke for over four decades, nor his long-term romantic partner, Evie Ellis, whom he visited in their shared Harlem apartment a few weeks a year, would have made sense, nor would have any of the anonymous women Duke saw occasionally on the road.[3] It was to be a close family night for the Duke.

Once inside, the pair was swiftly escorted to the second floor of the White House, where waiters attended to their refreshment needs. When asked what he wanted to drink, Duke asked for his usual "coke with sugar," and the mansion staff, though a mite baffled, delivered.[4] After Duke and Ruth were received by President and Mrs. Nixon and Vice President and Mrs. Agnew, the host gave them the grand tour of the family quarters. Referring back to an earlier remark the president had made at his inaugural ball ("As Duke Ellington would say, it don't mean a thing if it ain't got that swing"), the maestro chanced a question: "Mr. President, when you said that, did it imply that you were one of those graceful jitterbugs who used to inspire all the jazz bands down at the Rendezvous Ballroom at Balboa Beach in California—Stan Kenton's old home base?"

"No, Duke. I have never really been a dancer. I'm a watcher."

But from there, our new president went on to show us that he did have a genuine interest in music of the American idiom. While taking us around various rooms on the family's floor, he led us into one where there was an expensive stereo machine with many records and tapes. He proceeded to demonstrate all the audio possibilities—increasing the bass and the treble, one after the other, and showing how well the range was maintained at full and low volume. He was just like a kid with a new toy.[5]

Meanwhile, the dinner guests, consisting of mostly Ellington picks, were gathering in the Cross Hall as the twenty-four-piece Marine Band played appropriate Ellington selections under the direction of Colonel Albert F. Schoepper (who also served as a White House music consultant). There were Ellington's son, Mercer, and his daughter-in-law, his two grandchildren, and a nephew. There, too, were three of the people Duke most relied upon: Dr. Arthur Logan, his physician; Harry Carney, baritone saxophonist with the Ellington band for over forty years; and Thomas L. Whaley, copyist and conductor, with the band for twenty-eight years. In addition to a gaggle of government officials, there were a sizable number of Ellington friends and jazz-friendly clergy, and a formidable cross-section of the music profession, including songwriter Harold Arlen, Mrs. Count Basie (her husband on tour), Dave Brubeck, composer Richard Rodgers, and bandleaders Cab Calloway, Billy Eckstine, Dizzy Gillespie, and Benny Goodman. (See appendix 9 for the complete eighty-two-person dinner guest list.)

At 8:05, as planned, the president and first lady made a grand descent down the grand staircase with Duke and his sister. They paused for photographs one step from the lower landing. Mrs. Nixon wore a seafoam green lace gown by her dressmaker Countess Alexander of New York. Blond-wigged Ruth Ellington wore a Lilli Rubin outfit of beaded chiffon with a green chiffon coat. Fortunately, their different shades of green did not clash.

Top aide Haldeman, who would later characterize the evening as unbelievable, jotted in his diary: *High point was Duke's sister, who came down the stairs with him and the Nixons, in long flowing blonde hair.*[6] The *Chicago Daily Defender* reported that people were talking about the blonde-on-blonde images of Pat Nixon and Ruth Ellington as they posed for pictures with the president and the honoree.[7] Ruth's tresses flowed down her neck and dipped low over her forehead. All of this was accentuated by a long jeweled cigarette holder. Friends probably took no mind, the *Defender* surmised. They had come to expect tasteful sartorial statements from Ruth, who often attended classy Manhattan functions in support of Duke's interests. Like her brother, she was a nonconformist in her dress, but always elegantly so.

The four of them—Nixon and his wife, Duke and his sister—then proceeded to the Grand Hall and paused facing the East Room. The Marine Band played "Ruffles and Flourishes" and the presidential party was announced. As "Hail to the Chief" played, the principals moved into the East Room and stood on a reception line to welcome the guests. Ellington delayed the passage to the State Dining Room slightly by bestowing on each of his intimates four kisses, two on each cheek, according to his custom. Haldeman took note of this high point as well: *Duke kissed all the men twice, on each cheek (mother's kiss) as they went through the receiving line.* Nixon also took notice, and in between greeting the guests, he turned to Duke and asked, "Four kisses? Why four?"

"One for each cheek, Mr. President."

"Oh."

Duke later recalled that after the line had passed, "to my amazement, he turned to me, and I turned to him, and without a word being said, we exchanged four kisses. He seemed pleased. 'Now I am a member?' he asked.

'Yes, Mr. President, you are a member.'"[8]

The guests had been escorted out of the East Room to their places in the State Dining Room, and the presidential party followed suit. Inside, the company was seated at eleven round tables, seven or eight to a table, husbands and wives separated from one another. As for the seating of the guests (shown in detail on pages 76–77), the man in charge, head of the Social Entertainments Office, Sanford "Sandy" Fox (with input from Social Secretary Lucy Winchester) achieved a nominally balanced arrangement for eighty-four diners.[9]

According to the usual protocol, Sandy had spread the government officials around the State Dining Room, one each at seven tables, with two at four tables (spouses assuming the official mantle for the evening). Clergy and their spouses had been similarly dispersed, one each at seven tables, two at two tables; likewise Art Institute heads, one each at six, two at another table. In addition, Fox managed to seat guests reasonably well to the familiar "man-woman" pattern, achieving perfection at four tables and nearly so at five, with three alternate sex pairs each, no easy task given nine extra men.

Musicians and their spouses were scattered about the room, their placement obviously not a priority. Both the president and first lady, however, got more than their fair share of musical celebrities, three and four respectively, which no doubt accounted for the lively discussion at their tables.

The Ellington event posed a social challenge unlike any other in White House history up until that point. African Americans made up one-third of those to be seated (twenty-nine of eighty-four). Attention had to be paid to their distribution around the room. Fox certainly would have taken this into account in preparing the seating chart he submitted to the president and first lady for their review (a standard practice for Nixon and the two preceding administrations, according to Fox). The result was an irregular distribution across the room, but a reasonable one that would not likely draw too much attention to itself and be leaked to the press (and wasn't). Six tables seated three or more African Americans, with four at the first lady's table and five at the president's (which might have raised some eyebrows).

The only known modification to Fox's seating plan involved the president's table. African American gospel diva Mahalia Jackson seat was switched with that of Mrs. Edward R. Dudley, wife of a then sitting New York Supreme Court judge and, interestingly, the first black U.S. ambassador (Liberia 1949–1953). The rationale for the switch is unknown. Perhaps someone thought Mrs. Dudley's original table was lacking a musician.

As for the table decorations, the Johnson china and Vermeil flatware of the previous administration sat upon yellow tablecloths with embroidered organdy covers. The floral centerpieces on each table included yellow roses, yellow and white Marguerite daisies, Duchess spoon chrysanthemums, orange and white carnations, blue cornflowers, white sweet peas, gypsophila, orange lilies, and yellow, orange, and white snapdragons.[10]

With Ruth Ellington on his right, the president was joined by, among others, Benny Goodman, soul singer Lou Rawls, and trumpeter Dizzy Gillespie, the last of whom took the opportunity to speak to Nixon on several matters. He brought up economic conditions in South Carolina, where he was born, and the difficulties musicians were having getting royalties from the jukebox industry.

Dinner Seating Arrangement

Table 1

Ms. Gaye Ellington
Mr. Roger L. Stevens   Mr. Thomas Patterson
Mr. Stephen D. James   **1**   Rev. John Yaryan*
Mrs. John G. Gensel*   Mrs. Cab Calloway
Rep. Donald Rumsfeld^

Table 2

Mrs. John Yaryan*
Mr. John H. Johnson   Mr. Billy Eckstine
Mrs. Leslie Diamond   **2**   Mrs. Lou Rawls
Mr. Richard Rodgers   Mr. Duke Ellington
First Lady Pat Nixon^

Table 3

Mr. Otto Preminger
Mrs. Ethel Rich   Mrs. David Brubeck
Mr. Mercer Ellington   **3**   Rev. N. J. O'Connor*
Mrs. Richard Rodgers   Mrs. Harold Arlen
Vice President Spiro Agnew^

Table 4

Mr. Sigmund Galloway
Mr. Leslie Diamond   Mrs. Arthur Logan
Mrs. Robert Finch^   **4**   Mr. Harry Carney
Mr. John Walker III   Mrs. C. Julian Bartlett*

Table 5

Mrs. Bryant Kirkland
Atty. Gen. John Mitchell^   Mr. Edward Ellington II
Mrs. John Walker III   **5**   Mr. Bernard Flynn
Judge Edward R. Dudley   Mrs. Stanley Dance
Rev. John G. Gensel*

*Clergy
^Government official or spouse

Mr. Charles McWhorter

Mrs. John Mitchell^   Mrs. Willis Conover

Rev. C. Julian Bartlett*   **6**   Mr. Frank Shakespeare^

Mrs. Roger L. Stevens   Mrs. Mercer Ellington

Mr. Cab Calloway

Mrs. Benny Goodman

Mr. Harold Arlen   Mr. S. Dillon Ripley III

Mrs. Spiro Agnew^   **7**   Mrs. Billy Eckstine

Judge Thomas Weaver   Rev. Horace Donegan*

Labor Sec. George Schultz^

Mrs. Harry Carney   Mrs. William Basie

Rev. Harold Weicker*   **8**   Mr. Willis Conover

Mr. Fred Guy   Mr. David Brubeck

Mrs. S. Dillon Ripley III

President Richard Nixon^

Ms. Ruth Ellington   Mrs. Edward R. Dudley

Mr. Lou Rawls   **9**   Mr. John B. Gillespie

Mrs. John H. Johnson   Mrs. Donald Rumsfeld^

Mr. Benny Goodman

Mrs. Thomas Patterson

HEW Sec. Robert Finch^   Mr. H. Robert Udkoff

Mrs. Otto Preminger   **10**   Dr. Arthur Logan

Mr. Leonard Garment   Mrs. Daniel Moynihan^

Rev. Bryant Kirkland*

Mrs. H. Robert Udkoff   Asst. Daniel Moynihan^

Mr. Thomas Whaley   **11**   Ms. Mahalia Jackson

Mrs. George Schultz^   Mr. Stanley Dance

Nixon then said [to Dizzy], "You've represented the United States government several times [overseas]. What do you think about your making another trip?"

I said, "I wouldn't be interested in making another trip to play *for* somebody. But I would be interested in going to play *with* somebody. This means if I go to Cuba, I have to play *with* the Cubans. If I go to Africa, I have to play *with* the Africans, using music to further the feeling of togetherness and cooperation."

He said, "Well, do they have that caliber of musician over there?"

I said, "You don't realize the worldwide extent and breadth of our music. I'm liable to walk into a club in Afghanistan and hear a guy playing a solo he took off one of my records note for note. Sometimes you can find a better musician for a certain job in a place like Osaka than you can get in Philadelphia."[11] [Diz got his trips: to Africa in 1973 for Nixon and to Cuba in 1978 for President Carter. He played *with* the musicians.]

Recently converted to the Baha'i religion and never one to shy away from his causes, Dizzy gifted Nixon with an inscribed copy of the book *Baha'i Administration* that describes the religion's organizing principals. It's not clear whether Diz slipped the copy under the table or gave it to an aide for later delivery. In any case, Nixon thanked him.

Singer Rawls, for his part, talked to the president about soul food and told him the hors d'oeurves could have at least been fricasseed chitterlings on toothpicks. Nixon laughed.

At a nearby table, Ellington and Mrs. Nixon had the company of singer Billy Eckstine, composer Richard Rodgers, friend Leslie Diamond, and John H. Johnson, owner of *Ebony* and *Jet* magazines. Duke later recalled a conversation he had with the First Lady:

She told me her daughter had seen me in Woodward and Lothrop's [department store] while shopping earlier that day. [Indeed, she had. Someone had forgotten to pack Duke's pleated blue satin shirt, so he had to dash out and buy a conservative white shirt with studs and cufflinks.]

"Oh yes," I said, "and you have a beautiful daughter." After a pause, I ventured further. "Mrs. Nixon, have you heard of the White House Ordinance?"

"White House Ordinance," she said, turning and looking a little askance.

"Yes, Mrs. Nixon, there is law that says no first lady should be prettier than a certain degree, and you are exceeding the legal limit. Why, you can get a ticket for it!"

To my great astonishment, the first lady gave me a direct, accusing look and said, "I heard about *you*!"[12]

Animated conversation broke out as everyone discovered both common and uncommon interests. At one table, Daniel P. Moynihan, assistant to the president, discussed books and publishing with gospel singer Mahalia Jackson, while Duke's long-term copyist and conductor, Tom Whaley, explained the peculiarities of the music business to Mrs. George Schultz, wife of the Secretary of Labor. The Reverend Bryant Kirkland, who was responsible for the presentation of Ellington's Second Sacred Concert at the Fifth Avenue Presbyterian Church in New York, received an affirmative answer to the suggestion that Ms. Jackson should sing there. And how had she enjoyed recording that Columbia album [that included the hymn "Come Sunday"] with Duke Ellington?

"He didn't rehearse me nothin'," she replied forthrightly. "He said, 'Just open the Bible and sing.'"

The White House kitchen had prepared a banquet fit for a duke.[13] The Coquille of Seafood Neptune starter was followed by a main course of Roast Sirloin of Beef with Sauce Bordelaise, Potatoes Parmentier, and Salad Cressonnière. A Bernkoister Doktor 1967 white wine delicately complemented the seafood, while a Chateau Lafite Rothschild 1964 red bordeaux enhanced the beef sirloin. A Pol Roger 1961 sparkling

DINNER

Bernkasteler
Doktor
1967
Coquille of Seafood Neptune

Roast Sirloin of Beef Bordelaise

Chateau
Lafite-Rothschild
1962
Potatoes Parmentier

Mushrooms Provençale

Salad Cressonnière

Cheddar Cheese Mousse

Pol Roger
1961

Glace Nougatine

THE WHITE HOUSE
Tuesday, April 29, 1969

champagne inspired pallets for the Glace Nougatine desert. Interestingly, someone in the White House (the chef perhaps, or maybe even the president) scratched the initially selected wines—Puligny-Montrachet 1964 (fish) and Louis M. Martini Cabernet Sauvignon (meat)—for those that were served. A wise decision, most connoisseurs would agree.

As the guests were about to dine on their Seafood Neptune, a dozen violinists—the United States Army Strolling Strings—entered the room briskly. Taking up positions among the tables, they performed some of Ellington's most famous compositions. The diners first heard a medley that began with "In a Sentimental Mood" and ended with "Solitude." Next heard was "Sophisticated Lady." The Strings repeated their six-minute program before departing as gracefully as they had entered.

As the Glace Nougatine dessert was being served, Nixon stood, tapped his water glass with a spoon, and spoke warmly of the guest of honor's Washington, DC, background:

> To all of our guests here this evening, I think you would be interested to know that many years ago, the father of our guest of honor [James Edward Ellington], in this very room, serving as one of the butlers in the White House, helped to serve state dinners.
>
> Tonight, in honoring his son, I was trying to think of something that would be appropriate, something that has not been more adequately said, I think very well, by the music that we have heard. We have tried to convey our affection for Duke Ellington through this music, and later on in the East Room, when I will make the first presentation in this administration of the Medal of Freedom to Duke Ellington, I will have more to say in more extended remarks about what this day means to us and what it means to this House.
>
> But in this room, at this time, for these special guests, it occurred to me that the most appropriate thing for me to say would be this: I, and many others here, have been guests at state dinners. I have been here when an emperor has been toasted. I have

been here when we have raised our glasses to a king, to a queen, to presidents, and to prime ministers.

But in studying the history of all of the great dinners held in this room, never before has a duke been toasted.

So tonight I ask you to all rise and join me in raising our glasses to the greatest duke of them all. Duke Ellington.[14]

As reported in *Jet* magazine, Duke then responded by expressing his appreciation to the president for having given the affair in his honor.[15] Duke reminisced that he had always lived a good life, that his family had pampered him, and that his feet figuratively never touched the ground until he was eight years old. Ellington concluded with simple, moving sincerity, "There is no place I would rather be tonight, except in my mother's arms."

This was the first of many emotional moments in an extraordinary evening.

Guest Arrivals

Mr. and Mrs. Mercer Ellington.

Mr. and Mrs. Cab Calloway.

Mr. and Mrs. Benny Goodman.

Mr. and Mrs. Billy Eckstine.

Mr. and Mrs. John H. Johnson.

Mr. and Mrs. Stanley Dance.

John B. "Dizzy" Gillespie.

Duke and Ruth Ellington.

Having descended the grand staircase from the upstairs residence, the principals posed for photographers on the bottom step before stepping off to greet their guests as the Marine Band played "Hail to the Chief."

Sister Ruth and First Lady Pat looked on as Duke graciously bowed to the first guest in the second receiving line of the evening. The first line was for dinner guests; the second, for the entertainment-only guests.

Sister Ruth and First Lady Pat chatted with a guest as Duke bestowed his four-kiss reward on dancer Carmen de Lavallade as husband and fellow dancer Geoffrey Holder (*center foreground*) watched with interest.

President Nixon read the Medal of Honor Citation to honoree Edward Kennedy Ellington and those assembled in the East Room.

CHAPTER 6

The Ceremony

MEANWHILE, AS THE DINNER GUESTS were completing their banquet, guests who had been invited for the entertainment only (some 132 strong—see appendix 9) were being ushered into a small downstairs room full of cabinets displaying china used by the various presidents. Like those who came for dinner, many party guests had an Ellington touch (about half owed their gate card to Duke): musicians (composer-conductor Gunther Schuller and pianists Marian McPartland and Willie "the Lion" Smith), dancers (Geoffrey Holder and Carmen de Lavallade), and Newport Jazz Festival organizer George Wein. Attending also was a huge media contingent: representatives from the major newspapers (*Washington Post, Star, New York Times, Post,* and *Chicago Sun-Times*), African American newspapers (*Chicago Defender* and *New York Amsterdam News*) and magazines (*Time, Newsweek, Jet,* and *Ebony*), wire service journalists and photographers, and a slew of jazz writer-critics. Part of the last group, Whitney Balliett later described the scene:

> Pianist Earl Hines, sipping champagne as he stood with his back to the Canton China used by George Washington, watched a Navy Band trio made up of a drummer, saxophonist, and an

accordionist. "That's the damnedest accordion I've ever heard," he said. "It sounds like a *guitar*. It's just luck I'm here, and I'm very happy about it. Duke and I have been *very* close friends for a *long* time. I just finished an engagement at Blues Alley [jazz club] here, and tomorrow I'm off for South America."

Pianist Willie "the Lion" Smith, in his traditional garb of derby, horn-rimmed glasses, and cigar, drifted by looking like a well-slept owl, and saxophonist Gerry Mulligan and trumpeter Clark Terry, who were carrying their horns, began to play with the trio. [This did not surprise Balliett, who had said of Mulligan: "He would sit in with a tree full of cicadas."] Gunther Schuller, a fervent Ellington admirer and head of the New England Conservatory, came in, followed by jazz festival impresario George Wein. Pianist Marian McPartland was talking with Leonard Feather, jazz critic, in one corner. The music was booming and the guests had overflowed into an enormous arched hallway.[1]

The aides then hustled the visitors upstairs into the Great Hall just outside the East Room, where they formed the second receiving line of the evening—the "kissingest" one ever seen at the White House, said *Evening Star* reporter Eleni, and one of the few second lines seen during the Nixon years, the custom being scrapped in favor of VIP visits in the upstairs family quarters. President and Mrs. Nixon, Duke, and sister Ruth greeted guests near the door of the Blue Room. A short distance away, a contingent from the Marine Band played Ellington tunes. When long-term columnist with the *Chicago Sun-Times* Irving "Kup" Kupcinet and his wife passed through the receiving line, the president pulled two cigars he had stashed in his pocket and said, "You always gave me those cheap cigars when I appeared on your TV show. So I'm going to reciprocate by giving you two real Cubans." When the Kupcinets got to Pat, who hadn't heard her husband's comment, she looked at the cigars and exclaimed, "Oh, did you two have a baby!"[2] Not likely. Kup and his wife were both in their fifties at the time.

Duke bestowed his customary four-kiss reward, one kiss for each cheek, on nearly every passerby. When Whitney Balliett and his wife fronted Nixon in line, he told the president that

> he was doing a noble thing giving such a party, and Nixon uttered a perfect "Pshaw!"... From there, the guests were ushered into the East Room, the largest room in the White House, where several hundred chairs had been set up. TV and newsreel cameramen were packed into a screened-off area in the back of the room. The *New York Times* reported correctly that this was the first time the White House had ever allowed such an event to be televised. [The *Times* was unaware of the other precedent: the filming of such an event by the USIA for distribution overseas.]
>
> The ten-piece all-star band was waiting on a dais in the front of the room. Vice President Agnew was standing between the band and the audience, beaming and looking like a maitre d'. When the room was full, President and Mrs. Nixon, followed by Ellington and his sister, entered, and everyone stood. [Balliett confided he couldn't] resist such fillets of melodrama, and got a lump in his throat. The president, moving in a quick, wooden way, jumped up on the platform in front of the bandstand and, in his deepest rain-barrel voice [and with no notes], said,

> Sit down please, Ladies and Gentlemen. This is a very unusual and special evening in this great room. Before the entertainment begins, we have a presentation to make. I was looking at this [in his hands Nixon held an embossed certificate holder] . . . name on here and it says Edward Kennedy . . . Ellington.[3]

The stage pause drew the expected laughter, as Nixon motioned for Duke to join him on the platform. Spontaneous applause and shouted "yeahs" and "bravos" greeted Duke as he stood next to Nixon. "I think they like you," Nixon said. Then back to the assembled crowd, again without notes:

> For the first time during this administration, I have the honor of presenting the Presidential Medal of Freedom. And I think it is most appropriate that that medal be presented to Duke Ellington. When we think of freedom we think of many things, but Duke Ellington is one who has carried the message of freedom to all the nations of the world through music, through understanding—understanding that reaches over all national boundaries, and over all boundaries of prejudice, and over all boundaries of language. And because he has an unusual gift, a gift that he has shared with us—his own fellow citizens—and with all the citizens of the world, we believe this citation fits him particularly well. I will read it to you.

Nixon read the text (see chapter 1), emphasizing the last line—"In the royalty of American music, no man swings more or stands higher than the Duke"—and handed Ellington the certificate and the medal. Everyone stood and the room shook with applause. It was Duke's turn:

> Thank you very much, Mr. President. Thank you, Ladies and Gentlemen. This is the Presidential Medal of Freedom, and the word freedom is one, coincidentally, that we are using at the moment in our Sacred Concert. And of course we speak of freedom of expression, and speak of freedom generally as being something sweet and fat and things like that. But at the end, when we get down to the payoff, what we actually say is that ... we would like to mention the four major freedoms that my friend and the writer/arranger/composer Billy Strayhorn lived by and enjoyed:
>
> Freedom from hate unconditionally
>
> Freedom from self-pity

Freedom from fear of possibly doing something that may help someone else more than it would him

Freedom from the kind of pride that would make a man feel he is better than his brother

Taking the president by both hands, Duke leaned in close, whispered in his ear "I'll give you four kisses," and conferred once again, his celebrated four-kiss reward, at which the East Room crowd erupted gleefully. The press reported that Nixon was "taken aback," "embarrassed," but if he was, it wasn't because of unfamiliarity; more likely, he didn't expect to be kissed at the close of the medal ceremony.

Nixon then moved toward the piano on the riser, saying to Duke, "Stay up here. Stay with me," as he removed Paul Desmond's alto saxophone from the piano bench. Sensing that Nixon was going to sit down and play, the crowd reacted noisily. Pianists Dave Brubeck and George Wein guffawed visibly and loudly. The president stepped back to the microphone, raised his hand, and said,

Please don't go away. [Laughter in the audience.] Duke was asking earlier if I would play and I said I have never done so yet in the White House. But it did occur to me as I was looking at the magnificent program that has been prepared for us that one number was missing. You see . . . this is his birthday. Duke Ellington is ageless, but would you please stand and sing "Happy Birthday." And please, in the key of G!

Everybody sang and clapped enthusiastically at the song's end.

Others in the press secretary's office busied themselves with translating the president's and honoree's exchange of ceremonial remarks for immediate release to the press, which occurred at 10:36 p.m., in plenty of time for the morning newspapers. The president may not have liked socializing, but as Nixon aide Charles Stuart said, "If he had to have parties, he wanted to maximize their political benefit."

Mary Mayo sang "Prelude to a Kiss" backed by the all-star rhythm section: Hank Jones (*p, not pictured*), Milt Hinton (*b*), and Louis Bellson (*dms*).

❋

CHAPTER 7

The Concert

Nixon and Duke returned to their front-row center seats, Duke next to his sister, Ruth, both of whom were flanked by the President and Mrs. Nixon and Vice President and Mrs. Agnew. The band scurried from the wings to take their positions on the stage. Willis Conover, master of ceremonies for the evening, stepped up to the microphone at one side of the riser and faced the guests. In his sculpted baritone voice, he simply announced, "The Ellington Orchestra theme 'Take the "A" Train.'"[1]

Duke's Theme Song

"Take the 'A' Train"   The Band
Music/Lyrics by Billy Strayhorn (1941)

The evening would have been a first-class disappointment had Conover chosen to open with anything other than Duke's twenty-eight-year-old theme song. The maestro had opened with the theme at nearly every one of his appearances since its inception, and Conover had used it to open his own VOA jazz program for some twelve years. Ellington's

composing-arranging partner for over a quarter of a century, Billy Strayhorn outlined the song's origin to the band's chronicler Stanley Dance:

> One day, I was thinking about [bandleader Fletcher Henderson's]
> style, the way he wrote for trumpets, trombones, and saxophones,
> and I thought I would try something like that. Now this was a case
> of a combination of circumstances. At the end of 1940, there was
> the fight between the ASCAP [American Society of Compos-
> ers, Authors, and Publishers] and the radio, and at the beginning
> of 1941, all ASCAP music was off the air. When we opened at
> the Casa Marana, January 3, 1941, we had airtime every night but
> could not play our library [mostly written by Duke]. We had to
> play non-ASCAP material. Duke was in ASCAP, but I wasn't.
> So we had to write a new library, and "'A' Train" was one of the
> numbers. The reason we gave it that title was because they were
> building the Sixth Avenue subway at that time, and they added
> new trains, including the D train, which came up to Harlem, to
> 145th Street, and then turned off and went to the Bronx, but the
> A train kept straight on up to 200-and-something Street. People
> got confused. They'd take the D train, and it would go to Harlem
> and 145th Street, but the next stop would be on Eighth Avenue
> under the Polo Grounds, and the one after that would be in the
> Bronx. So I said I was writing directions—take the A train to
> Sugar Hill [up in Harlem].[2]

Everything about Strayhorn's catchy number became famous and
widely imitated: the Duke Ellington opening piano vamp (doodeley-
oooh ... doodeley-oooh doot doot ... doodeley-oooh ... doodeley-oooh
doot doot); the Ray Nance trumpet solo, whose licks are copied by trumpet players to this very day;[3] and the Swing Era fade-out (a saxophone-
whispered theme discretely punctuated by the brass).

Conductor Whaley gave the downbeat and pianist Hank Jones didn't
disappoint: He opened with a spot-on imitation of Duke's introductory

vamp, which was met with immediate shouts of recognition and scattered applause. Like so many nervous horses at Hialeah on opening day, the band charged out of the starting gate with one of the most rambunctious small-group "'A' Train" performances on record. The daylong anticipation, the celebratory foreplay, and the familiarity of the tune all contributed to the excitement of the moment. Ten musicians sounded like fifteen, thanks to the two-trumpet power of former Ellingtonians Bill Berry and Clark Terry, matched by the two-trombone duo of Urbie Green and J. J. Johnson.

After the band stated the theme, Berry took the first solo, and damn if he didn't reference the one Ray Nance took on the first recording some twenty-eight years earlier. Green soloed next—competent and forceful—and the band rode "The 'A' Train" out with Clark Terry bubbling on top in his unmistakable trumpet voice. The audience roared as the last note sounded. They had settled in, oblivious to the austere painted gazes of George and Martha Washington looking down from the Gilbert Stuart portraits on the wall, and the three 650-pound cut-crystal chandeliers hanging over their heads. The evening had begun, and from the first number alone, they knew it was going to be a good one. What they didn't know was that it would be a long one, too. The concert would cover twenty-eight numbers, seventeen of which are acknowledged jazz standards,[4] and last almost an hour and a half.

An Ellington Nine-Tune Medley

Conover returned to his microphone:

An interviewer recently asked Duke Ellington, "Mr. Ellington, what is your favorite image of yourself?" And he said, "My favorite image of myself is when I wake up in the morning and room service is knocking at my door. [The audience laughed, as Conover cocked his eyebrow, looked over at Ellington, and said, "Remember?"] Each of us who are not members of his orchestra,

but are nonetheless friends, has a particular image of Duke Ellington—part of that image will be demonstrated now through a
medley of some of the songs he has written.

"I Got It Bad (and That Ain't Good)"	Trombonist Urbie Green
Lyrics by Paul Francis Webster (1941)	Rhythm Section

More than anything, Ellington longed for a Broadway hit musical, one
that he could score—one that would launch his songs as no other medium could—but it proved elusive. He came close with *Jump for Joy*:

> In 1941 a team of scholarly Hollywood writers decided to at-
> tempt to correct the race situation in the U.S. through a form
> of theatrical propaganda. This culminated in . . . *Jump for Joy*, a
> show that would take Uncle Tom out of the theater, eliminate
> the stereotyped image that had been exploited by Hollywood and
> Broadway, and say things that would make the audience think.
> The original script had Uncle Tom on his deathbed with all his
> children dancing around him singing . . . there was a Hollywood
> producer on one side of the bed and a Broadway producer on the
> other side, and both were trying to keep him alive by injecting
> adrenaline into his arms![5]

Although *Jump for Joy* ran for only three months in Los Angeles, it
demonstrated, as Duke's son, Mercer, later recalled, what a black musical
could and should be and, not insignificantly, how quickly Ellington could
write for a purpose.[6] The night before first rehearsal, Duke composed a
handful of classics on the night train into Los Angeles that included "I
Got It Bad (and That Ain't Good)," one of Ellington's most lyrical and
elegant ballads.

Nearly three decades later at the White House, trombonist Urbie

Green, backed by the all-star rhythm section, pianist Hank Jones, guitarist Jim Hall, bassist Milt Hinton, and former Ellington drummer Louis Bellson, traced the sumptuous contours of the well-known melody, octave leaps and all, in fine fashion. His usual strong and earthy self, Urbie still managed to suggest the smooth upper-register playing of jazz bone men like Juan Tizol and Tommy Dorsey.

Never one to lavish unwarranted praise, guest Whitney Balliett singled out Green's gorgeous solo as one of the evening's memorable ones.[7] The audience responded warmly—after all, it was only the first song in the medley, with much, much more to come.

———✳———

"Chelsea Bridge"   **Alto Saxophonist Paul Desmond**
Music by Billy Strayhorn (1941)   **Rhythm Section**

The second number of the medley was the first impressionistic piece written by "Strays" (as Duke called him) directly for the orchestra as a result of the ASCAP radio ban. Inspired by the James Whistler painting *Battersea Bridge*, the song's title was a slip of memory at the 1941 recording session—a fortuitous lapse, most would agree.[8] Strays's dreamscape, with harmonies reminiscent of French composer Maurice Ravel, is a most intriguingly complex thirty-two-bar AABA song.[9, 10]

The original recording of "Chelsea Bridge" featured the tenor sax of Ben Webster in pretty mode. Alto saxophonist Paul Desmond took on the assignment to see if he could measure up.

Several critics in the White House audience considered Desmond's take on Strays's exquisite miniature as close to perfection as one could get. Desmond, on the other hand, was grossly perturbed. As biographer Doug Ramsey later revealed:

Desmond was not happy with his feature on "Chelsea Bridge." When they came to the song's middle section [commonly called the bridge], bassist Milt Hinton forgot the complicated harmonic changes and went into an unrelated pattern. Desmond managed to keep his composure and preserve the melody line. It is unlikely that non-musicians in the audience knew anything had gone wrong, but Paul had been convinced it had been a disaster.[11]

True, non-musicians would never have detected the mistake that evening, but after repeatedly listening to the concert CD, most people would notice the faux pas. Desmond covered up splendidly, but perhaps his absence from the music scene—since the breakup of the classic Dave Brubeck Quartet in December 1967—created a touch of insecurity. As we shall learn, his harsh inner critic contributed to the delayed release of the concert CD.

———✳———

"Satin Doll"   Trombonist J. J. Johnson
Music by Billy Strayhorn (1953)   Rhythm Section
Lyrics by Johnny Mercer (1958)

With glib tongue planted firmly in cheek, Ellington usually introduced the next song at clubs and concerts as follows:

> The next song is dedicated to the most beautiful lady here. We will not point her out because we do not want her to feel conspicuous. We will just let her sit there and continue to feel guilty.[12]

The members of the Ellington Orchestra would then swing out with one of their most memorable finger-snapping numbers. It was, in fact, the band's last bona fide commercial hit. First written by Duke and Strays (mostly the latter) and recorded in 1953 when Ellington signed on with Capitol Records, the tune was outfitted with lyrics by Strays and Mercer (mostly the latter) in 1958.[13] Still, "Satin Doll" languished, not really taking off until a then-unknown jazz pianist nudged Duke in the ribs:

> Whenever Duke came in [to the Hickory House club, Duke's favorite New York steakhouse], Billy Taylor, who was playing piano . . . dug back into his mental file of Ellingtonia and tried to play something obscure or one of the old things that Duke might not remember. One night Taylor played "Satin Doll." Duke called him over and said, "Hey, man, that's a nice little arrangement."
>
> Billy replied, "Thanks, Duke. I'm glad you like it. We get a lot of requests for it."
>
> Duke nodded. "I'll have to put that back in the book. You've got it sounding very good." . . . From that time on, Duke stayed with the song, playing it wherever he went, until other bands and singers picked it up, laying on it until it became a jazz [and popular] standard.[14]

American song historian Alec Wilder, usually a lukewarm cheerleader of Ellington songs, in this case had uncharacteristic high praise: "It's a soft-spoken, underplayed little song with a marvelous, perfect Mercer lyric, and it truly swings."[15]

Such a well-known tune didn't require any introduction, even at the White House. Pianist Jones simply chorded the patented opening vamp Duke had crafted years before, and the crowd reacted immediately— they knew what was coming—and trombonist J. J. Johnson delivered. His burnished legato treatment of the easily swinging melody gave his performance most of its charm. After the trombone master limned the tune that most people could whistle from memory, as critic Hollie I. West of the *Washington Post* heard it, "Johnson broke away from his tune, laying a bluesy rocking rendition that brought cries of 'yeah, yeah.'"[16] Jazz critic Dan Morgenstern also described the solo as "bluesy"[17]; Doug Ramsey called it "booting."[18] When "Johnson broke away from his tune," drummer Bellson added to the excitement by switching from brushes to sticks, one keeping time on the ride cymbal, the other counter beating the snare drum's rim.

"The 'A' Train" inaugural aside, this was the first special moment of the concert, and the East Room crowd let J. J. and his rhythm mates know it with their finger snapping and hand clapping throughout the number, and with their boisterous applause at the end. You might have thought it was the concert finale, not just the third in a nine-number medley.

———✳———

"Sophisticated Lady"   Saxophonist Gerry Mulligan
Lyrics by Irving Mills and Mitchell Parrish (1933)   **Rhythm Section**

When music publisher Irving Mills first heard Duke Ellington's band, he realized that the musicians' complex jazz arrangements could become the basis of successful popular songs. The publisher proposed a partnership to Ellington, and a contract was signed in 1926 that allowed Mills's name to appear on the credits for Ellington's songs, thus assuring Mills not only the publisher's share of royalties but also a portion of the songwriters'.[19] The contract remained in effect for thirteen years, and even though Ellington ultimately sued for release, he was, as critic Gary Giddins has pointed out, quite explicit about Mills's contributions to the band: the historic engagement at the Cotton Club, record contracts, motion picture deals, European tours, acceptance into ASCAP, and several other victories over Jim Crow.[20] Indeed, Mills was invaluable, but his name didn't really belong on the composer credit line.

Beginning with his first recording in 1932, according to biographer Hasse, Ellington preferred to perform "Sophisticated Lady" as an instrumental, but the song is also famous as a vocal. This harmonically rich ballad, with a high contrasting and ingenious bridge, became a vehicle for Lawrence Brown's sentimental trombone and Otto Hardwick's florid alto saxophone. The piece's authorship is disputed—Ellington, Hardwick, and Brown have all been credited. Ellington said he wrote it as a composite tribute to three high school teachers: "They taught all winter and toured Europe in the summer. To me, that was sophistication."[21]

In 1933, lyrics by Mitchell Parish of "Star Dust" fame were added. "Sentimental didactic" is how Philip Furia described them; "Scarcely lyrical," said Alec Wilder; and Ellington himself called them "not entirely fitted to my original conception." Despite so many cooks, lyric weaknesses, and the song's difficult bridge (which George Gershwin famously said he wished he had written), "Sophisticated Lady" became a pop standard.[22]

Movie director Otto Preminger, in the East Room audience that night, had wanted to use "Lady" for the main theme of his mid-1940s movie *Laura*. The film's composer objected and finally won over the director with an alternate theme he wrote (now known by nearly everyone) that better suited *Laura*'s brooding ambience.[23]

Also seated in the East Room audience was Harry Carney, Ellington's virtuoso baritone saxophonist who had been with him nonstop since 1927. The maestro featured him countless times on "Sophisticated Lady," and his reverential melodic embellishments, transcendent basso-profundo tones, and held-note ending had become almost as legendary as the song itself. Not too surprisingly, all-star baritone saxophonist Mulligan drew the challenge.

Shouts of recognition greeted the opening notes that emanated from Jeru's bass horn. An air of tension must have filled in the room. Most knew Carney was there. How close would Jeru come to the well-known virtuoso's version? How would he measure up? He held his ground. He could maneuver around his horn with the best of them. The attending critics (Balliett, Morgenstern, and West) concluded that Mulligan's rendition resembled Carney's.[24] At one juncture, Jeru executed a Carney-reminiscent triple-tongue flutter but chose not to imitate his sustained high-note ending. Time restrictions likely prevented him from doing so.

Over in less than two minutes, the number received spirited applause from the president and his guests.

——— ✳ ———

"Just Squeeze Me"   **Trumpeters Bill Berry, Clark Terry**
Lyrics by Lee Gaines (1946)   **The Band**

Like so many of Duke's works, "Just Squeeze Me" grew from a modest start as an instrumental melody to a popular song. It was originally recorded in 1941 by a small Ellington unit under the title "Subtle Slough." Half a decade later, Lee Gaines, the bass singer of the vocal quintet Delta Rhythm Boys, penned the lyrics. From that point on, the tune became a playful vocal feature for singer-trumpeter Ray "Floor Show" Nance.[25]

Over the years, singers have rendered "Squeeze Me" more as a sultry ballad than a novelty number. Not so for Duke's seventieth birthday. The arrangement took its cue from the lighthearted Nance vocal and showcased the dueling plunger-muted trumpets of Bill "Beez" Berry and Clark "CT" Terry. The duo harmonized the charming melody over a loping riff set down by guitarist Jim Hall and pianist Jones (a perfect arrangement for a children's jazz record). Nixon talked animatedly to Duke during the horn men's initial presentation, and no wonder, as Terry later remembered,

> When we did "Squeeze Me," I got out the plunger mute—the plumber's friend—and Nixon was nudging his wife, pointing at it, and saying, "Look at that! Look, it's a toilet plunger! Look at that!" I guess he hadn't seen a whole lot of jazz bands.[26]

The president, not to mention the two-hundred-plus guests in the East Room, was not prepared for what happened next as the duo began their trumpet dialogue. Beez's first solo was pleasant and low key. His next offering—whether intentional or not—raised the volume and threw down the gauntlet, challenging Terry. As everyone in the jazz world knew, musically, you didn't play games with CT. Terry's riposte: an exhilarating, escalating wah-wah scream that figuratively lifted the East Room crowd out of their chairs gasping for air. Beez responded admirably, but CT had been primed, ready to launch his arsenal of trumpet tricks.

> Jazz has a vocabulary of vocal effects, including portamento, both rising and falling [CT employed a jangled rising portamento in his first retaliation]; the blurry distorted trumpet sound that is referred to as a growl; constricted half-valve effects that Dizzy Gillespie . . . used to telling effect; and even the articulation of notes through the use of a rubber plunger, called the wah-wah effect. Clark Terry has carried vocal effects on trumpet probably further than any player in jazz history, and sometimes you can understand the words his horn is saying: profane, specific, and funny.[27]

Over audience shouts and laughter, Beez and CT exchanged four trumpet statements that, according to critic Morgenstern, delighted even the non-jazz fans in the audience.[28] CT's puckish trumpet vocalizations, the attending critics agreed, stood out as the concert high point (rivaled only by pianist Earl Hines's masterful solo, which would occur later in the program).[29]

At song's reprieve, the full band joined the loping rhythm that Hall and Jones had set at the beginning while the brass duo sweetly harmonized the catchy melody. Long and hard applause followed, delaying the start of the next tune in the medley.

Noted wit Paul Desmond, who marveled at the perfection of Terry's playing on this and other numbers that night, later remarked, "When we get back to New York, I'm going to ask him to come over to my place and make a mistake."[30]

————✳————

"I Let a Song Go Out of My Heart"   The Band
Lyrics by Henry Nemo and John Redmond (1938)

Duke commented on the next song's origins in his memoir:

> "I Let a Song Go Out of My Heart," written in a little Memphis
> hotel, was originally in the Cotton Club Parades of 1938, but Irving
> Mills decided it should come out and be replaced with . . . "Swing-
> time for Honolulu." But the band played "I Let a Song" on the
> radio every night, and so did Benny Goodman from the Penn-
> sylvania Hotel. He also recorded it, and "I Let a Song" got to be
> a big number that year.
>
> After we left the Cotton Club, we went touring, and when
> we came back to New York, we went into the Apollo Theatre
> on 125th Street. In preparing my big song of the season for the
> Apollo, I decided to do a new arrangement with a rather strong
> countermelody. Opening day, I soon learned that the audience,
> as always, wanted to hear the version that they had heard on the
> air. So we . . . went back to the old arrangement, and that's the
> way it stayed.[31]

The following year, 1939, the new arrangement was reworked and
recorded as "Never No Lament," which led to yet another song: "Don't
Get Around Much Anymore."

The band sketched "I Let a Song" and the following two songs—call
them Duke's World War II hits—in true medley fashion, each lasting
about a minute. As Conover had said, the night was about Duke the
song composer, not about the musicians. These three numbers lived up
to that promise, and as such, were greeted by the East Room crowd with,
if not enthusiasm, nostalgic respect, as many in the room reflected on
the joys and tears of their war years.

———✳———

"Do Nothing Till You Hear from Me"   The Band
Lyrics by S. K. "Bob" Russell (1943)

In a process frequently repeated in Ellington lore, the main theme of "Concerto for Cootie" was borrowed from a figure that trumpet player Cootie Williams used as a warm-up exercise. Bob Russell then added lyrics to the instrumental, and the combination turned into the hit song "Do Nothing Till You Hear from Me." How musically efficient: nothing is thrown away—everything is put to good use.

"Don't Get Around Much Anymore"   The Band
Lyrics by S. K. "Bob" Russell (1942)

Song historians Philip Furia and Michael Lasser described the way Russell's touching lyrics perfectly evoked the melancholy tone of the day:

> As America changed during WWII, its love songs became more introspective and reflective, perhaps because the characters that sang in them were always alone. The ballads of these years were a direct reflection of what the women left behind were living through. Few songs caught that mood with greater poignancy than "Don't Get Around Much Anymore."
>
> The song's melody has a smoky but sad quality that sustains Bob Russell's tense, cryptic lyric. It is a song for the shadows. While others go on dates or dance on crowded floors, the singer prefers solitude. As bad as it is, it's better than a night of solicitude and companionship without her lover. Even though the song's sentiments are intensely personal, it almost never uses "I," as if she denies her identity during these dark days of separation. Finally, she makes herself go to a club, though she only gets "as far as the door." What stops her is the thought that old friends will

ask about him: "They'd have asked me about you." The elliptical lyric is filled with gaps and suggestions that make the song more poignant and must have brought its original listeners even closer to their own stark emotions.[32]

"Don't Get Around" and Duke's other wartime hits "I Let a Song" and "Do Nothing" scaled the charts—going platinum in today's lingo—resulting in a substantial contribution to the Ellington Orchestra's coffers:

In 1943 we were playing the Hurricane Club on Forty-ninth and Broadway in New York . . . Midway through the Hurricane engagement, I found myself a little short of cash, so I went up to the William Morris Agency . . . for the purpose of borrowing five hundred dollars. While I was exchanging greetings with some of the executives, an office boy passed and saw me.

"Oh, Mr. Ellington," he said, "I have some mail for you, too."

"Is that so?" I said disinterestedly.

He handed me about a dozen envelopes, which I proceeded to peel through casually until I came to one with a transparent window from RCA Victor. I opened it and took a quick glance at the check inside. The figure $2,250 is what I thought I saw as I slid it back in the envelope. To myself I said, "Hey, if this is $2,250, I don't need to make this touch up here, but maybe my eyes deceived me and it's really $22.50. So I pulled the check out again and it said $22,500! By the time I got my head back in my collar, I was at the elevator exit on the first floor rushing to get a taxi. Man, what a surprise! What a feeling! I could breathe without inhaling for the next three months![33]

———✳———

"In a Mellotone"   **The Band**
Lyrics by Milt Gabler (1940)

Finally, something for the band to stretch out on: the loose and eminently danceable "In a Mellotone." The tune developed almost spontaneously as a riff that the Ellington Orchestra used to play on the chord pattern of the Artie Shaw vehicle "Rose Room." Like Ellington's "C-Jam Blues" and "Perdido," this swinging riff with its contrasting call-and-response patterns has become a popular jam session vehicle. Small wonder: After you hear just the title, this tune almost plays itself in your head. Five notes, five syllables—"In a Mel-Lo Tone"—da da de da daah, and so on, with note values changing on subsequent repeats.

For the lyric, Duke tapped another unusual collaborator, Milt Gabler (uncle to comedian Billy Crystal). Best known at the time as the owner of the Commodore Record Shop and record label, Gabler would become co-owner of Decca Records in the 1950s, and produce numerous jazz records, but also the historic "Rock Around the Clock" by Bill Haley.

Taken at a relaxed jog, the all-star band played the theme (the call) while J. J. scattered tasty fills on his trombone (the response). At times, things seemed inverted, J. J. out front soloing with the band kicking him along with a backing "da da de da daah" riff. All the frontline melody players took their slice of the mellow pie while Hinton and Bellson held steady rhythmic compass: Desmond (smooth as usual but not as keen-ing); Berry (strong and consistent, backed by the "Mellotone" riff by the band); Green (in characteristic tailgate mode); Hall (first time heard as soloist); Mulligan (bouncy as usual, backed by a new riff by the band); and crowd-pleaser Terry (percolating to start but stratospheric high notes and mocking vocal effects at the end). The band closed out the long and spirited stamping number in raucous faux-Dixie style to great applause. At seven minutes, it was the longest number of the night—that is, until the after-show jam session.

At medley's end, Conover stepped to his microphone without notes:

The songs were "I Got It Bad (and That Ain't Good)," "Chelsea Bridge," "Satin Doll," "Sophisticated Lady," "Just Squeeze Me," and then "I Let a Song Go Out of My Heart," "Do Nothing Till You Hear from Me," "Don't Get Around Much Anymore," and "In a Mellotone." I think. [Laughter and applause.]

A Trilogy

Conover announced the next number, a bass and guitar duet on Ellington's "In a Sentimental Mood," and the audience responded with oooohs and aaahs.

———✳———

"In a Sentimental Mood"	**Guitarist Jim Hall**
Lyrics by Irving Mills and Manny Kurtz (1935)	**Bassist Hinton**

This song, like many in the Duke Ellington catalog, had an improbable inspiration.

> Ellington was in Durham, North Carolina, at a party where two women were fighting. Ellington put one girl at each end of the piano and told them he had written a new song dedicated to them. He improvised a tune while the girls cooled it off. It was later published as "In a Sentimental Mood."[34]

Quite a beginning for a gorgeous ballad variously described as "very lovely and delightful" (Alec Wilder), "yearning and haunting" (John Edward Hasse), and "uncompromising sophistication" (Gunther Schuller).[35] This sinuous yet bluesy tune was perhaps the first Ellington work to really catch the attention of Tin Pan Alley: Watch out George Gershwin, Cole Porter, and all the rest. There's a new kid on the block to contend with.

A polite stillness settled over the East Room during guitarist Hall's reading of "Mood." He opened unaccompanied (later joined by bassist Hinton), and many in the audience no doubt strained to hear his rendition of Duke's sinewy ballad, usually voiced by saxophone; a difficult task for any guitarist, really. The plucked instrument does not always lend itself to the demands of songs like this one, whose notes swell, ebb, and linger. Moreover, Hall is an acquired taste like German wines and may not have overwhelmed many in the audience that night, although he received appreciative applause at the close of his two-minute segment. Repeated hearings of the recorded concert make it clear that Hall acquitted himself admirably on a most challenging number.

———✳———

"Prelude to a Kiss"   **The Band**
Lyrics by Irving Mills and Irving Gordon (1938)

Conover introduced the next song in a somewhat pedantic manner:

> A song may be played simply. Or sung lyrically or arranged harmonically, or completely torn down and then rebuilt as musical architect Gerry Mulligan has done to Duke Ellington's "Prelude to a Kiss."

The last of the well-known Ellington tunes with a lyric credit for Irving Mills, "Prelude to a Kiss" was a musician favorite but somewhat of a late bloomer as far as the public was concerned. Song historian Alec Wilder commented:

> "Prelude" is another chromatic idea supported by very gratifying, satisfying harmony and, except for a totally inept instrumental release [bridge], comes close to being a song. Even the lyric by Irving Gordon has a few moments, though the image of a "flower crying for the dew" somehow fails.[36]

Still, as Ellington biographer Hasse concluded, "Prelude" ranks as one of the maestro's most esteemed ballads, even though its chromatic melody has tripped up many a singer.[37] But arranger Gerry Mulligan looked at the ballad's score and saw it differently. As jazz critic Hollie I. West reported in the *Washington Post* the next day,

> Ellington heard a radically different version of "Prelude." Last night's rendition was a special arrangement by Gerry Mulligan, who wrote it in medium-up tempo, featuring abundant counter play between the arranger and Desmond, Green, and Johnson. The theme was a circuitous ascending and descending unison line played by Mulligan and Desmond at the beginning and end of the song.[38]

Indeed, even after the heads-up from Conover, when the first strains of Mulligan's piquant interpretation of the usually placid "Prelude" rolled out, a surprised Ellington sat upright. Once he recognized the song, he relaxed back in his chair with an amused look on his face.[39] The other critics called the arrangement "ingenious" (Balliett), "highly original" (Morgenstern), and "zesty" (Ramsey).[40]

Many jazz fans and certainly many musicians in the audience (despite being forewarned by Conover) wouldn't have had a clue. Most would have thought the number anything other than "Prelude"—perhaps a 1950s West Coast jazz number off a Shorty Rogers and His Giants album.

Mulligan and Desmond soloed first, improvising in tandem, weaving separate contrapuntal lines over bass and drums accompaniment, as they did, for example on their 1962 *Two of a Mind* album (Bluebird, 2003). Trombonists Green and Johnson took over and—why not—continued in the contrapuntal mode (quite humorously, in fact). The next polyphonic duo, Terry and Mulligan, likewise improvised in counterpoint, reminiscent of Jeru at his peak 1950s popularity in duet with trumpet partner Chet Baker.

While some in the audience might have considered this unusual arrangement of "Prelude" out of character with the evening's purpose—the celebration of Ellington songs—it nonetheless served as a contrasting interlude (always a good idea in any concert). It also provided a reminder to everyone that jazz is not a slavish discipline devoted to exact replication of past classics. Quite the opposite, revered pieces act as springboards for fresh interpretations, and in that, Jeru succeeded splendidly.

Seated in the audience, columnist Earl Wilson of the *New York Post* concluded that as far as he was concerned, Mulligan probably was second only to Duke and the Nixons in interest. He seemed to play with his eyes closed all the time. When Wilson put the question to the sax man after the concert, he answered in typical elliptical fashion. "Yes I do, except when I have to read music. Then I also play with my eyes closed."[41]

———✻———

"Ring Dem Bells"   **The Band**
Lyrics by Irving Mills (1930)

"Ring Dem Bells" marked the beginning of Irving Mills's taking credit as lyricist on some Ellington pieces, eventually totaling sixty of them. No one knows if he wrote the text himself or hired someone under contract—or if Duke occasionally contributed. Later, son Mercer Ellington would say flatly that Mills did not write any of the lyrics but took 75 percent of the royalties. This indeed was the contract agreement Mills had with his father.[42] Mercer, all of eleven years old at the time, later remembered:

> The piano was in our living room, but even when Pop played ["Bells] as softly as possible, with the door closed, the strains would drift through the apartment as we slept. Beside my memory of him there with a pencil in his hand, I can remember seeing the sheet music for "Ring Dem Bells" around. He would do the writing, and band member Juan Tizol would be given the job of

copying off the parts. This number became a great favorite with other musicians, and Pop used it in the movie *Check and Double Check*. It was a favorite of mine, too. And I used to be able to sing all the parts.[43]

The all-star band punched out an up-tempo version of "Ring Dem Bells" as if it were a Broadway show pit band and "Bells" was the closer. Conover missed a trick: he could have added a line of tap-dancing chorus girls for effect. The band played variations of the theme to back sequential solos by Desmond and Mulligan before laying out for the finish, another tandem improvisation by Terry and Mulligan. All and all, another East Room crowd pleaser.

Guest Pianists

Conover at the microphone again: "That was Duke Ellington's "Ring Dem Bells," spelled *t-h-e-m*. Now we hear from three guest pianists. The first plays a medley of three Ellington songs: 'Drop Me off in Harlem'—"

Three knocks from backstage interrupt him.

A quick wit, Conover quipped, "Mr. Lombardo, please!" [a reference to rival bandleader Guy Lombardo]. The audience laughed.

He continued, "Followed by 'All Too Soon' and then 'It Don't Mean a Thing (If It Ain't Got That Swing).'"

———✳———

"Drop Me Off in Harlem"   Pianist Billy Taylor
Lyrics by Nick and Charles Kenny (1933)   Bassist Hinton
                                      Drummer Bellson

Duke wrote Billy Taylor's first number with a most improbable pair of collaborators: Nick and Charles Kenny of "Love Letters in the Sand" fame (successfully delivered by pop singer Pat Boone in 1957).

If "Harlem" seemed unfamiliar to many in the East Room that night, that's because it was. The tune had seldom been heard since first being recorded in 1933. An Ellingtonian like Billy Taylor wouldn't let a gem like this slip into obscurity. And while singer Ella Fitzgerald's songbook treatment was lovely, soft, supple—even sexy[44]—Billy's version was an upbeat romper. It's easy to imagine that such a rousing interpretation would have compelled other musicians present, maybe even Duke himself, to open the piano bench or visit that back storage room to sift through the song sheets and give "Harlem" a try.

Taylor introduced the tune with a basso-rhythmic pattern that gave way to a bouncy statement of the melody over an infectious Latin beat supplied by drummer Bellson. The audience would have had a difficult time sitting still for this one. It ended quickly and segued into the next number without applause.

———✳———

"All Too Soon"   **Pianist Billy Taylor**
Lyrics by Carl Sigman (1940)   **Bassist Hinton**
                                                      Drummer Bellson

"All Too Soon," one of the best examples of Ellington's melodic creativity, was written and recorded as an instrumental in 1940. The lyrics were added later by Carl Sigman, whose credits include "Crazy She Calls Me" and "My Heart Cries for You." Many, like critic Gary Giddins, consider the song as well as "Warm Valley" to be Ellington's most gorgeous nocturnes.[45]

Keeping with its customary slow tempo, Billy Taylor decorated the melody with his signature ringing block chords and feathery arpeggio runs, the gentle mood enhanced by occasional brush flutters on the snare drum by Bellson. Over all too soon, the number gave way to a fast-tempo swinger. In his set, Taylor would employ most of the arrows in his musical quiver. Who could blame him? It was his first time at the

White House, and he was playing for Duke, the man he most admired in the field of music.

——— ✳ ———

"It Don't Mean a Thing"   Pianist Billy Taylor
Lyrics by Irving Mills (1932)   Bassist Hinton
                                              Drummer Bellson

The instruction booklet for the Swing Era—if one could say such exists—was embodied in the sheet music for this tune. Ellington's band (and his first permanent singer, Ivie Anderson) had been declaring "It Don't Mean a Thing (If It Ain't Got That Swing)" four years before the mythical start of the Swing Era at the Palomar Ballroom in Los Angeles, California, on August 21, 1935. The apocryphal tale goes something like this: After a poorly received cross-country tour, a dejected Benny Goodman and his ragtag musicians arrived at the Palomar Ballroom in California fully expecting to disband after the engagement. Unbeknownst to Benny, the "hot" numbers he had been playing on his midnight-hour weekly radio show in New York City had struck a resonant chord with a prime-time teen audience on the West Coast. Benny had wisely carried Duke's instruction booklet in his hip pocket, pulling it out when all else had failed to save the day, and launched what was to become the Swing Era.

In August 1931, during intermissions at Chicago's Lincoln Tavern, Duke composed and arranged "Swing" and then recorded it six months later. The piece, wrote Ellington, became "famous as the expression of a sentiment which prevailed among jazz musicians at that time."[46] The title, in fact, had been a credo of trumpeter Bubber Miley's.

The number is as well known for its opening call—Duke's titular injunction—as its response—the famed "doo-wah doo-wah doo-wah" riff—which instrumentalists and vocalists have both endeavored to stamp with their own individual mark.

Taylor probably caught the East Room guests by surprise as he jumped from the tranquil "All Too Soon" into a fast-tempo version of "Swing" that featured boppish single-note runs in both hands, left hand chasing the right hand up and down the keyboard. A winner was not declared. This homage to pianist Bud Powell gave way to rapid thick chords banging out the theme—both call and doo-wah response. The trio received boisterous applause for its quality performance. Bassist Hinton and drummer Bellson seemed as pleased as everyone else over their support given to pianist Taylor, as evidenced by their exchange of congratulatory smiles and hand slaps at the conclusion.

As Billy stepped off the riser to make room for the second guest pianist, very few of those gathered in the East Room that April night would have known that the concert had just passed its halfway mark timewise, with another twelve songs to come.

———✳———

"Things Ain't What They Used to Be"	Pianist Dave Brubeck
Music by Mercer Ellington	Bassist Hinton
Lyrics by T. Persons (1941)	Drummer Bellson

Conover returned to the microphone: "Our second guest pianist [whom Conover chose not to name], augmented by two saxophonists, plays 'Time's A-Wastin',' or 'Things Ain't What They Used to Be.'"

Duke described the song's origins in his memoir:

During this period (1940–1941), we produced some very good music. Because of the ASCAP [radio ban], I could not play any of my own compositions, and this prompted the great activity of Billy Strayhorn, Juan Tizol, and [my son] Mercer Ellington, which in one way or another led to . . . a number of instrumentals that have become standards, including my son's "Things Ain't What They Used to Be."[47]

For his only number, pianist Dave Brubeck selected "Things" and invited Desmond and Mulligan to join him, a gesture that had to please fans of the fabled classic Brubeck Quartet. This would be one of the few times (perhaps the only time) Dave and Paul played together since the quartet disbanded in December 1967.

Backed by rhythm-mates Hinton and Bellson, Brubeck started "Things" off at a cantering gate. The saxophones joined him for one of the shortest statements of the theme on record (let's get to our solos, boys!). Desmond's alto improvisation began as usual—lilting and melancholic—but then turned uncharacteristically hot, several glissandos thrust upwards, bringing Duke out of his chair. According to critic Doug Ramsey, in the audience directly behind Cab Calloway, who was sitting close to Duke,

> Duke had been lounging comfortably as he listened. He sat bolt upright when, on "Things," with Brubeck at the piano, Desmond played a stunningly accurate impression of Johnny Hodges, Ellington's star alto player of forty-one years. "Hey," Duke said, and turned to Calloway with a grin, a reaction that pleased Desmond enormously when I described it to him.[48]

Mulligan followed in typical trampoline-like fashion, and then it was Brubeck time. The pianist ran off several single note lines before the ghost of pianist Erroll Garner appeared with his left-hand chomp-chomp-chomp, spooking Brubeck to get "bombastic"—namely, to tuck in the chin, dig in, and lay down those heavy, pounding frat-house chords that critics hated, but the pianist and his many fans loved: "The word 'bombastic' keeps coming up as if it were some trap I keep falling in to. Damn it, when I'm bombastic, I have my reasons. I want to be bombastic. Take it or leave it."[49]

With a full head of steam built up, Brubeck was ready to keep the party going all night long, but Jeru mistakenly assumed the pianist had musically nodded to close out the number and began the "Things" theme on his baritone. Brubeck and Desmond quickly joined Jeru and it was all over—except for the applause, which was considerable.

———✳———

"Perdido"	Pianist Earl Hines
Music with Juan Tizol	Bassist Hinton
Lyrics by E. Drake and Langsfelder (1942)	Drummer Bellson

For new material during the ASCAP ban, Duke also turned to valve trombonist Juan Tizol, who contributed several exotic numbers and a tightly swung "Perdido." Although the Spanish word *perdido* means "lost" or "missing," the title inspiration may lie elsewhere: Perdido Street is just off the French Quarter in New Orleans.

Another jam session favorite to rival "Mellotone," this boppish number matches three notes to three syllables, repeats them seven times with slight variations, so grab your axe and let's go. And that's just what pianist Earl Hines did. The critics raved:[50]

Hollie I. West: "The audience . . . responded most during the concert to a brief appearance by pianist Earl Hines who played a fiery version of 'Perdido.' His light and brilliant improvisations brought gospel singer Mahalia Jackson to her feet while Special Assistant for Urban Affairs Daniel P. Moynihan craned his neck to get a better view of the pianist. Billy Eckstine, the singer who formerly performed with Hines said, 'Do it, Baby, do it.'"

Stanley Dance: "Hines brought the concert to its peak in three thrilling choruses of 'Perdido.' Such excited, shouted approval as greeted this performance can seldom have been heard in the White House before . . . Friends of his Chicago years converged on Hines [afterward] to congratulate him. Mahalia Jackson, who had been excited by his 'Perdido,' embraced him and reminded him of when he tried to get her to sing the blues. Billy Eckstine, whom Hines originally brought to fame, came to bestow a jazz encomium. 'You dirty old man,' he said admiringly. 'I told [singer] Lou Rawls one number was all you needed. "Let him alone and you'll see," I said. And one number did it.'"

Dan Morgenstern: "But it was Hines who broke it up with just three choruses of a romping 'Perdido,' assisted by Hinton and Bellson—a moment of musical magic."

Leonard Feather: "Almost stole the show." [An understatement.]

Doug Ramsey: "[Hines] in two daring minutes of 'Perdido' tapped the essence of jazz; [perfectly captured by] the grins on the faces of Hinton and Bellson when Earl Hines was in full flight."

Tom Whaley: "Everybody was talking about Earl Hines. Billy Taylor was great, and Dave Brubeck was great, but Earl Hines— that was *all*!"

So what exactly sparked these excited responses to Hines keyboard pyrotechnics? It wasn't just the fastest-of-the-night tempo (although that was part of it to be sure). No, it was a flash moment midway in his solo when upper-register notes seemed to fly off the keyboard every which way as if they were coming from an antique player piano whose roll had spun madly out of control. Still in charge, Hines followed this brief episode of superhuman virtuosity at the same feverish tempo he had used at the start. The last note struck didn't have a chance to reverberate before the East Room exploded with the loudest sustained cacophony of shouts, cries, stomps, and applause heard all evening. Bassist Hinton stood upright behind his bass, dramatically wiped his brow, and pointed excitedly and repeatedly in Hines direction as he stepped down off the riser.

President Nixon had to feel as overwhelmed as everyone else. After the show, he invited the father of modern jazz piano upstairs to his private quarters for a chat about matters musical, the only all-star, other than Duke, to be so honored.[51]

A visual vignette, albeit brief, of the Hines "Perdido" moment replete with the facial grins of Hinton and Bellson can be seen on *In Tune with History: A Musical and Historical Journey through the White House* (White House Historical Association).

Two Pieces

Fatha stepped off the riser to make way for the returning band members. The buzz caused by his performance had not subdued, so Conover wisely let the next numbers announce themselves.

"Warm Valley"   **The Band**
Lyrics by S. K. "Bob" Russell (1941)

"Warm Valley" describes a scene not geographical, but rather anatomical (readers are invited to use their imaginations). This is the second in the pair of songs that Gary Giddins has called Ellington's most gorgeous nocturnes, the first being "All Too Soon."[52] Few would disagree. "Valley" was the first orchestral ballad feature for the lyrical alto of Johnny Hodges; it even served as the band's closing theme on radio for a while.

This number called for saxophone, that's for sure, and the band's baritone saxophonist got the call. Mulligan carried the melody by himself, with choice backing by pianist Jones and occasional splashes of color from the band. Jeru is the sole soloist as well, and it would not be fair to compare his outstanding effort to the well-known treatment by Duke's celestial alto saxophonist Johnny Hodges.

———✽———

"Caravan"	The Band
Music with Irving Mills and Juan Tizol (1933)	Bassist Hinton
	Drummer Bellson

Valve trombonist Juan Tizol developed and orchestrated "Caravan." Despite decades of constant use for every small nightclub and burlesque act, to say nothing of honky-tonk and frat-house jam sessions, this song has survived a myriad of treatments to remain one of the most appealing of Tizol's several Middle Eastern–tinged works. While the serpentine melody conjures "an image, perhaps, of a Middle Eastern snake charmer's trick, or a camel caravan undulating across the rolling sand dunes," its composer hails from the other side of the world: Puerto Rico.[53]

Drummer Bellson, under the East Room spotlight for the first time, initiated a loud, rather active exotic rhythm using sticks with sleigh bells attached. After the musicians slithered through "Caravan," they left the riser, instruments in hand, and the room grew silent for Milt Hinton's unaccompanied bass solo, which set the stage for a flawlessly designed drum solo by Bellson, a "fully baked solo," Whitney Balliett would say.

With a firm sense of contrast and construction, Bellson built his two-plus-minute solo: a rapid tattoo on his high-hat cymbal (tickety tickety tickety tick) peppered with bass drum "bombs," then a snare drum roll and more high-hat cymbal fluttering, up to a snare-and-bass drum crescendo, and down to another stint with sticks and high hat. Bellson concluded by extracting the full range of sounds from various pitched tom-toms (that he altered with elbow pressure), giving lie to the notion that the drum kit is strictly a percussive instrument. The band took the theme out, and Bellson returned for a caroming coda—a reprieve of his solo in miniature.

The audience responded with booming applause, taking its cue in part from band members, who had turned in the direction of the bowing drummer, nodding their heads and clapping enthusiastically.

The Singers' Turn

Conover prepped the audience for what was coming next: "The musical instrument is an echo of the human voice, but Duke Ellington often uses the human voice wordlessly as a musical instrument."

———✳———

"Mood Indigo"	Singer Mary Mayo
Music with Barney Bigard (1930)	The Band
Lyrics by Irving Mills (1931)	

A 1931 composition originally called "Dreamy Blues"—which Ellington claimed to have written in fifteen to twenty minutes while waiting for his mother to cook him dinner—put Duke on the map as far as the public was concerned.[54] The melody was stated by a trio—straight-muted trumpet, plunger-muted trombone, and clarinet—but the composer deliberately reversed the traditional roles, giving trombonist Tricky Sam Nanton the highest part and clarinetist Barney Bigard the lowest. The result was as otherworldly as the tune's title implied and caused a sensation when initially performed on the radio. Retitled "Mood Indigo," it was the band's first big commercial hit and most requested number for almost forty years. Mitchell Parish of "Star Dust" fame actually wrote the lyrics, but lost out on the royalties because he was a songwriter contracted to, guess who, Mills Music.

Duke wrote his part in about twenty minutes and arranged the number, both true, but he also had an invaluable contribution from clarinetist Bigard:

> Duke had a date for a small group recording that in fact was supposed to be my group. We would record for all kinds of companies in those days and put the band under any kind of name with one of the sidemen signing in as leader. That was to avoid contract

complications. All the bands did it. Anyway, I brought what I had of the number to the date and we tried to work it out. We just used Tricky [trombonist Sam Nanton], [trumpeter] Artie Whetsol, and myself, along with the rhythm section. Duke figured out a first strain and I gave him some ideas for it too. He wrote out a three-part harmony for the horns, we added my second strain and recorded it. Whetsol had the lead, I had the second, and Tricky Sam had the third. We didn't think anything of it and all of a sudden it began to get popular and that was it.

I missed the boat for twenty-eight years on royalties. I didn't get a dime. It was all under Ellington and Mills's name. You see in those days—just to show how stupid we were—we would write a number and sell it to Mills for twenty-five or fifty dollars. If we had kept the numbers with our names on, we would have had royalties for years. Now it has finally been legally cleared up for "Mood Indigo," and I do get royalties for it.[55]

Exemplified in the first chorus of "Mood," Ellington's cryptic orchestration—voiced for Nanton (plunger-muted trombone), Whetsol (straight-muted trumpet), and Bigard (clarinet)—prompted this oft-quoted observation by arranger, conductor, and pianist Andre Previn:

[Bandleader] Stan Kenton can stand in front of a thousand fiddles and a thousand brasses and make a dramatic gesture and every studio arranger can nod his head and say, "Oh, yes, that's done like this." But Duke merely lifts a finger, three horns make a sound, and I don't know what it is.[56]

While Previn and his studio arranger friends discerned the inversion that put the trombone on top and the clarinet on bottom, the Ellington effect continued to mystify them. No one knew better than Duke the sonorities of his players on their respective instruments. That "Mood" quality was due to them and nobody else, as Duke himself discovered when the principals left the band.

Take the trumpet part Artie Whetsol played on "Mood Indigo": to play that high D, to stay on it and sustain it up here, haunted trumpet players for many years to the extent that they never wanted to play the lead part. That was what drove [trumpeter] Wallace Jones into becoming a funeral director! He said the reason he was no longer staying in show business was very simple— "Mood Indigo."[57]

Duke wrote in his memoir:

To give "Mood" a little additional luster for those people who remember it from years ago, we play it with the bass clarinet down at the bottom instead of the ordinary clarinet, and they always feel it is exactly the way it was forty years ago.[58]

In other words, the unique New Orleans woody clarinet sound of Barney Bigard had to be replaced by baritone saxophonist Harry Carney on bass clarinet to approximate the illusory eerie tone of the original recording.

Mary Mayo, a pure-voiced singer possessed of accurate pitch, was an excellent Conover selection to cover the song Duke and his orchestra played four times at the Mayflower Hotel for President Eisenhower some fifteen years prior. Midway in the song, Mayo put her wordless vocalese to good use—wrapping an obbligato around a bronze ornament from trombonist J. J. Johnson—and then again at the close, a tribute to the famed three-part opening with trombone on top (Johnson), trumpet in the middle (Berry), and voice (Mayo) on the bottom where the clarinet (Bigard) used to be. Ethereal indeed! Fans of this tune had to be pleased; their applause indicated as such.

———✳———

"Prelude to a Kiss"	**Singer Mary Mayo**
Lyrics by Irving Mills and Irving Gordon (1938)	**Rhythm Section**

Conover programmed "Prelude" twice. Instead, he could have chosen "Solitude," which is similar in renown, mood, and difficulty, but for some reason he chose not to. Guests who attended the dinner, at least, got to hear the U.S. Army Strolling Strings play "Solitude." Perhaps Conover, like song historian Wilfred Sheed, would vote "Prelude" the most beautiful song ever written, except for the one problem with the words. Or perhaps session singer Mayo was simply more comfortable with the song—she certainly navigated its tricky melodic waters with ease. More likely, Conover believed that after Mulligan's earlier medium-tempo impressionistic sketch, the audience deserved a customary reading of the ordinarily dreamy ballad.

———✳———

"I Didn't Know about You"	**Singer Mary Mayo**
Lyrics by S. K. "Bob" Russell (1944)	**Rhythm Section**

Like so many other Ellington songs, "I Didn't Know about You" had an instrumental origin. Duke recorded it as a harmonically interesting vehicle for Johnny Hodges's saxophone in July 1942 as "Sentimental Lady." (It might have also been known as "Home" at one time). After a confab with lyricist Bob Russell and a slight change in melody, it emerged as "I Didn't Know about You" in 1944. This was the fourth and the last winner for the Ellington-Russell hit-making juggernaut that gave a wartime America something to hum. "Warm Valley," "Don't Get Around Much Anymore," and "Do Nothing Till You Hear from Me" all preceded "I Didn't Know about You." They would try again in 1960 with "Like Love" based on an Ellington theme from the Otto Preminger film *Anatomy of a Murder*, but with considerably less success than they achieved with their 1940s hits.

———✳———

"Praise God and Dance" (1968)   **Singer Mary Mayo**
Lyrics by Duke Ellington   **The Band**

Conover announced the next two songs: "Duke Ellington has said there is only one perfect being and that is God. All the rest of us are simply varying degrees of imperfection. He has also said this in two other ways."

For the next three numbers, the band set aside their secular Ellington songbooks and slipped their Ellington Sacred Concert hymnals on their music stands. Along with singer Mayo, the band offered up "Praise God and Dance" from the Second Sacred Concert that premiered at St. John's Cathedral in New York City on January 19, 1968. Unlike the First Sacred Concert held three years earlier at Grace Cathedral in San Francisco, the second consisted of all new material, although it shared some themes with the first.[59] Based on the 150th Psalm, the "Praise God" hymn closed out the Second Sacred Concert in dramatic fashion:

> Here the whole company was used, and after an impressively sincere introduction by singer Alice Babs, the performance proceeded in a series of joyful explosions, like a Roman candle. Saxophonist Paul Gonsalves, clarinetist Jimmy Hamilton, and trumpeter Cat Anderson were the chief soloists. At St. John's, two sets of dancers had surprised the audience. One line, erupting down the center aisle, colorfully dressed, and coached by Geoffrey Holder, moved with gestures symbolic of worship in the idiom of modern dance. The second, issuing from behind the band, was swinging all the way with steps and rhythms right out of the Savoy Ballroom.[60]

Willis Conover missed another trick by not including an accompanying dance number. Dancers Geoffrey Holder and his wife, Carmen de Lavallade, who had been Duke's Madam Zajj in the TV musical *A Drum Is a Woman*, were in the audience and could have easily coaxed some attendees to join them in a snake line once around the East Room. Congregants at Duke's Sacred Concerts regularly burst into the aisles on their own to join the professional dancers.

As for the hymn, Alice Babs, the Swedish singer who usually sang the song, commented on its weight and beauty:

> It has a gravity that conveys the deepest message. And the melody line is so pure. Like Bach, I can give it the same power I give to Bach. In church, at home, his are the songs I sing.

Again, as on her first three numbers, Mayo acquitted herself well, as everyone expected.

The clergy most responsible for staging Duke's Sacred Concerts at their facilities were in the audience that night, seated up front in the second row (see appendix 9). Reverend Gensel, a particular favorite of Ellington, even officiated at the last rites of Billy Strayhorn. Duke insisted the White House send invitations to all seven clerics, most of whom brought their wives and, as we shall see anon, danced at the after party. Conover chose not to acknowledge their presence from the riser that night; it would have been a nice touch if he had.

---***---

"Come Sunday" (1943)	Singer Joe Williams
Lyrics by Duke Ellington	**The Band**

"Come Sunday," which Gary Giddins has rightly crowned Duke's supreme contribution to the American hymnal,[61] was first introduced in 1943 at Carnegie Hall as a wordless spiritual theme in *Black, Brown and*

Beige, Ellington's first voyage into extended composition. This ambitious work never achieved a regular position in his repertoire, and "Come Sunday" languished as a result, at least for a spell.[62]

In 1958, Duke collaborated with gospel singer Mahalia Jackson for the Columbia album *Black, Brown and Beige* (actually, an abridged version of the 1943 production). Outfitted with lyrics by Duke—some say his best—the haunting refrain was given its most magnificent reading ever by the gospel diva.[63]

Five years later, a group of Chicago citizens organized an exposition to celebrate the centennial of the Emancipation Proclamation. For this occasion, Ellington created a musical revue called *My People*, which included "Sunday."

Two years after that, in 1965, the song was canonized at the White House as part of President Johnson's Arts Festival and at Ellington's First Sacred Concert premier at Grace Cathedral Church in San Francisco, which toured internationally thereafter, totaling close to fifty performances.

Even with its impressive resume, "Sunday" was due another White House appearance, this time by blues and ballad singer Joe Williams. He loved singing Ellington songs and included at least one in nearly every show. He sang "Sunday" at an earlier Ellington tribute in the summer of 1963 in New York City (Duke's fortieth year in the music business) and again on record in 1966: *Presenting Joe Williams: Thad Jones/Mel Lewis* (Blue Note).[64]

Mahalia Jackson's rendering of this lovely hymn is unsurpassed. But on the male side of the ledger, no one has come close to matching the depth and poignancy that Williams has lent to the song. One of the critics in attendance that night, Leonard Feather, characterized Joe's version as "deeply moving."[65] Critic Morgenstern noted, "Williams [is] singing as movingly as I've ever heard him."[66] Society columnist Earl Wilson concluded that the most touching point in the concert was when Joe Williams sang, "Lord above, God Almighty above, please look down and see my people through."[67] After the concert, when complimented for his moving version of the song, Williams, wearing a necklace with a pendant containing a picture of Martin Luther King, said, "How could you not sing it right, with those words of Duke's."[68]

Joe would sing the same hymn at Count Basie's funeral on April 28, 1984, at the Abyssinian Baptist Church in Harlem.

———✳———

"Heritage" (1963)   Singer Joe Williams
Lyrics by Duke Ellington   The Band

The *My People* musical revue of 1963 included old songs like "Come Sunday" but also new songs like "Heritage," also known as "My Mother, My Father." Two years later, Ellington featured the song at the premier of the First Sacred Concert at Grace Cathedral in San Francisco. In his introduction, Duke captured its universal nostalgic appeal:

> We took the liberty of adding a number tonight . . . inspired by the Fourth Commandment . . . to honor . . . well, it's more like everybody's type of song because it sort of honors thy fathers and mothers to the point of never referring to them in the past tense.[69]

Bringing the same amount of conviction and richness to "Heritage" as he did to "Come Sunday," Williams sang slowly and thoughtfully, with the feel of an elegy. According to Doug Ramsey, there wasn't a dry eye in the East Room when he finished.[70] Joe's passionate reading of this warm tribute to family brought to mind Ellington's remark earlier in the evening about the sanctity of his mother's arms.

As with "Come Sunday," Williams would revisit "Heritage" in a studio date for Fantasy Records accompanied by the Cannonball Adderley Quintet (*Joe Williams Live*, 1973) and again, memorably so, at Duke's funeral on Memorial Day, May 27, 1974.

Ellington had to be pleased that "Heritage" and "Praise God and Dance," both penned in the 1960s, had been included in the program, not so much because they were nonsecular, but because they were contemporary. Duke always preferred (when finances permitted) to showcase his current work and leave past successes to the past. Conover knew this of course, and shaded his selections accordingly, although omitting Ellington evergreens like "C-Jam Blues," "Solitude," "Rockin' in Rhythm," and "I'm Beginning to See the Light" from the program might have perturbed some audience members.

———✳———

"Jump for Joy"   **Singer Joe Williams**
Lyrics by Sid Kuller and Paul Francis Webster (1941)   **The Band**

A swinger from the satirical musical of 1941 of the same name, "Jump for Joy" closed out the band concert in truly joyous fashion. Ellington wrote this number on the overnight train from Salt Lake City to Los Angeles, along with another hit from the musical, "I Got It Bad," but unlike that one, "Jump" is imbued with a rhythmic bounce and sway that could only have come from a ride on board a clickety-clacking express train sweeping across the heartland. Willis Conover could not have chosen a better match for this song. Joe's caramel baritone perfectly enveloped the song's gospel ardor and secular esprit.

He had previously recorded "Jump" in 1963 backed by, among others, his all-star bandmates Hank Jones, Urbie Green, Milt Hinton, and Clark Terry. Given Joe's love of Ellingtonia, he must have sung the song a hundred times after that 1963 studio date. Whether it was this past familiarity with the tune, or the animated bouncing tempo set by conductor Whaley, or the band's sensing the concert finish line, Joe was out front but still solidly "in the pocket" for an all-out swinging climax to the concert.

> Come little baby, and jump for joy   [Joe]
>
> Bop bop bop   [Band]

At the conclusion of "Jump," signaling the close of the concert, the musicians gathered around Conover at the center of the riser. He took the microphone and shouted "May I present" several times over a steady appreciative roar from the 235 souls gathered in the East Room. Conover finally broke through and began introducing the all-stars. As he announced each one, Duke stood up, bowed, and blew kisses, and the musicians in turn responded with warm smiles.

The members of the audience doled out generous applause for each musician, adding loud cheers when they heard Clark Terry's name. Both Earl Hines and Mary Mayo received an especially enthusiastic crowd response as well.

Duke at the Keys

After introducing himself, Conover continued, "And perhaps the host and hostess are willing to introduce the composer . . . Ladies and Gentlemen, the president of the United States and the first lady." [Applause.] Nixon stepped up on the riser:

> Ladies and Gentlemen. After seeing and hearing this great array of stars, there is absolutely nothing that could top it, except . . . just one. I think we ought to hear from the Duke, too.

As was planned a month or so prior, the birthday honoree took the stage for his "impromptu" number, the one he had practiced at the mahogany Steinway concert grand piano earlier in the afternoon. Suave, debonair, and elegant as always, Ellington spoke humbly, quietly:

> Thank you, Mr. President. That is the greatest compliment I ever had—to say that I am eligible to follow this much artistry [as we

have heard tonight]. [Applause.] I am somewhat of a courageous nature, however . . . I shall pick a name and see if I can improvise on it . . . something, you know, very gentle, graceful, and something like princess—Pat.

———✳———

"Pat" **Pianist Duke Ellington**

Ellington had two instruments: the orchestra and the piano. He composed at the latter and used it in performance to introduce numbers, set the tempo, feed ideas to his bandsmen, and accompany their solos. If his piano playing generally took a backseat to his four main careers (composer, bandleader, showman, and publicist-promoter), many consider him a fine instrumentalist. As jazz journalist Ralph Gleason succinctly opined,

> Make no mistake about it: In addition to all the other things Duke Ellington was, and was superbly, he was also one hell of a piano player. Anytime.[71]

Indeed, in Rizzo's book *The Fifty Greatest Jazz Pianists of All Time*, Duke is ranked thirty-eighth. John Edward Hasse, one of his biographers, characterized his playing thus:

> His piano sound was deep and resonant; his touch remarkable, his use of all registers of the piano exceptional . . . His style was versatile, ranging from Harlem rent-shouts and down-home blues to poetic prefaces and impressionistic interludes, often laced with dissonant clusters of notes. He could jump instantly from elegant to earthy.[72]

As usual, jazz critic Whitney Balliett was a bit more poetic:

[Duke] has taken the Harlem style apart and rebuilt it, with Gothic flourishes, into an infinitely more imposing structure. He has replaced the ump-chump ump-chump of the left hand with startling offbeat chords and generous basso-profundo booms. He has added populous dissonances and far-out chords. And into these, he has worked crooked arpeggios—directionless, seemingly drunken ones—and handsome upper-register necklaces of notes that poke harmless fun at [stridemaster] James P. Johnson's lacy right-hand garlands. As such, Ellington's piano style has had a good deal of subtle influence, particularly on pianists Thelonious Monk and Cecil Taylor . . . prodding soloists with disconcerting, far-out chords, rumbling behind a lazy trombone section, out-Monking Monk when the spirit was on him.[73]

The pianist who was capable of laying down weird thundering chords that could influence Monk and Taylor also had a lighter, ruminative side—a Billy Strayhorn side, if you will—that was capable of producing lovely, impressionistic sketches.

After introducing "Pat," the maestro swiftly moved to the piano bench, leaned forward, and essayed an introspective three-minute piece. According to the jazz scribes in attendance, his performance was . . .

indeed gentle and graceful, with serene melodic and harmonic qualities not entirely to be grasped at one hearing, as is so often the case with his piano solos. [Dance]

a slow, Debussy-like melody that brought the room to dead silence. [Balliett]

a brief, pensive, extemporized solo, and the concert was over. [Feather]

full of serenity and the wizardry of Ellington's harmonies. Mrs.

Nixon, who looked distracted through much of the evening, paid close attention. [Ramsey]

Warm applause followed Ellington to his seat, and the president retook the stage:

The evening is still young. [Laughter.] I just received from Mr. Conover the information that if we will all rather gradually move to that room next door, and there will be refreshments there . . . and music, this room will be cleared, the band will return and they will have a jam session and dancing for all those who want. How about it?

A large cheer rang out as Nixon bid his guests a buoyant good night. He and wife Pat swiftly departed for the second floor of the residence. It was exactly 12:15.

Invited as an entertainment-only guest, pianist Willie "the Lion" Smith (shown here surveying the East Room jam session scene) joined his 1920s pupil Duke at the piano.

CHAPTER 8

The Jam Session

THE WHITE HOUSE STAFFERS SNAPPED into action and started clearing the East Room to accommodate "a jam session and dancing for all those who want."[1] Press estimates put the attendance at close to 200; in reality the crowd numbered some 235, counting the dinner guests, entertainment-only guests, and a smattering of working press and musicians from the Marine and Navy bands (see appendix 9). Unlike the dinner, where the guests were overwhelmingly Ellington picks, the crowd assembled for the jam session split about half and half between Duke's and the president's selections. This split resulted from a sizable number of Ellington invitees (53 out of 135) sending in their regrets, and their places filled (at the eleventh hour) by Nixon apparatchiks (who undoubtedly thought they had died and gone to heaven—see appendices 7 and 8).

During the East Room makeover, the ebullient crowd of government officials, clergy, art institution heads, composers, musicians, members of the press, and friends of the principals milled about, their finery on full display. Dancer Geoffrey Holder wore a self-designed black velvet cutaway, singer Billy Eckstine sported a lavender dinner shirt, and Lou Rawls an Edwardian shirt with three-inch cuffs and neck ruffles. A dozen women had chosen Chiffon for the evening: dancer Carmen de Lavallade (white pleated); Mrs. Otto Preminger and singer Mahalia Jackson (yellow); Ruth Ellington (green and white by Lilli Rubin); Mrs. John H. Johnson (royal blue with yards of chiffon by Burke-Amey); Mrs. John Silvera (aqua); Mrs. Billy Eckstein (white with seed pearls and red bulge beads); Mrs. Milton Hinton (Teal Traina emerald green); Mrs. Irv Kupcinet, wife of the *Chicago Sun-Times* columnist (Burke Amey side-fastened sheath); Mrs. Billy Taylor (Rudi Gernreich purple jersey); and Nora Holt of the *New York Amsterdam News* (iridescent sequin gown designed and made for her in Shanghai in 1932).[2]

Some in the crowd joined all-stars Paul Desmond and Urbie Green and critic Doug Ramsey and headed for the bar. Vice President Agnew told columnist Earl Wilson, "You know, I can play a little Duke Ellington on the piano, too," and then he sat down at the Marine Band's piano in the entrance hall while partygoers gathered around and listened to the "surprise guest pianist" play his Ellington favorites "Sophisticated Lady" and "In a Sentimental Mood."[3] Others, notably Billy Eckstine and Louis Bellson, cavorted in the lower corridors of the White House. Mahalia Jackson, resplendent in flowing yellow chiffon, held court with admirers, but ducked questions about her remarriage to nearby escort Sigmund Calloway.

Still others discussed their favorite Ellington tunes.[4] Smithsonian Head Dillon Ripley and Protocol Chief Emil Mosbacher and his wife all voted for "Mood Indigo." Presidential Assistant Daniel P. Moynihan said "East St. Louis Toodle-oo" was his, and the wife of the Guyanese Ambassador Lady Carter said "Satin Doll." Ellington himself moved easily from cluster to cluster, slapping friends on the back, signing autographs, and taking a quick puff on a cigarette when offered. When he neared Whitney Balliett and his wife, Nancy, she said to him, "I was so glad you kissed President Nixon. I think he liked that." Ellington replied, "I always kiss my friends. So now he belongs."[5]

Nixon sent word to Leonard Garment that he should bring Fatha Hines upstairs to the family quarters for a nightcap.

Hines and Nixon sat around for a while, reminiscing. Hines . . . talked about the early joys of his long life in jazz. Nixon, the political utilitarian, told about what he [had] learned from the years of piano lessons and practicing [he'd] endured as a kid. By the time Hines . . . got downstairs [after the fifteen-minute chat], the chandeliered East Room had been transformed into the old Cotton Club.[6]

The jam session band had formed: One half included the all-stars, complemented by Dizzy Gillespie and, for a spell, both Dr. Harold Taylor of Sarah Lawrence College on bongos and Leonard Garment on clarinet (but no Benny Goodman); and the other half, members of the Marine Band, still in their formal scarlet tunics, and the downstairs Navy Band trio, still in their dress blues, who looked as if they were in Valhalla. Years would pass before Benny Goodman forgave Garment for not instructing him to bring his clarinet.

The grand piano with the golden eagle legs that Steinway & Sons had presented to the White House in 1938 switched players many times, some alone, some in tandem: from Ellington to his mentor Willie "the Lion" Smith (still bedecked in derby despite Cab Calloway's lecture to observe decorum and remove the topper)[7] to Marian McPartland ("Isn't this something," she laughed, putting a drink on the piano top) to festival producer George Wein to Dave Brubeck to Billy Taylor to Leonard Feather. Fatha Hines was called to participate in the jam session, but he begged off because he was leaving for a South American tour a few hours later. Amateur pianist Vice President Agnew likewise begged off because, as he told a friend, "I felt too outclassed."[8] An appreciative crowd that included National Security Advisor Henry Kissinger, drink in hand, clustered around the piano nodding their approval.

The duo of Duke and the Lion at the piano had to tug at both their hearts, as well as the hearts of the jazz cognoscenti clustered nearby. In the 1920s Lion had befriended the slightly younger man in the Big Apple and helped show him the ropes.[9] And here they were, almost five decades later, the two of them, once again together at the keyboard in a most improbable setting a long, long way from the Capital Palace on Lenox Avenue in Harlem. Ellington learned a lot from the cigar-chomping pianist, telling a reporter at the party that he had influenced him more than anyone else. "The Lion is just a great intangible force that you can't put your finger on but that you can't resist."[10]

Showmanship, for example. Duke would lift his hands off the keyboard like his mentor with a flourish to draw people's attention. The Lion summed up his musical credo for a reporter, "There's nothing like a good melody. That's why today's young musicians can't last. Everyone wants to hum something."[11] A sentiment Ellington would not challenge, especially the good melody part. The maestro paid tribute to his friend, only two years his senior, when he composed and recorded "Portrait of the Lion" in 1939.

Fearing his Harlem friend would monopolize the keyboard all night long, Duke urged Marian McPartland—who spent the evening shuttling between the White House and her gig at Blues Alley—to take her turn at the grand piano. Once she was on the riser, the Lion said to her, "I suppose you want to play."

"Yeah, I'd like to," Marian responded, moving in a little.

"Okay," Willie said as he walked off in a sulk. Ellington stood nearby chuckling to himself.

After a decent interval at the keys, McPartland zipped back to Blues Alley, where she greeted her guests with, "Sorry I'm late. I'm also doubling at the White House."[12]

Meanwhile, at the jam session, Fatha Hines stood off to the side of the piano chatting with Reverend Weicker, who had been invited to the party by the evening's honoree for his involvement in the recently staged Sacred Music Concerts. Eleven months later, at the reverend's wedding reception, Hines and his quartet performed for two hundred guests at the Colony Club in Spanish Harlem.[13]

Joe Williams, Billy Eckstine, and Lou Rawls all gathered at the microphone at one point, cutting each other on blues classics "Every Day," "Stormy Monday," and "It's a Lowdown Dirty Shame." They held court for nearly half an hour.

Duke led off the dancing with Carmen de Lavallade after the chairs had been pushed back. Guests joined in, dancing the popcorn, frug, monkey, and unnameables in front of the bandstand, in the aisles, and between the chairs. The president's personal secretary since 1951, Rose Mary Woods, yelled "This is a groove," kicked up her heels, and soon had musicians and Nixonians dancing, including first daughter Trisha, who executed a passable frug with an African American guest while Joe Williams warbled "They call it Stormy Monday (But Tuesday Is Just as Bad)." Urbie Green cut a slice of William's musical pie, executing a bluesy solo on his trombone. Benny Goodman no doubt winced when event instigator Leonard Garment showed off his musical skills on clarinet, riding atop the ensemble in fine New Orleans style on a slow tempo version of "When the Saints Go Marching In."

Gerry Mulligan, who would jam with zoo monkeys if given the chance, never left the bandstand, backing up all comers on his baritone saxophone, including an impromptu Clark Terry and Dizzy Gillespie trumpet duo. From all reports, wife of the baritone master, actress Sandy Dennis, didn't seem to mind. Willis Conover and USIA boss Frank Shakespeare stood close by in obvious awe. Members of the clergy joined in with energy and surprising ability. "This must be that Ecumenical Strut," a musician thoughtfully observed. Ellington danced in turn with Rose Mary Woods, Mrs. Logan, his sister, Reverend Yaryan's wife, Mrs. Joe Williams, and AP feature reporter Mary Campbell, and then went over to his personal physician, Dr. Arthur Logan, who was sitting in one of the leftover gilded chairs. The doctor took his pulse and pushed Ellington back on the floor for more dancing and posing for the cameras.

Many in the crowd took note of conspicuous absences.[14] Jazz vibraphonist Lionel Hampton, for example—the one African American musician who went all out for Nixon in every election campaign he was involved in: House, Senate, vice president (twice), and president (twice).[15] Few knew Hamp and his band were on tour in Europe for the State Department. Others noted the absence of black members of Congress, although Ernest Pettinaud, a Jamaican and long-term maitre d' of the House of Representatives restaurant had made the cut, along with his wife. Also not there, but (wrongly) thought to be on the list that the guest of honor had submitted to the White House, was Clifford Alexander Jr., Dr. Logan's son-in-law.[16] As the *New York Times* reported a year and a half earlier on August 4, 1967, Duke was a beaming guest in the second row of the East Room, when President Johnson swore Mr. Alexander in as the Chairman of the Equal Employment Opportunity Commission. President Nixon, succumbing to pressure from Republican Senate Leader Everett Dirksen, had recently announced that Alexander would not be renamed to the chairmanship. He promptly resigned from his post, causing an uproar in the African American community. Duke wisely kept Alexander off his guest list, knowing the president would not have invited him anyway. However sad, for political reasons, Alexander was effectively denied the opportunity to witness another bright moment in the East Room with Duke and his father-in-law.

Though many in the East Room that night would not have known, also absent were Swing Era jazz pianists Mary Lou Williams and Teddy Wilson (the latter a member of the famed 1940s Benny Goodman Quintet with Lionel Hampton and Gene Krupa). Both keyboard artists were on Duke's list and invited, but sent regrets. A shame really, since both would have beefed up the group of '20s and '30s pianists in attendance: Willie "the Lion" Smith, Earl "Fatha" Hines, and Duke Ellington to contrast and compare with the modernists Dave Brubeck, Hank Jones, Marian McPartland, and Billy Taylor, not to mention competent but lesser lights Leonard Feather and George Wein. The piano lineup at the Duke tribute was not as jaw-dropping impressive as that presented at President Carter's South Lawn Jazz Festival in 1978—from ragtimer Eubie Blake to ultra-modernist Cecil Taylor, with Mary Lou Williams,

Teddy Wilson, Dick Hyman, Billy Taylor, McCoy Tyner, and Herbie Hancock in between—but the first White House assemblage of jazz keyboard masters nonetheless did the jazz art world proud. This group would have been prouder still had Mary Lou Williams and Teddy Wilson been able to attend Duke's birthday party.

Also invited but absent—though not known to the partiers—was a stunning array of well-known singers:

Marian Anderson	Bing Crosby	Maurice Chevalier
Louis Armstrong	Dean Martin	Leslie Uggams
Diahann Carroll	Frank Sinatra	Rosemary Clooney

Imagine the excitement in the room if Louis "Pops" Armstrong had joined the likes of Billy Eckstine, Lou Rawls, and Joe Williams at the microphone for an extended round of the blues. Or if Pops had joined Bing for a duet of the sort they had been doing on radio and TV and in film for the past three decades. And what if Frank and Dean had gotten into the act with their patented Las Vegas schtick? Or if the glamorous songbirds—Diahann Carroll, Rosemary Clooney, and Leslie Uggams—had taken over the mic for a spell? But the fantasy topper of them all would have been the spectacle of Pops joining his heirs Dizzy and Clark in a trumpet rondo. Would the jam session have been more spectacular, more memorable? Would it have generated greater press coverage? Never to know of course. It was probably best that the guests on hand that night were kept in the dark about those invitees who sent in their regrets. After all, by all accounts, the Ellington night was never to be topped as it was.

As the party roared on well past the midnight hour, photographers swarmed around the room taking pictures of musicians, dancers, and bystanders from every possible angle. White House photographer Ollie Atkins followed suit but unlike the others, he focused his camera's lens on administration officials, particularly the president's personal secretary, Rose Mary Woods. Atkins clicked away as his party muse danced in turn with Duke and several other partners, and (essentially) by herself. These latter photos show the auburn-haired beauty in controlled abandon, oblivious to everything but the music, expressing pure sensual joy.

Thirteen years prior at the 1956 Newport Jazz Festival, a platinum blond in a black cocktail dress had ignited a late-night crowd and the Ellington Orchestra with her wild spontaneous dance during tenor sax man Paul Gonsalves's legendary twenty-seven-chorus improvisation.[17] Her photo appeared in newspapers and magazines—even on the back cover of the Columbia LP album that captured the excitement of that once-in-a-lifetime event. While few knew her real name, the "girl who launched 7,000 cheers" became justly famous, forever linked with Ellington's late-career comeback that began at Newport '56.

Had anyone other than Ollie Atkins—such as a cameraman from a newspaper, magazine, or wire service—taken pictures of Woods under the rapturous spell of the infectious rhythms emanating from the East Room jam band and published them in a daily newspaper or weekly magazine, the nascent Nixon administration would have had a cause célèbre on its hands. The press would have immediately compared Ms. Woods to her long-ago Newport counterpart and kept the story alive for weeks. Since Atkins's photos were for the historical record (releasable to the public only by authorization of the president), Ms. Woods retained her anonymity, at least for a while. Four years later, her name would be immortalized after an improbable encounter with an unruly tape machine that ostensibly caused an eighteen-and-a-half-minute gap in a critical Watergate tape. Another side of Ms. Woods public persona lives on through the photographs taken by Ollie Atkins at the mansion that special April night, a number of which are included in this book.

According to the *Afro-American* newspaper, many guests remarked, "This is the way it should be . . . black and white dancing together," while others were trying to remember another occasion where this many black guests had assembled at the White House at one time for a dinner gathering. Many could not recall such an occasion.[18] (Because, in fact, there had never been one.) The party went on and on, prompting Mrs.

Logan to say, "If this thing doesn't break up soon, I'm going to head for the Lincoln bedroom." Thankfully to some, Mercer Ellington brought the jamming to a halt with a gentle reminder to his father. "Pops, we're booked on an 8:15 a.m. flight later this morning because we've got a date in Oklahoma City tonight."[19]

The party broke up sometime after 2 a.m. "Good morning" was the thing to say as the guests departed for home in the sprinkling of rain that had begun to fall, making the pavement look glossy in the reflection of the White House lights. Singers Billy Eckstine, Joe Williams, and Lou Rawls with their arms around one another's shoulders, continued the party, singing the blues as they left the mansion. Paul Desmond and Urbie Green, who had taken full advantage of the open bar, solicitously helped one another out of the White House entrance and into a taxi as three o'clock approached. Willis Conover escorted Willie "the Lion" to a cab, where the derby-topped pianist asked if there were any late-night clubs featuring jazz and urged Willis to join him. Conover begged off.

Returning to his hotel in a White House limousine, Duke held his medal under his coat and commented to his publicist, Joe Morgen, "With how much more respect can one civilized person treat another than the president in honoring me and acknowledging me and my reason for being—my greatest honor." Back at the hotel, Ellington quickly changed into his traveling clothes. While making his farewells in the crowded suite, he stuffed telegrams and birthday cards into his coat pockets. He had a plane to catch. He would get a little sleep in Oklahoma City, where he and the band had an engagement in less than eighteen hours: a dance for a high school prom at the Civic Center Music Hall.

As for the president and first lady during the downstairs revelry, the latter confided to friends, "We sat upstairs and listened." For how long is not known.

During and after the party, reporters from the local newspapers and national magazines (most prominently *Jet* magazine) queried musicians and others on Duke and the importance of the evening. Their effusive comments follow:[20]

Ruth Ellington: "The artists on the program were superlative. The thing that moved me the most was that Willis Conover . . . was astute enough to project the philosophy of our life by ending the program with 'Praise God.' After all, God is responsible for all that we have. The most gracious act of the evening was that of the president when he sat down to play 'Happy Birthday' on the piano."

Tom Whaley: "It's great, but the man should have been honored years ago. He is the greatest living. He is the most peaceful man in the world."

Gerry Mulligan: "It's an honor to be asked to honor the Duke. That's the way we all feel about him."

J. J. Johnson: "I can't think of anyone in the field of music and the arts more deserving of such a tribute. Duke has given so many people so many years of pleasure."

Hank Jones: "This man has contributed so much. He has an endless flow of ideas and has maintained his musical integrity. More than that, he created the climate for change by taking his music and making it the great common denominator. If you can exchange ideas musically, then you can change ideas politically, socially and so on. We are all richer for Duke doing this. He doesn't demand respect. He commands respect."

Clark Terry: "The president has done a great thing for a great person while he is alive and can enjoy the tribute. Tell Duke he is a great man. Let's all shout it from the mountaintop."

Joe Williams: "[Duke's] contribution to the music of the world will last for centuries and here we are in the White House to honor him. I can't possibly be more pleased. My wife [Jill Hughes, who photographed the cover of Duke's *My People* album] is here with me and is thrilled to death . . . I think by recognizing Duke Ellington, the president also recognizes the proud heritage and the contributions of black people to America and the world."

Louis Bellson: "This was a great tribute to a great man. It was well deserved and the president handled the affair in a deserving manner. I was really happy to be a part of it."

Billy Taylor: "Duke has been the musical ambassador for this country for many years. He is a composer who takes his hat off to no one. He is really a phenomenon of our times. His music expresses the feelings of the '20s, '30s, '40s right up until today . . . He epitomizes excellence in the presentation of his music all over the world—the kind of thing that those of us in the black race are very proud of and those of us who are just Americans are just as proud . . . It is fitting that the musicians who were asked to serenade Duke came from all kinds of ethnic backgrounds."

Dave Brubeck: "Duke has really been my idol all my life and I think this is a tremendous occasion for all of us who think so much of Duke. I consider him one of the most important Americans and he should be honored in this way . . . The royalty of Europe has honored Duke many times but this is the first time a jazz musician has been so honored in the United States . . . Jazz is not the first good music to have a strange place of origin. It's good for people to recall that much of the great music that Bach wrote . . . came from bawdy songs and beer houses."

Earl Hines: "I've often wondered why this country didn't give him the same recognition he received many years ago in Europe. It is so late for this honor, although I am happy that our country has finally caught up . . . I'm thrilled to be on this program to honor this great man with so many outstanding musicians, to help celebrate his great birthday . . . all he needs now is his own TV show."

Lou Rawls: "This is a groove. We should have more things like this. I think I'll tell the president that later tonight."

Billy Eckstine: "Duke is one of the great thrills of my life. I'm happy that the president is paying tribute to my idol. This great human being has been my guiding light. He gave the guys like me a chance, and showed that the black man can have dignity in moving any obstacle."

Mahalia Jackson: "I want to say that he [the president] really made history tonight."

Songwriter Harold Arlen: "Can you imagine Coolidge doing this?"

Director Otto Preminger: "I know that half the people here tonight, including me, didn't vote for Mr. Nixon. But after this, we all have a new appreciation of him."

Columnist Irv Kupcinet: "It was Woodstock in black-tie."

Nancy Balliett: "A friend had told me before the party, 'Nancy, it doesn't matter who the president is . . . when you hear them playing "Hail to the Chief," you'll be overwhelmed,' and I was. I couldn't believe the combination of characters and the warmth and camaraderie of that evening, all because of Ellington's music. And I loved it that Duke mentioned Billy Strayhorn, his writing partner. The artists were at ease because they had 'been everywhere, seen all,' and were at ease wherever they went. They just happened to be at the White House. They hugged and embraced and the evening was filled with smiles."

White House butler: "I have never seen the House like this. It sure has lots of soul tonight."

Black musician from California: "I voted against Nixon three times since 1960, but after tonight, he could run for Grand Dragon of the Ku Klux Klan and I'd be for him."

A veteran observer of state functions: "I haven't had this much fun at the White House in forty years."

Jazz musicians as they packed up their instruments to leave: "Man, this was some kind of great."

Mrs. Bess Abell, the White House social secretary during the Lyndon Johnson administration: "My God, I thought he was ours." [Duke had been invited to the White House so many times (eight actually) by LBJ either as a dinner guest or musician that Mrs. Abell took it for granted that he was an LBJ man or at least a Democrat.]

"SMILE OF ACHIEVEMENT–Duke Ellington glowed as brightly as a White House chandelier as he acknowledged the award from President Richard Nixon." Cover photo and caption from the June 1969 USIA *Photo Bulletin*. The enclosed four-page article was titled "Presidential 'Do' for the Duke."

CHAPTER 9

An Affair to Remember

THIS SINGULAR WHITE HOUSE JAZZ event reverberated throughout the jazz arts community like none other before. It was about recognition, about respect, and about honor. It reverberates still.

Leonard Feather: "It would have been easy to write off the whole affair cynically as a political ploy. True, it redounded to the president's benefit . . . nevertheless, what took place that night transcended questions of either politics or race . . . Respectability was the name of the game, and respectability is what Ellington, more than any other man living or dead, had brought to jazz in his music, his bearing, and his impact on society."[1]

Doug Ramsey [in a letter to the president]: "In honoring Mr. Ellington, the most distinguished and respected of jazz artists, you heartened musicians everywhere who often feel their creative efforts are ignored, and indeed, in the eyes of the world, you added stature to the art form itself."[2]

Phyl Garland: "Jazz even in its complex Ellingtonian modes has been dismissed by the establishment as mere "entertainment," considered fleeting and frivolous. One cannot help but conclude that this has been because jazz, beneath its obvious European trappings, is essentially a *black* art. In light of this past, the White House tribute brought a belated stamp of official approval to America's finest artistic creation."[3]

The morning after the party, Nixon was ecstatic.[4] Six months later, he was still enraptured. Upon learning that Duke was preparing to set out on State Department–sponsored trips to Burma and Yugoslavia in early 1970, the president sent a letter to Duke dated October 2 praising his talent and enthusiasm and wishing him every success in his latest venture as an Ambassador of Goodwill.[5]

It was Nixon's intention to drop the sobriquet "Ambassador of Goodwill" on both Duke and Lionel Hampton—the latter already in the Republican camp, the former still in need of cultivation. The grandiose moniker was never realized due to State Department concerns with proliferation of titles. Nixon successfully crowned singer Pearl Bailey Ambassador of Love, however.

Two months later on December 3, the chief executive made his feelings known publicly at an East Room musicale with trumpeter Al Hirt and the 5th Dimension vocal group. President Nixon joined the performers on the stage and said,

> Only one other night has there been the excitement of such music in this room, and that was the great jazz of Duke Ellington. This is in the same category. That was a great night and this is a great one. [He turned to the musicians] I hope you'll all live as long as the Duke and be as good as he is.[6]

A year and a half later on June 4, 1971, the cheerleader in chief phoned the maestro at his apartment in New York:[7]

Nixon: "I just wanted to wish you well on your trip to Russia . . . I want you to know that I can't think of anybody that will do a better job for this country in the Soviet Union than you will. I'm just delighted that you can take the trip and give them that old style back there." [Ellington probably gasped when he heard his music being described as old style, but it's inaudible on the tapped oval office phone line.]

Duke: "Thank you, Mr. President. I want to wish you a joyous post-anniversary" [referring to a White House event that had taken place two months before].

Nixon: "We never have an affair that people don't remember the day you were here. That Ellington night will never be topped."

Duke: "It was beautiful."

Indeed, ten years later, Nixon still felt the same:

Except for the POW dinner in 1973, which was a unique historical event, I think that the most memorable of all our White House social occasions was Duke Ellington's seventieth birthday on April 29, 1969, when I presented him with the country's highest honor, the Medal of Freedom.[8]

The president and those in the jazz art world in attendance that night were not the only ones who had come to the same conclusion. Almost a year after the fete, Thomas Meehan of the *New York Times* wrote,

The party for Duke Ellington last year . . . was one of the gayest White House evenings in years. Those who brought it to life, however, weren't the Nixons or other administration people but out-of-towners who had come to Washington especially for the party—specifically, Ellington's free-wheeling friends from the world of jazz.[9]

About the same time, a staff writer for the *Los Angeles Times* had this to say:

> It is generally acknowledged that the Nixon White House has had [social] high spots that rank with those of any other administration. The most outstanding example was a birthday party Mr. Nixon threw for Duke Ellington, an evening that undoubtedly will be remembered as one of the most glittering in the history of the White House. But the big sparklers that evening were not members of the administration, but the greats of the jazz world who came to town especially for the occasion.[10]

Most seem to agree: A Nixon party had matched, maybe even topped the excitement and glamour of those held by the previous two administrations. The Kennedy parties with Jackie at the helm often swung until four o'clock in the morning, and President Johnson was known to keep dancing at late-night shindigs until everyone else in the room was ready to drop from exhaustion. But at least for one night, there was magic at a Nixon soiree—though he and wife, Pat, missed the last third—and that is the way it would always be remembered.

The day following the tribute, Nixon instructed his aides to find out if the concert could be made public domestically (the White House Communications Agency had taped the whole affair for the archives). Here was a chance for Nixon to match (if not trump) what President Kennedy had done after his much-publicized East Room concert by Spanish cellist Pablo Casals on November 13, 1961. A week after that event, the ABC and NBC radio networks broadcast a recording of Casals performance, marking the first time a White House musicale had been heard by the general public.[11] Moreover, four months later, wider public dissemination of the concert was achieved through a Columbia LP titled *A Concert at the White House* with flattering photos and liner notes (another White House first).[12]

For the Ellington concert, Columbia Records was again more than willing. Frank Stanton, head of CBS, offered to have the album pressed, packaged, promoted, and distributed at no charge, with profits of album sales divided equally between the Musicians Union Trust Fund and a Billy Strayhorn Scholarship Fund. Ellington approved, but some of the musicians refused to give their permission for its release, among them altoist Paul Desmond, who despised his performance on "Chelsea Bridge," and guitarist Jim Hall, who despised Nixon administration policies. More than two decades after Desmond's death, Hall finally agreed to the music's release. The concert album, issued under the Blue Note label, reached the public in 2002.[13]

Okay, there would be no domestic radio broadcast or Columbia LP of the concert, but Nixon never thought highly of the Casals concert anyway (only the publicity bonanza it received)—or of any Kennedy social events, for that matter—as he told aide H. R. Haldeman later in his first term:

> Jackie Kennedy received bravos for years because she brought Pablo Casals to the White House to play his cello forty years after his prime. When we look over the list of people that we have had to the White House, they make the Johnson years appear almost barbaric and the Kennedy years very thin indeed.[14]

Nixon was prepared, however; he had his hole cards: newspaper coverage, network television coverage, international radio broadcasts over the VOA, and an internationally distributed documentary film. Take that, Jack Kennedy!

Domestic Media Coverage

Newspaper/Magazine Coverage

As biographer Cohen has noted, no other occasion during Ellington's life elicited so much newspaper coverage as the White House tribute dinner.[15] And no wonder—a media swarm numbering over forty had descended on the East Room: noted columnists and journalists from both mainstream and African American newspapers and magazines; prominent jazz writer-critics, multiple wire service journalists, and (seemingly) countless photographers. Next-day newspaper editors ran with the copy, obviously intrigued by the Horatio Alger story of a lower- to middle-class black born at the dawn of the twentieth century overcoming all to become a world-renown composer-bandleader, only to be awarded the nation's highest civilian honor in the manor where his father once served as a part-time butler.

The story ran in most of the nation's top circulation newspapers, as shown in appendix 11. Of the seventy-nine state capital and populous city newspapers surveyed, sixty-three carried the story, twenty placed it on the front page, and thirty appended an event photo.

The tone of the coverage in African American papers was prideful (how could it not be?—Ellington was the first black to receive the nation's top civilian honor) yet cautionary. In the *Chicago Daily Defender*, Washington beat columnist Ethel L. Payne wrote soon after the event:

> The present occupants of the White House have taken a leaf from the social handbook of the two previous administrations. For the 70th birthday of Duke Ellington, all the stops were pulled out. The guest list read like pages of "Who's Who," the entertainment was top drawer, and for President Nixon, it was a welcome respite from the storm over race relations. Not since the famous 1963 reception that JFK hosted for 1,000 guests has the White House been so a-glitter.[16]

Two days later, Ms. Payne further reflected:

> It was nice to discover that the president wasn't a two-headed monster, but a fellow who could be jolly and human and could play "Happy Birthday to You" in the key of G . . . It would have been nice [if he had invited more black politicians], but all in all,

it was a good show and for the time being, Mr. Nixon has picked up a few brownie points.[17]

The *New Pittsburgh Courier* echoed these same sentiments almost three weeks later:

President Nixon garnered many brownie points with his salute to Duke Ellington the other week. With the star-studded guests arriving from all over the U.S., the new administration desperately had need of some points.[18]

But there were two sides to that celebratory medal, illuminated in two separate columns by the same writer, in the *Baltimore Afro-American*:

Duke and His Friend Dick

Not only was this a fine tribute to a great American, carried out in a manner that exhibited an all-out effort on the part of the president to make it more than just another dinner fete, but it additionally gave millions of people a chance to see a more human side of the president.[19]

Icing on the Cake

Do not fall into the mistaken notion that a party given by the Nixons, attended by blacks and whites together, has solved anything in this country or abroad nor does it necessarily portend better days. Keep your eyes on the ball. Watch the issues. Listen to Nixon's words as carefully as you have listened to Duke's music. This is a time for serious evaluation and action and this country must not be influenced by the icing on the cake.[20]

Beneath the celebratory glow, the black press and indeed the black community feared that programs initiated under the previous Johnson administration to help the poor and blacks would be thrust aside, and that the unprecedented high positions achieved by blacks in the previous administration would not be duplicated in Nixon's.

TELEVISION COVERAGE

Print media coverage of the event was extensive, no question, but television coverage surely had the greater impact. For the first time, a broad swath of the American public witnessed an East Room entertainment on their nightly network news. They had seen news conferences, arrival and departure ceremonies, weddings and solemn occasions, but never an East Room soiree on television.

The NBC and ABC networks both devoted a generous three minutes to the Ellington honors at the close of their April 30 broadcasts. Both spotlighted the medal ceremony and the singing of "Happy Birthday," but otherwise differed.[21] NBC chose to open with studio commentary by news anchor David Brinkley:

> Duke Ellington may be classified as a great national resource since he has done as much for American popular music as anybody, more than most, and has been doing it longer. He is still playing at seventy, and still enjoying it. One morning a while ago, somebody greeted him on the street and said it was a fine day, and Ellington answered, "Any day I wake up is a fine day." Last night he was a guest of honor at the White House where he won the highest award the government gives to civilians. President Nixon gave him the Medal of Freedom.

The scene shifts to the East Room with Nixon on the dais reading the last line of the award—"In the royalty of American music, no man swings more or stands higher than the Duke"—and then handing Ellington the certificate and medal amid substantial applause. The scene cuts to the all-star band playing the last strains of "'A' Train" with Clark Terry's merry solo floating on top of the ensemble, followed by energetic applause (scene lasts about one minute).

A ten-second vignette follows: Duke kissing Nixon, twice on each cheek, and then uproarious applause, then laughter. Next scene, Nixon is up on the riser, about to play the piano, and says, "Duke Ellington is ageless, but would you please all stand and sing 'Happy Birthday.' And please, in the key of G!" Laughter as Nixon sits down and begins playing. After the crowd sings the second "happy birthday to you," the scene shifts back to the studio. The segment and program ends with wry smiles on the faces of Brinkley and cohost Chet Huntley. "Good night, Chet." "Good night, David."

Howard K. Smith in the *ABC Evening News* studio:

The White House at night is ordinarily a sedate place, but last night it was far different from all other nights. ABC's Tom Jarriel has the story of a birthday party for a man whose first two names are Edward Kennedy.

Guests arriving at the White House diplomatic entrance followed by guests mingling in the East Room are shown as Tom Jarriel narrates:

This Edward Kennedy's last name is Ellington and he's better known as Duke. The musical genius was the honored guest at the White House on his seventieth birthday. The guest list was selected from Ellington's many musical friends, like vocalist Cab Calloway and composer-conductor Benny Goodman, men who have been playing Ellington's music now for nearly a generation. In a special ceremony in the East Room, the same room where Duke Ellington's father once served as butler, President Nixon presented Ellington with the nation's Medal of Freedom.

Up on the riser for the medal ceremony, Nixon faces the audience and speaks. "I was looking at this name on here [certificate holder] and it says Edward Kennedy . . . Ellington." [Laughter.] Nixon gestures to Duke in the front row to join him on the riser. Duke steps up. Next shot, Duke grabs Nixon's hands, leans forward, and kisses him twice on each cheek as the audience roars. Nixon (with Ellington in tow) moves toward the piano as Jarriel narrates:

> The president has said he digs Ellington and the feeling came to be mutual last night. There was all kind of musical talent around, but before the jazz greats took over the bandstand, the president played a special number for his captive audience. It was his premier performance as a White House pianist.

At this point the camera captures pianists Dave Brubeck and George Wein guffawing at the president's antics. Back to the bandstand, a smiling Nixon invites everyone to stand and sing "Happy Birthday" to the ageless Duke Ellington.

The audience eagerly rises and bellows out the short song, accompanied by Nixon at the piano. Shots of the jam session in full swing are now seen and heard, including Duke dancing with Carmen de Lavallade, as Jarriel narrates:

> After an hour of formal jazz, the Nixons opened the dance floor and turned the ceremonial room over to a jam session. The players rotated fast and the dancers kept going into the early hours of the morning, long after the Nixons had vanished from the scene. Down [in] front [of the stage] there was a swing time as the music charmed everyone from diplomats to military aides, from cabinet members to clarinet players.

The music plays on as the TV camera focuses on Gilbert Stuart's portrait of George Washington. Jarriel continues, "The only disapproving face in the hall was one frozen in oil and deaf to the music. Tom Jarriel of *ABC News* at the White House A-Go-Go."

What a spectacle! A jovial Nixon behaving more like an activity director on a cruise ship than the serious-minded, tough-as-nails president usually seen on the nightly TV news. The irony of it all, the architect of the anti-black southern strategy, and now the nation's chief executive, awarding the highest civilian award in the land to a black man, who in turn kisses him four times, and then accompanies a birthday sing-along to said black man from the piano bench, all to a soundtrack of swinging jazz, boisterous laughter, and wild applause. Madison Avenue could not have concocted a better promotional video for Nixon, Duke, and jazz, but at only three minutes long and seen only once, the overall effect, though staggering on repeated viewings, was likely more subliminal than actual. Nonetheless, if a poll of the estimated ten to twenty million people who saw the clips could have been taken the next day, all three—Nixon, Ellington, and jazz—would have shown higher positives, but history provides no such record.

(TV news clips of the Ellington evening can be seen at various locations around the United States, notably the Library of Congress in Washington, DC, courtesy of the Vanderbilt Television News Archive.)

International Media Coverage

MAGAZINE

Other than repeated mentions by Willis Conover on his daily *Music USA* broadcasts, the rest of the world beyond America's shores first learned of the event in the July 1969 issue of the *Photo Bulletin*—a monthly USIA photo-essay magazine that was furnished to USIS posts overseas. The *Bulletin*'s lead story "Presidential 'Do' for the Duke" featured a full-length cover photo of the principals standing on the East Room riser with the following caption: "SMILE OF ACHIEVEMENT—Duke Ellington glows as brightly as a White House chandelier as he acknowledges award from President Nixon."[22] The four-page article opened with this:

In the royalty of American music no man swings more or stands higher than the Duke," Richard Nixon declared to a glittering assemblage of jazz musicians and Washington officialdom as he

presented his first Presidential Medal of Freedom. "The Duke,"
of course, is Edward Kennedy Ellington, who was honored with
a state dinner at the White House—where his father was once a
part-time butler—on the 70th anniversary of his birth, April 29.
Vice President and Mrs. Spiro Agnew . . . and Ellington's sister
joined in the applause as he accepted the highest civilian award
of the United States Government. Flanked by President and
Mrs. Nixon, he greeted the 80 dinner guests; another 100 arrived
later to share a nostalgic sampling from the prolific composer's
repertoire (including "Mood Indigo," "Don't Get Around Much
Anymore"). Ellington had never met President Nixon before
this signal recognition of his 46-year contribution to public pleasure. But he was no stranger to the Executive Mansion; he once
discussed his distinctly American musical idiom with the late
President Dwight D. Eisenhower; talked of their mutual interest
with piano player President Harry Truman and was invited there
frequently by President Lyndon B. Johnson, who appointed him
to the National Council on the Arts.

Seven photos, some with captions, some not, followed: (1) a photo of
Duke receiving his award in front of a standing audience, applauding;
(2) Duke and the president in the reception line; (3) the all-star band on
the riser; (4) Duke dancing with Carmen de Lavallade; (5) Nixon at the
piano playing "Happy Birthday"; (6) Nixon leaving the piano and Duke
applauding; and (7) Willie "the Lion" Smith with Duke at the piano.

While distribution and readership statistics are not available for this
particular issue of the *Bulletin*, the print run was likely in the thousands,
and the overall readership some ten thousand. Ellington was well known
in various parts of the world as a result of his European concert trips,
State Department tours (to South Asia and the Middle East in 1963 and
to Africa in 1967), and the *Music USA* broadcasts by Willis Conover on
the VOA with "'A' Train" as the opening theme, followed by the spinning

of Duke's platters from time to time, and the occasional in-person interview. Moreover, the July 1969 issue was not the first time Ellington graced the *Photo Bulletin* pages. In November 1964, a day in the life of the composer was featured in a two-page article titled "Star-Crossed Ellington." Two 1965 *Bulletins* featured photos of Duke and the orchestra, the first in concert at the Fifth Avenue Presbyterian Church in New York City, and the second with Lady Bird Johnson in the South Lawn bandstand at the Festival of the Arts. Duke Ellington was a worldwide celebrity even before the White House shindig, more so afterward.

Documentary Film

Richard Nixon was the first president to allow motion picture cameras in the White House to film entertainers in performance for domestic television and, separately, for overseas distribution by the USIA. Nixon's two immediate predecessors, presidents Kennedy and Johnson, filmed several social events inside the mansion that featured entertainment, but none were broadcast on television or screened in public theaters.[23]

This absence of precedent raises the question then, who first suggested filming the Ellington event? A precedent of sorts may have existed, however. As mentioned earlier, JFK tape-recorded his Pablo Casals concert for dissemination to the public by radio and a Columbia LP, for which he received enormous praise. This groundbreaking happenstance did not escape the Camelot-obsessed eyes of Nixon or of Frank Shakespeare, president of CBS (Columbia Records) at the time, who would become Nixon's television advisor during the 1968 campaign and his USIA director after the election. Both were television savvy and quite familiar with the USIA. As vice president, Nixon was present at the creation of the agency and starred in a USIA film that documented his famous trip to South America in 1958. The USIA had produced the documentary *Richard M. Nixon—The New President* that began circulating after his election to introduce the new commander in chief to television viewers around the world. Two weeks after taking office, Nixon had ordered the USIA to send a slickly produced copy of his inaugural speech to every American embassy.[24] John F. Kennedy did, so should he.

Keenly aware of USIA capabilities, the idea for the USIA film could have come from the president himself, but if it had originated with Shakespeare (or anyone else), Nixon would have approved of it in a flash. He had built his 1968 presidential campaign on television, and he would build his presidency on the medium as well. Filming Duke's grand night would fit right in with that strategy. Besides generating publicity, as seen from the president's perspective, the film would be as much about him as Ellington, and it would garner him the respect he thought he deserved from people still enamored with the Kennedy mystique.

Informed of the president's decision, and with only five short weeks to go, the USIA turned to the accomplished and trusted filmmaker Sidney J. Stiber. Over the previous twenty years, he had written or produced some five hundred films for television, industrial, and government clients, including twenty-five for the USIA, among them an award-winning short on poet Robert Frost and a documentary on Vice President Nixon's famed trip to South America in 1958.

On the afternoon of the event, Stiber and his assistant set up a stationary 35 mm camera on the platform reserved for the television networks and still photographers at the back of the East Room.[25] The producer manned the fixed camera during the proceedings, while his assistant roamed the establishment with a mobile camera to capture the arrival of guests as they entered the White House, and later on as they danced at the jam session. Back at his New York studios the next day, Stiber drafted the script and then wisely showed it to Stanley Dance (USIA had wanted Ellington's biographer to do the scripting), who gave the manuscript a thumbs-up, no changes required.

With foreign audiences in mind, and from the ninety-some minutes of raw footage he shot, the producer shaped his seventeen-and-a-half-minute film for overall dramatic effect by shifting sequences—Duke's piano solo, the award ceremony, and the singing of "Happy Birthday"—to the end of the film, as shown on the next page:[26]

Prologue	2.1 min.
Preliminaries:	1.1 min.
Title/Guest Arrival	
Telegrams/Letters	
Nixon/Duke Arrival	
Souvenir Program	
Concert	3.1 min.
Jam Session	2.7 min.
Duke Piano Solo	3.4 min.
Medal Ceremony:	4.8 min.
Nixon Medal Speech	
Duke Freedom Speech	
Duke/Nixon Kiss	
Birthday Sing-Along	
End Credits	0.3 min.
TOTAL LENGTH	17.5 min.

First seen and heard in the prologue is the Ellington Orchestra playing for dancers at a crowded nightspot, followed by a Sacred Music Concert rehearsal and performance at a Midwest college campus. These scenes serve as a visual backdrop for Willis Conover's narration that establishes the purpose of the White House tribute and sets the stage for the pageantry and bonhomie to come:

Duke Ellington . . . pianist, orchestra leader, and arranger . . . is one of this century's most creative, prolific, and versatile musicians. His music transcends categories and delights millions, of all ages, in all kinds of contexts all over the world. The scope of his music enables him to move with easy authority from crowded dance floors to college campuses, where he often presents his Sacred Music Concert, an expression of religious belief in his own musical idiom. Because of the happiness he has brought the world through his compositions and performances, it was fitting that he should be honored on his seventieth birthday in the White House, by the president of his country.

The title *Duke Ellington at the White House* appears over a still shot of the most famous building in the United States. The camera then documents the arrival of the evening's guests as they pass through the canopied lower entrance to the mansion. Conover narrates:

> Among the distinguished guests: Secretary of Labor and Mrs. George Schultz, Duke Ellington's son, Mercer, with members of his family; musical stage star Cab Calloway with Mrs. Calloway; clarinetist Benny Goodman and his wife; singer Billy Eckstine and Mrs. Eckstine; Dr. and Mrs. Arthur Logan; magazine publisher John and Mrs. Johnson. Other guests include leaders in the fields of art [Stanley Dance] and religion; trumpeter Dizzy Gillespie; the guest of honor Duke Ellington and his sister Ruth Ellington.

Seen next is a mound of scattered letters and telegrams (Duke loaned the photo to Stiber) as Conover intones: "Birthday greetings have come from every continent, but none are warmer than those of President and Mrs. Nixon."

The arrival of the principals follows: President and Mrs. Nixon and honoree Ellington and sister Ruth pose for photographs at the bottom step of the grand staircase leading from the upstairs quarters before they step off to greet their invited guests. Next seen: a close-up of the souvenir program booklet (that Stiber no doubt picked up the night of the tribute). The pages turn as Conover explains: "Tonight, a special program of Ellington compositions is played by a handpicked band representative of the profession in which he excels."

The concert begins with the all-star band on the East Room stage blasting out the final chorus of Duke's theme. Applause. Coverage of the concert continues, absent narration, with a montage of various artists:

guitarist Jim Hall playing "In a Sentimental Mood." Applause. Pianist Billy Taylor's two-handed take on "It Don't Mean a Thing (If It Ain't Got That Swing)." Applause. Mary Mayo sings a snippet of "Mood Indigo" with a trombone obbligato by J. J. Johnson, followed by a Louis Bellson drum solo on "Caravan." Another applause wipe brings on pianist Earl Hine's feverish take on "Perdido," accompanied by his smiling rhythm-mates bassist Milt Hinton and drummer Bellson. Applause, then singer Joe Williams and the band close out the concert with the buoyant last chorus of "Jump for Joy." Applause.

Next, on the bandstand surrounded by the all-stars, President Nixon announces, "This room will be cleared. The band will return and they will have a jam session and dancing for all those who want—how about it?!"

Unlike the concert, the jam session is filmed mostly by the mobile camera, yielding a Felliniesque montage of dancers, bystanders, partiers— folks not usually seen together—government officials, clergy, academics, writers, jazz musicians, many with their wives—white and black—all in close proximity to one another dressed in their finest, moving to a late-night jazzy soundtrack and having a good time. Only the music the band produces is heard; narrator Conover is appropriately silent.

The session opens with Joe Williams at the microphone, backed by a mixed band of all-stars with uniformed marine and navy musicians, and several guest musicians (Dizzy Gillespie, Leonard Garment, and others). Joe Williams sings "It's a Dirty Low Down Shame" with singer Lou Rawls nearby, ready to join in. The camera never loses touch with the evening's honoree as he dances into view for several seconds. Dave Brubeck and George Wein are shown together at the piano, followed by a dance-floor sequence: Duke dancing with Rose Mary Woods, then HEW Secretary Finch with his wife, then back to rug-cutter Ellington with a new partner. Representing the departed president and first lady, daughter Trisha dances up a storm with an African American partner. Up on the riser, the camera captures a rather vigorous four-kiss exchange between Brubeck and Duke as Brubeck and Wein relinquish their places at the piano bench to a pair of old-time piano masters. The camera lingers on the keyboard duo of Duke and Willie "the Lion" Smith, clearly fascinated with the visage of the derby-hatted, cigar-chomping Lion. Trombonist Urbie Green takes center stage soloing on an unnamed blues that gives way to the full band playing a slow version of the "Saints." Front and center, both visually and audibly, is event instigator and part-time clarinetist Leonard Garment playing with an authority that had to please nearly everyone in the East Room save for Benny Goodman. As the jam session comes to a close, the camera pans back and forth between Duke, dancers, and musicians (the marine tenor saxophonist and trumpeter Dizzy Gillespie prominent). Dissolve to a shot of President Nixon on the riser again, hand extended to a seated Ellington, saying, "I think we ought to hear from the Duke, too." The honoree steps up to the microphone, announces he will improvise something gentle and graceful for the First Lady. Duke moves to the piano and plays "Pat" in its three-minute entirety. He walks off the riser to his seat amid sustained applause. Dissolve.

Unburdened by network television time constraints, the medal ceremony is presented next in its entirety, including Ellington's warmly delivered four-freedoms speech the networks left out. Not counting the prologue, preliminaries, and end credits, the ceremony constitutes one-third of the film's running time. The remaining two-thirds is devoted to the music—concert, jam session, and Duke's piano solo—to the delight of jazz fans of course, although most would have wanted more.

But it is the comparatively short jam session that stands out, the takeaway emotional highlight of the film. Unusual for the time—and perhaps for all time—the camera documents authentic camaraderie between people at an official White House function—black and white—having fun, dancing together, with the evening's honoree in the lead with multiple partners. The congeniality on the dance floor is mirrored on the bandstand. The mixing of the races, yes, but also the mixing of marine, navy, and civilian musicians with celebrated jazz musicians, all very jazz-like, very democratic, very American.

As borne out in the film footage from which the documentary was cut, Ellington's free-wheeling friends—the big sparklers from out of town—were the ones who set the tone for the good time had by all.[27] Said another way, the concert and guest musicians didn't just provide the music for the party. They were the party.

From a USIA perspective, Sidney Stiber produced the perfect propaganda film. Whether this was his or others' intent, or serendipity, doesn't matter. The documentary served U.S. goals at the time. The drumbeat from the Soviet propaganda machine, especially in Africa and Latin America, constantly lambasted the United States over the treatment of its minority citizens, and had to be countered.[28] Stiber assembled a direct cinema-style documentary that served the purpose. It not only demonstrated harmony between the races rarely seen on news broadcasts during the turbulent '60s, but also convincingly told the backstory of a black man rising from societal bottoms to attain high achievement and be honored for such at the highest level of government. The film owes its success in this regard to the relative lack of narration; over 70 percent is actual live sound. The viewer is thus allowed to come to his or her own conclusion, which adds to the film's authenticity.

The first indication that the USIA had a hit on its hands came sooner than expected at the Moscow International Film Festival in July 1969. Bruce Herschensohn, director of the USIA Motion Picture and Television Division, led a U.S. contingent to Moscow that included Willis Conover and Leonard Garment. He arranged for a noncompetitive screening of the Ellington documentary (Kubrick's *2001* was the official U.S. feature entry that year) and reported the audience reaction back to Washington:

> This was shown to a smaller group than usually viewed festival films, but the reaction was spontaneous, friendly and enthusiastic. He [Herschensohn] discovered that they were interested not only

in the music but in the fact that this glittering occasion was fully integrated, that a Negro was being honored for his special contributions to American culture, and that the President's warmth and sense of humor was evident. He says nobody considered it a great movie but the event it portrayed came through very strongly and positively.[29]

In early October, after a one-month internal agency review, the USIA air-pouched English-language 16 mm test prints of *Duke Ellington at the White House* to USIS posts in 119 countries around the globe:[30, 31]

Africa	36
Europe	27 (9 to Communist nations)
Far East/South Asia	26
South/Central America	23
Middle East	7

USIS posts were informed to forward orders for more print and language versions, in 16 mm and 35 mm format, to the agency within three weeks of receipt of the test prints. Three African posts immediately responded as requested; their evaluations follow:

Malawi

The film helps add to President Nixon's image as an individual. It also has other human-interest elements since its setting seems rather informal and realistic. A good program picture that would appeal to all segments of the population. The test print is adequate.[32]

Mali

Jazz buffs at the radio and in the army will want more music than this film offers, but they will enjoy seeing it anyway. *Duke Ellington at the White House* will serve a [USIS] post objective with special and general [theater] audiences; its value in Africa is obvious. Post will present film to OCINAM [Malian office in charge of distribution and exhibition of foreign films] for possible theater use of 35 mm version once we have a copy in French. Request one 16 mm copy of the French version.[33]

Tanzania

While it is hard to imagine jazz in the White House, this film shows that on Duke Ellington's birthday, the President and his guests were able to relax and have a good time as they paid a fitting tribute to the Duke, who appeared to enjoy the evening very much. Somehow, despite tuxedos and the solemnity of the surroundings, musicians and dignitaries mingled and had a good time. President Nixon is very human and engaging in his role as host, but the First Lady was neglected by the cameramen. Duke Ellington's description of four important freedoms is sincere and moving. Even his kissing the president after receiving the Medal of Freedom does not seem out of place. It is unfortunate that the famous musicians are not identified while they play. The post wishes to order three additional 16 mm English prints and two 35 mm English prints. Five 16 mm Swahilli prints are requested, if available.[34]

Responses from the remaining 116 countries are not available from archival records. At least the three surviving evaluations above are telling.

At about the same time of the African responses, the Ellington documentary began to be noticed back home, receiving a CINE Golden Eagle Award nomination (more on this later) and government approval for submission to film festivals overseas.[35]

In December the film was slated to be shown at the National Academy of Television Arts and Sciences conference at Fordham University, but was inexplicably canceled in favor of an animated cartoon on the Apollo 12 lunar landing[36] (well, maybe the latter *was* more important).

The first public notice of how the film was faring overseas came in a January 1970 *New York Times* article headlined "*Silent Majority*, USIA Film, Fails to Stir Foreigners," which reported on other countries' lackluster responses to the Nixon administration's defense of its Vietnam War policies posited in the documentary. The article continued by saying, "In contrast to *The Silent Majority*, a film titled *Duke Ellington at the White House* had been very well received" by foreign audiences.[37] USIA head Frank Shakespeare learned this firsthand several months later in Portugal:

> The *Duke Ellington at the White House* film has been a great success. It is referred to by the Portuguese as a "real" rather than a "propaganda" picture and has been appreciated and effective. Perhaps we should make more actuality films . . . since the actuality factor doubtless accounts for the adjective "real."[38]

At the end of April, Shakespeare testified to Congress about the agency's increased use of television to reach an ever-wider audience for its documentaries:

> The USIA produces many documentary films for theatrical use; in addition to traditional use of those films [showings at USIS posts, festivals, and elsewhere], we are giving increasing emphasis to placement of these films on television all over the world. Our documentary film *Czechoslovakia 1968*, which just received an Academy Award, has had extensive placement. This is also true of our film *An Impression of John Steinbeck, Writer*, which was an Academy Award nominee. Other programs enjoying substantial television exposure include *Duke Ellington at the White House*, and the NASA films on the Apollo missions that we adapted for international programming in twenty-two languages.[39]

What the new USIA head was alluding to in his testimony was the significant expansion of television worldwide in the prior decade that had greatly expanded the agency's reach beyond its traditional means, which had been the subject of a contemporaneous *New York Sunday Times* article:

> [USIA films] are telecast by more than 90 countries ... it operates more than 200 libraries and reading rooms in 83 countries, their shelves filled with 1.9 million books [and sizeable film collections]. At least 23 million persons use these facilities each year.[40]

Greater use of television had increased the number of potential worldwide viewers of USIA films beyond tens of millions to hundreds of millions.

In May more good stateside news: Council on International Non-Theatrical Events (CINE) awarded its Golden Eagle certificate to *Duke Ellington at the White House*.[41] Of the fifty-six films the U.S. government entered into the competition, twenty won a Golden Eagle, seven of them produced by the USIA. One of course was the Ellington documentary. The import of this award increased the awareness of any winning film (much like the Academy Oscar) and in the case of the Ellington film improved its chances of being shown at foreign film festivals and in foreign theaters.

The USIA archival record does not include placement and distribution statistics for the Ellington documentary. However, such statistics can be assumed similar to those of *Czechoslovakia 1968*, a USIA documentary that received worldwide attention at the same time as Ellington's. The film had the following distribution:[42]

16 mm	158 prints to 117 countries
35 mm	71 prints to 57 countries

Thirty-one countries placed the show on television at least once and in a number of instances on several stations with repeat telecasts. Eighteen counties placed it in commercial theaters. These *Czechoslovakia 1968* statistics came from an early assessment (November 1969) and were no doubt much increased after the film won an Academy Award in March 1970. Moreover, repeat telecasts, where they can be arranged, can be an effective means of reaching an audience. For example, *The Silent Majority* film mentioned above was shown twenty-eight times to seven million people over Mexican television.[43]

As for film festivals, statistics for individual films are not known, only in the aggregate. In 1970, the USIA submitted films to forty-nine festivals around the world.[44] Duke's film was probably submitted to a goodly number of festivals based on its CINE Golden Eagle Award, but certainly not to all.

The number of people worldwide who viewed *Duke Ellington at the White House* during its first run showings in 1969–1970 at USIS posts, embassies, theaters, in the field, at festivals, and over television is difficult to estimate even if all factors are known. But assuming the film garnered significant television play, it is likely that far more people beyond America's borders saw the seventeen-and-a-half-minute documentary than the ten to twenty million American viewers who saw the three-minute nightly news broadcasts the day after the event. It is the subsequent showings during the 1971–1974 period that would explode the film's watch count. These showings would have been stimulated by Willis Conover's constant references to the event on his VOA show, and the publicity generated by (1) the Ellington Orchestra around-the-globe tour on behalf of the State Department in 1971–1973 (more on this later), (2) the worldwide celebrations of Duke's seventy-fifth birthday on April 29, 1974, and (3) his passing on May 24, 1974, shortly thereafter. The cumulative total would not be measured in the tens of millions of viewers, but (possibly) hundreds of millions.

Bruce Herschensohn recalled that when he was head of the Motion Picture and Television branch at the USIA and went on foreign trips, he received positive reports about the film and witnessed excellent reactions at screenings.[45] Lastly, film producer Sidney J. Stiber recollected he was told several times by USIA officials that his film had been seen by four hundred million people worldwide, making his documentary—at even a quarter of that number—the mostly widely viewed musicale in White House history.[46]

ELLINGTON ON THE VOA 1969–1974

President Nixon knew when he authorized Willis Conover to coordinate the entertainment for the Ellington evening that he was getting a competent, knowledgeable jazz insider who could reliably stage an East Room event worthy of the honoree and the nascent Nixon administration. The president probably did not know, however, that he was getting in the bargain a crack publicist who would ceaselessly promote the Ellington event on his daily one-hour *Music USA* program over the VOA for the remainder of the president's term in office. Conover obtained (as he had for President Johnson's musicales) a sound recording of the evening's happenings—the ceremony and concert—which he repeatedly broadcast, along with liberal dollops of Ellington's other music, to his overseas listeners.

The Johnson administration was the first to allow the VOA to broadcast sound recordings of its after-dinner entertainments, and Conover took full advantage, featuring Johnson White House performances by prominent jazz stars, including Duke Ellington, on his *Music USA* program, as shown below:[47]

Herb Alpert and the Tijuana Brass (broadcast twice)
Dave Brubeck Quartet (broadcast twice)
Tony Bennett
Charlie Byrd Trio
Duke Ellington Orchestra, Festival of the Arts (broadcast twice)
Chad Mitchell Trio/Stan Getz Quartet
North Texas State Lab Band with Duke Ellington
Sarah Vaughan (broadcast twice)

Having featured Ellington in performance at the Johnson White House three times on *Music USA*, the jazz voice of the VOA was primed to do so again for Nixon. On the day of the event, Conover broadcast a prerecorded birthday salute to the maestro in his usual terse baritone:

Today, April 29, 1969, is the birthday of Duke Ellington.

Today, on his birthday, Duke Ellington is a guest of honor at the White House in Washington, DC.

Today, the president of the United States and Mrs. Nixon are paying tribute to Duke Ellington in the company of his friends and family and creative peers—first at a dinner in the State Dining Room and then at a concert by outstanding American musicians playing Ellington's music in the East Room of the White House.

Today, we at the *Jazz Hour* join Ellington's admirers around the world in saluting him on his birthday.[48]

A medley of Ellington songs followed, including "Heritage (My Mother, My Father)," an elegy Joe Williams sang that evening at the celebration, and a fifteen-minute excerpt from a previously recorded Sacred Concert.

A month later, the performance recorded at the White House on April 29, excerpted into three parts, was broadcast to the world on three consecutive days, May 28, 29, and 30.[49] Conover's listening audience (numbering in the tens of millions) heard everything from the president's and honoree's remarks at the medal ceremony, to the East Room crowd singing "Happy Birthday," to the ninety-minute-long concert, including audience reactions, Conover's comments, and Nixon's final exhortation to clear the East Room for a jam session. The recording was broadcast complete, uncut, and unedited, except for Conover's introductory and explanatory voice-overs: basically an "actuality" audio documentary, as

USIA chief Frank Shakespeare might have said. A repeat broadcast of the program occurred two months later on July 3, 4, and 5.[50]

Later that year on December 6, Conover broadcast Duke's closing improvised piano solo "Pat" on a segment devoted to Ellington songs.[51] Further, two other jazz performances at the Nixon White House in 1969 soon made their way to the VOA airwaves: the Modern Jazz Quartet on December 5, which Conover had a hand in setting up, and trumpeter Al Hirt and the 5th Dimension popular vocal group on January 17, 1970.[52] Neither broadcast repeated. And strangely, no other artist performance at the Nixon White House was broadcast over the VOA (singers Pearl Bailey and Peggy Lee, and pianists Bobby Short and Billy Taylor, for example).

In 1970, Conover reshaped the Ellington recording to fit two *Music USA* segments by omitting extraneous material and unused space on the original three-excerpt version. The two-segment, two-day version was broadcast three times in 1970—July 31 and August 1, September 29 and 30, and October 9 and 16, and once the following year—October 15 and 22—and once the year after on August 15 and 16.[53]

Anticipating Ellington's seventy-fifth birthday on April 29, 1974, the *Music USA* host upped the ante and created a four-day celebratory sound print of the Ellington White House tribute.[54] This time Conover spread the event over four days—April 23, 24, 25, and 26—filling the empty space he created with additional voice-over throughout and, on the first day, a sample of Ellingtonia: the orchestra with symphonic backing on "She Too Pretty to Be Blue," followed by the maestro's hip monologue on "Peter and the Wolf" and an Ellington piano trio performance.

On Duke's actual birthday, Conover replayed portions of the Ellington evening—the ceremony speeches, the "Happy Birthday" sing-along, and Duke's piano solo "Pat"—followed by a recitation of some of the honors Ellington had received over the years, and an in-studio interview with the maestro at the piano.[55] The host asked his guest the all-too-familiar questions, What advice did he have for up-and-coming musicians and could he play a recent composition for the listening audience? Duke complied, offering a piano rendition of a number off his recent *Afro-Eurasian Eclipse* LP. Conover played the LP version followed by "Satin Doll." At the sign-off, Willis dedicated the program to "the man who brought America to the world through his music."

Conover's many rebroadcasts of the Ellington evening might seem excessive, especially when compared to the recorded performances of other jazz artists that, at best, garnered only one repeat broadcast. But the airtime devoted to the evening paled in comparison to that given to Ellington's other recorded music, be it a newly released LP (*Latin American Suite*, for example) or a compilation of tracks from various LPs to fit a given theme (1940s, for example). When Conover featured other artists—singers or instrumentalists—he would often select their rendition of an Ellington composition, such as "Rockin' in Rhythm," "Satin Doll," or "Duke's Place (C-Jam Blues)." The hours of Ellingtonia broadcast over *Music USA* by year is given in the table below:[56]

Year	All-Ellington Programs (hrs)	Ellington Compositions by Others (hrs)
1969	35	3
1970	19	5
1971	17	2
1972	12	3
1973	75	5
1974	66	4

The annual on-air hours available to the *Music USA* host numbered 290 (no broadcasting on Sunday, and only half an hour on most Saturdays). In 1969, Conover allotted 13 percent of his annual airspace to Ellington, a lesser percentage in 1970, 1971, and 1972. He stepped it up considerably in 1973 and 1974 when the VOA almost became the VOE, totaling 28 percent and 24 percent of the airspace, respectively. Conover obviously had in mind Duke's seventy-fifth-birthday anniversary in 1974 when he developed his 1973 playlists, but could have been motivated as well by outward signs (if not insider knowledge) of the maestro's ill health, which ultimately led to his passing in May 1974. Duke's death no doubt influenced Conover's choices in the latter half of that year.

Conover complemented his Ellington-favored scheduling by opening and closing his program with the Duke's "'A' Train" theme and, in addition, making regular on-air announcements detailing the wheres and whens of Ellington and his orchestra during their State Department tours. (Conover did this for all touring musicians.) All of this benefited the Ellington entourage immensely, helping to fill the auditoriums, theaters, and stadiums at their concerts in various foreign lands. And it added luster to the maestro's personality, or as biographer Cohen put it, "Ellington's birthday appearance at the White House lent additional status to his presence."[57] This too filled the seats at concerts.

———✳———

The specific benefit to the president or to the U.S. government from Ellington's music on the VOA, or the repeated broadcasting of the Ellington evening is more difficult to assess, and beyond the scope of this book. There is, however, consensus as to the overall benefits to the government, as noted by biographer Cohen:

> *Music USA* represented the "most effective propaganda coup" in VOA's history, a show that inspired 1,400 fan clubs in ninety countries. The show's popularity loomed especially large in Eastern Europe. Thanks to the VOA, Yugoslavia . . . had thousands, probably tens of thousands fans of American jazz . . . Like internationally touring American musicians such as Ellington and Armstrong, Conover's show balanced the worldwide image of overwhelming

and sometimes ill-used American power with examples of American creativity, soul, and grace. Culture did not represent the most important weapon in the eventual American Cold War victory, but it played a powerful role. Through the promotion and display of American music and genius, American ideas of political and artistic freedom seeped into authoritarian Communist, and socialist-led countries, and an interest in American life was nurtured.[58]

As examples of American creativity, soul, and grace, nobody did it better, and deserved plaudits more than Edward Kennedy Ellington and Willis Conover.

Ironically, it took the release of the Blue Note CD *1969 All-Star White House Tribute to Duke Ellington* thirty-three years later for the U.S. public to hear the music played at one of the most stellar social events ever held at the executive mansion. And what they heard was an abridged version of what tens of millions of overseas *Music USA* listeners had heard. Americans heard the all-star concert all right, but no speeches by the principals, no singing of "Happy Birthday," no Conover commentary, and no East Room crowd reaction. In other words, no peripheral aural excitement of the kind that elevated a previous Ellington concert recording, *Newport '56*, to become an all-time classic.

As mentioned earlier, the delayed release of the concert CD occurred because Paul Desmond and Jim Hall opposed its initial release. But did they know that the whole world—Conover's world at any rate—would hear the concert anyway? And that President Nixon would accumulate a brownie point or two; after all, it was Nixon who awarded the nation's highest honor to Duke Ellington, which Conover's audience would have agreed was long, long overdue.

Finally, according to Ellington film expert Klaus Stratemann, the VOA produced a ninety-minute audiotape of the Ellington evening as a radio-station handout.[59] The number of such tapes distributed by the VOA, and to what countries and stations are not known.

Impact on Ellington and Jazz

The excitement of Duke's birthday bash no doubt influenced Nixon to schedule subsequent jazz soirees. At some point, after listening to the featured musicians that night, he told Leonard Garment, "If this is jazz, we should have more of it at the White House."[60] President Nixon would host thirteen jazz events during his tenure (see appendix 12), close to equaling the record held by his predecessor, LBJ. Overall, the Nixon administration held 118 social events featuring music of all kinds (see appendix 13). Mainstream popular music fare was the main entrée served at half the events; the other half: classical, 22 percent; jazz, 10 percent; theatrical, 10 percent; film/book, 5 percent; and country, 3 percent. Nixon overindulged in classical (no surprise there), slighted country, but fairly presented jazz.

In addition to the Ellington tribute, Nixon held two other ground-breaking jazz events (though not recognized at the time): He was the first president to invite authentic New Orleans jazz musicians—namely, the Dixieland bands fronted by trumpeter Al Hirt (December 3, 1969)[61] and by clarinetist Pete Fountain (July 15, 1972)—to perform on the nation's premier stage, the latter for a visiting head of state, Mexican President Echeverria. Nixon instructed staff to invite the first great influence in jazz, trumpeter Louis Armstrong, to the White House. But Louis passed before the deal could be consummated.

The impact of that Ellington night had another payoff for jazz. Nixon employed more jazz musicians as cultural ambassadors than any other president. Most of those he dispatched overseas also performed at the White House (see appendix 14). In addition to launching Ellington and his orchestra on their around-the-world tour in 1971 and 1972 (discussed further below), the Nixon State Department dispatched all-stars Dave Brubeck, Earl Hines, and Gerry Mulligan to Europe in 1970 and Eastern Europe in 1971. All-star rhythm-mates Milt Hinton and Louis Bellson—in the company of singer Pearl Bailey, who would perform twice for Nixon—all got their tickets stamped for a cultural exchange trip to the Middle East in 1974. After his dinner-table conversation with the president, the original jazz ambassador Dizzy Gillespie secured two more overseas trips: Europe in 1970 and Africa in 1973. While bandleader Count Basie couldn't make Duke's birthday bash (his wife attended on his behalf), the Count and his swinging band nonetheless toured Eastern Europe in 1972.

For Ellington, receiving the nation's highest honor was greatly appreciated, of course, but it didn't really change much; he continued doing what he always did: pursue his musical mistress. The years following his White House tribute didn't differ from those immediately preceding it: barnstorming one-nighters, festivals, State Department tours, Sacred Concerts, new songs, new extended compositions, and awards and honors of all sorts from cities, states, countries, universities, clubs, and magazines.

The publicity surrounding the White House tribute and the impact it had on the president resulted in an immediate payoff for Duke and his orchestra: an extensive and lucrative diplomatic tour around the world on behalf of the State Department.[62] In early 1970, Ellington and the band toured Burma and Laos. The *Guardian* newspaper in Burma called the Ellington performances

> a welcome goodwill gesture by the U.S.A. The very fact that our select audience was entertained by the man who was conferred with the highest honor by the U.S. president, should be proof enough of the goodwill the U.S. Government seeks to show Burma.[63]

A few months later, the Ellington Orchestra managed a state visit to Yugoslavia. The peripatetic musical diplomats then visited the Soviet Union during September and October 1971, which many considered to be their most important and publicized State Department tour ever. Other jazz figures had preceded Ellington to the Soviet Union—Benny Goodman (1962), Earl Hines (1966), and Charles Lloyd (1967)—but Ellington was the most famous single American cultural figure to tour the country. As soon as that trip ended, the Ellington Orchestra toured seventeen European countries, including Poland, Yugoslavia, and Hungary.

In the latter part of October, Duke and the band began a twenty-four-day, thirteen-country Latin American tour. A short stop in New York City to catch their collective breath, and then the men boarded a jumbo jet for the Orient. By the time Ellington returned from the Asian excursion in February 1972, he had visited over forty countries during the preceding five months. Ellington's last dates outside the United States—a five-and-a-half-week tour of Europe with a week in Africa—occurred in 1973. Both parties benefited greatly: Nixon got what he wanted and needed, an exemplary goodwill ambassador. Duke got a solid half-year payday for his men, inspiration for future compositions, and kudos for jazz itself as a worthy emissary of the United States.

In anticipation of his seventy-fifth birthday in 1974, *DownBeat* magazine's April 25 issue published tribute quotes from over two hundred musicians from all styles and eras of jazz.[64] On his birthday, the world seemingly stood still to mark the event in grand style.

Stanford University presented a three-day symposium examining Ellington's "contribution to music." Ellington's Orchestra [without its hospitalized maestro] appeared at a Concert of Sacred Music at St. Peter's Church in New York City, just a couple of blocks from the hospital . . . The Voice of America paid tribute to Ellington "on every news, discussion, educational, cultural and music—classical and pop as well as jazz—program" . . . Willis Conover, of the *Music USA* program, assembled fifty radio programs featuring exclusively Ellington music that aired throughout 1974. [USIA] films about Ellington were shown in 189 posts in 108 countries around the world. Sixteen different USIA magazines published in twenty-five languages featured Ellington articles and photographs. Photo exhibits and live concerts by local musicians were scheduled to take place at the U.S. embassies of the more than fifty countries that Ellington and the orchestra had visited on behalf of the State Department.[65]

His whirlwind life came to an end one month later, on May 24, 1974.

Honors

The honors didn't stop after his death. His hometown of Washington, DC, named a building, arts school, and bridge after him. The U.S. Postal Service issued a commemorative stamp on April 29, 1986. The Smithsonian Institution acquired a massive collection of Ellingtonia (documents, compositions, photos, tapes, and awards) in 1988, made possible by a $500,000 grant from the U.S. Congress.

In 1999, commemorating the centennial year of his birth, the Pulitzer Prize was bestowed posthumously on Edward Kennedy Ellington in recognition of his musical genius, which evoked aesthetically the principals of democracy through the medium of jazz, and thus made indelible his contribution to art and culture. Although Duke missed out on this prestigious award while he was alive—to the chagrin of many in the jazz arts community—he graciously accepted his Grammy Lifetime Achievement Award in 1966 and his nomination to the Songwriters Hall of Fame in 1971. Importantly and deservedly, Ellington received a major storyline (second only to Louis Armstrong's) in Ken Burn's 2000 TV documentary, *Jazz*, introducing a new segment of the American population (those not even born at the time of his East Room tribute) to the maestro's music and import.

Finally, on January 26, 2009, the United States Mint issued a quarter featuring Duke, making him the first musician—and the first African American—to appear by himself on a circulating (as opposed to a commemorative) U.S. coin. Ellington's image appeared on the tails side of the quarter honoring the District of Columbia, while George Washington remained on the heads side, according to protocol.

Thereafter, Willis Conover continued his weekly VOA jazz broadcasts—with a few interruptions—for another twenty-seven years and arranged a total of forty White House jazz events for every president after Nixon up to and including Bill Clinton.[66] Considering that he organized the jazz for the LBJ inaugural, the V of the VOA could claim a most unusual achievement: jazz impresario to seven presidents, LBJ to Clinton, 1965–1996. For this, and all his accomplishments, Willis received a *DownBeat* Lifetime Achievement Award in 1995.

As for the other event instigators, Joe Morgen remained Duke's publicist until the maestro's death in 1974, and Charles McWhorter accepted Nixon's offer to serve on the National Council of the Arts (1970–1976). Thereafter, he held high posts on the boards of numerous music, arts, and dance companies, including the American Ballet Theater.[67] Leonard Garment, in his capacity as Nixon's liaison to the National Endowment for the Arts (NEA) and Humanities (NEH), worked with those agencies to increase their annual appropriation. NEA funding grew from $9 million in 1969 to $80 million in 1974—a stunning accomplishment considering that its appropriation for 2012 is only $150 million. After his stint in the White House, Garment became chairman of the Brooklyn Academy of Music and then helped found the Jazz Museum in Harlem. He was awarded the National Medal of Arts by President George W. Bush in 2005 as an arts advocate and patron.[68]

Many of the all-stars would return to the White House.[69] Fatha Hines played for presidents Ford and Carter. Billy Taylor, in addition to two more gigs for Nixon, performed for Ford, Clinton (twice), and George W. Bush. Brubeck, whose classic quartet played for Lyndon Johnson, would get another invite from President Reagan, and then receive the Presidential Medal of the Arts from President Clinton. Milt Hinton returned two more times for Nixon and once for Carter. Drummer Louis Bellson, in the company of his wife, Pearl Bailey, would accompany her thrice (for Nixon, Ford, and Carter). Clark Terry, who performed for Lady Bird Johnson and presidents Carter and Clinton, would make a final appearance for George W. Bush. Joe Williams sang "Every Day I Have the Blues" one more time at the Clinton White House.

Some of the guest musicians appeared as well. Billy Eckstine sang for President Carter, and Lou Rawls for President Clinton. Benny Goodman brought his clarinet to play for President Reagan, and Dizzy Gillespie, who was the first jazz artist to tour for the State Department under President Eisenhower, got the call twice from President Carter and once from President Reagan. Benny received his Grammy Lifetime Achievement Award in 1986; three years later, Dizzy mantled his award. Lastly, President Bill Clinton tapped Marian McPartland for another go at the East Room piano.

Photograph of the East Room—the largest room in the White House—with several hundred chairs set up prior to the Medal of Freedom ceremony, concert, and late-night festivities. The screened-off area in the back was reserved for motion-picture camera operators and still-picture photographers and their equipment. This would be the first time in history that the White House allowed a musicale to be filmed for broadcast over television—a commonplace occurrence today. In addition, it was the first time such an event was filmed for a documentary to be distributed overseas by the USIA.

The banquet over and a second reception line formed for the entertainment-only guests, Vice President and Mrs. Agnew engaged in chit chat with early-seated guests as all-star band members huddled next to the stage (guitarist Jim Hall most visible).

Dinner and entertainment-only guests packed the East Room to capacity and awaited the start of the Medal of Freedom ceremony. Front and center, Mr. and Mrs. John H. Johnson, publishers of *Ebony* and *Jet* magazines; to their right, clergy members instrumental in staging Ellington's Sacred Concerts.

The ceremony began with the president reading the Medal of Freedom citation. He gave particular emphasis to the last line: "In the royalty of American music, no man swings more or stands higher than the Duke."

The president handed the citation certificate to Duke and then took receipt of the Medal of Freedom from a White House aide with Ellington looking on.

President Nixon showed Ellington the Medal of Freedom in its case while the audience applauded. He then handed the encased Medal to the honoree. Below, this UPI photo accompanied stories in various U.S. newspapers the next day.

With citation and medal in his possession, Ellington literally beamed as the East Room shook with applause from a standing audience.

Ellington responded warmly to his award, thanking the president and posthumously his writing and arranging partner, Billy Strayhorn, citing the latter's major freedoms:

Freedom from hate unconditionally

Freedom from self-pity

Freedom from fear of possibly doing something that may help someone else more than it would him

Freedom from the kind of pride that would make a man feel he is better than his brother

Taking the president by both hands, Duke leaned in close and conferred his celebrated four-kiss reward. The East Room crowd erupted gleefully—as did, no doubt, intrepid editors who didn't shy away from publishing a potentially incendiary UPI photo in their next-day newspapers.

Duke and the president smilingly acknowledge the boisterous East Room crowd's reaction to Duke's "one for each cheek" ritualistic kiss.

After the kiss, President Nixon moved toward the piano on the riser, saying to Duke, "Stay up here. Stay with me." Sensing that Nixon was going to sit down and play, the crowd reacted noisily. The president stepped back to the microphone, raised his hand, and said, "Please don't go away . . . You see . . . this is his birthday. Duke Ellington is ageless, but would you please stand and sing 'Happy Birthday.' And please, in the key of G!"

President Nixon played "Happy Birthday" on the piano to the ageless Duke as everybody in the East Room stood and sang the timeless song to "Dear Edward." The assembled clapped enthusiastically at song's end.

Urbie Green, backed by the all-star rhythm section, traced the sumptuous contours of "I Got It Bad (And That Ain't Good)," originally written for *Jump for Joy*.

Paul Desmond offered his take on Billy Strayhorn's impressionistic "Chelsea Bridge."

J. J. Johnson swung out on a bluesy rocking version of "Satin Doll," propelled by a hand-clapping, finger-snapping audience.

Shouts greeted Gerry Mulligan's opening notes on "Sophisticated Lady," a brief homage to Duke's baritone saxophonist Harry Carney in the audience.

The Clark Terry and Bill Berry trumpet duo harmonized "Don't Squeeze Me." CT's puckish, screaming solo lifted the East Room crowd out of their chairs.

Earl Hines ripped off a fiery version of "Perdido" that brought the audience to their feet.

Mary Mayo voiced the familiar "Mood Indigo" backed by a tasty line from trombonist J. J. Johnson.

Joe Williams's deeply moving "Come Sunday" brought tears to some audience members' eyes.

Duke closed out the concert with "Pat," a new composition dedicated to the First Lady.

Duke took a bow at the conclusion of his brief, pensive extemporized tribute to the First Lady. Warm applause followed him to his seat. Concert over.

All eyes turned toward Dave Brubeck as Willis Conover (*far right*) introduced the players at concert's end. *Left to right*: Dave Brubeck (*p*), Hank Jones (*p*), Mary Mayo (*v*), Jim Hall (*g*), Billy Taylor (*p*), Paul Desmond (*as*), Gerry Mulligan (*bs*), Joe Williams (*v*), Clark Terry (*tp*), Tom Whaley (*c*), Bill Berry (*tp*), Urbie Green (*tb*), J. J. Johnson (*tb*), Louis Bellson (*dms*), and Milt Hinton (*b*). Earl Hines (*p, not pictured*).

Dinner-guest and singer Lou Rawls took advantage of the open microphone and sang some lowdown blues accompanied by all-stars Milt Hinton and Clark Terry, dinner-guest Dizzy Gillespie, and marine and navy tenor saxmen. Rawls would soon be joined at the microphone by singers Billy Eckstine and Joe Williams.

Event instigator and programmer Willis Conover (*far right*) and USIA Director Frank Shakespeare watched the trumpet master duo of Clark Terry (*foreground*) and Dizzy Gillespie (*behind Terry*) with trombonist Urbie Green at the microphone.

Not to be denied, navy musicians joined the jam band on drummer Louis Bellson's bongos (the ones he featured in "Caravan" during the concert).

Asked why he played with his eyes closed, Gerry Mulligan answered, "Yes I do . . . except when I have to read music. Then I also play with my eyes closed."

Dinner-guest Dizzy Gillespie showing off the world's most famous trumpet cheeks.

All-star Dave Brubeck and festival impresario and pianist George Wein took their turn at the piano.

A heart-tugging moment for all concerned, Duke and his mentor Willie "the Lion" Smith once again shared a piano bench—a long way from 1920s Harlem.

Duke danced with multiple partners. Shown here with Carmen de Lavallade (*top left*); the president's secretary, Rose Mary Woods (*top right*); and a woman identified as Mrs. Joe Williams (*bottom*), with Dr. Arthur Logan nearby.

While the president and first lady retired to the upstairs quarters to listen to the downstairs revelry, first daughter Trisha stayed behind to dance the frug with an unknown guest.

White House photographer Ollie Atkins caught the president's secretary, Rose Mary Woods, in controlled abandon, oblivious to everything but the music, expressing pure sensual joy.

Duke Ellington greeted by jazz fans upon his arrival at Moscow Airport on September 11, 1971. He opened in Leningrad two days later, the first concert in a five-week tour of the Soviet Union sponsored by the State Department.

Ethiopian Emperor Haile Selassie I toasted Ellington during a reception in his honor at the Jubilee Palace in Adda Abba, Ethiopia, on November 20, 1973. Two evening concerts followed the reception, and then Duke and his orchestra flew off to Zambia for another concert before returning home. This would be the maestro's final visit to the African continent.

A general view inside the Cathedral of St. John the Divine in New York City, as people gathered for the funeral of Edward Kennedy Ellington on May 27, 1974. Fifteen thousand guests packed the church while another twenty-five thousand or so people milled outside. Stanley Dance delivered the eulogy. Ella Fitzgerald sang "Solitude" and "Just a Closer Walk with Thee." And as he did at the seventieth-birthday tribute for Duke at the White House, Joe Williams sang "My Mother, My Father (Heritage)."

Ruth Ellington Boatwright (sister) and Mercer Ellington (son) joined hands in front of a poster depicting a stamp honoring Duke Ellington in New York, April 29, 1986. The stamp was issued to mark Ellington's eighty-seventh birthday.

One side of the District of Columbia quarter featuring district native son Duke Ellington. U.S. Mint and DC officials celebrated the release of the coin on February 24, 2009, during a ceremony at the Smithsonian's National Museum of American History. Ellington is the first black American to be prominently featured on a U.S. coin in circulation.

Denied while still alive, Duke finally received his Pulitzer. Columbia University Provost Jonathan B. Cole presented daughter-in-law Lene Ellington and grandson Paul Ellington with the 1999 Pulitzer Prize Special Edition on April 29, 1999.

"It's very too bad," composer Aaron Copland was quoted as saying. The *New York Times* protested the injustice of it all. Jazz critics were highly displeased. The only one seemingly unruffled was Ellington himself. The sixty-six-year-old composer told *Newsweek*, "I've absolutely no disappointment . . . Fate's trying to keep me from becoming too famous too young . . . As long as I can hear my music, I don't care if I ever win a prize." (*DownBeat* magazine, June 17, 1965.)

Appendices

———————— ✳ ————————

Early Jazz Events
at the White House

Washington Navy Yard Jazz Band

IN MAY AND JUNE OF 1921, the recently inaugurated president and Mrs. Harding held four well-attended meet-and-greet garden parties on the White House grounds. The Marine Band played in concert on the South Lawn at all four, while the Washington Navy Yard Jazz Band played for dancing in the East Room for the first three (the last party being staged for soldiers from Walter Reed Hospital).

The *Chicago Daily Tribune* ran this headline on May 19, 1921: "White House Gets First Taste of Jazz: 2,000 Attend Party." The *Tribune* further reported:

> The marine band was in attendance on the lawn, playing selections which ranged from "The Pilgrims' Chorus" to "The End of the Perfect Day," while the Navy Band from the yard played the gayest of jazz music in the East Room. Mrs. Harding herself passing the word among the younger set as it filed decorously past the presidential party ... And for the first time in the history of the White House garden parties, there was dancing in the East Room.[1]

This was the first time "jazz" and "White House" appeared in the same sentence in an American newspaper. And it was the Navy Yard

Jazz Band from Washington—not the better-known Boston or Great Lakes Navy Yard Jazz bands—that participated in this historic coupling.

Both northern bands—Boston and Great Lakes—formed in 1917, the same year jazz was first recorded. These bands engaged in publicity tours on behalf of the navy during WWI to assist wartime recruiting and fundraising through the sale of Liberty War Bonds.[2]

The Washington Navy Yard Jazz Band started later, in the spring of 1918, and held its inaugural public concert in early July, providing the music for a benefit military baseball game at American League Park.[3] By August, press releases in Washington newspapers drew attention to the band's appearance at a Navy Yard Employees Field Day at Central High School, noting that the nation's capital band had already "gained quite a reputation" and had become "famous."[4] Despite the band's presumed notoriety, its public performance schedule eased as the war drew down. One of its only events occurred in May 1919, when the band accompanied dancing in the streets of Washington on Navy Carnival Day.[5]

But changes were afoot.

That same month, Charles Benter was appointed bandmaster at the Navy Yard, a position he would hold until 1942. More than anyone else, he was responsible for the Washington Yard Band (full orchestra and smaller units) becoming the official band of the U.S. Navy (so ordered by President Coolidge in 1925).[6] Benter's arrival at the Yard coincided with the return of many bandsmen to civilian life after WWI. He immediately set out to attract and enlist the best musicians he could find by letting his musicians wear civilian clothes during off-duty hours, offering higher pay, granting permission to live off base, and, one might surmise, allowing those interested in jazz to play it.

The rebuilding began. In late July, as reported in the *Washington Post* under the headline "Yeoman (F) and Marinettes Pass in Final Review," the Washington Navy Yard Jazz Band provided the music at a mustering-out ceremony for women combatants on the Ellipse behind the White House. Much to the delight of the assembled crowd, the band featured the widely popular "The Alcoholic Blues," penned earlier in the year after prohibition was enacted by Tin Pan Alley pioneer Albert Von Tilzer (lyrics by Edward Laska).[7]

The newspapers and archival records for 1920 have a dearth of information on the Washington band. The thin record we do have shows that the band began its long association with radio as a small orchestra (which likely played some jazz) broadcasting from a hangar at the Anacostia Naval Air Station.[8]

It probably took Benter some time—perhaps a year—to assemble a unit suitable for continuous public engagements. By early 1921, the archival records show, the band was ready, and it was booked to furnish music for Friday night dances at Congressional Club debutante balls on January 14 and 28 and February 11 and 25. The January appearances were noted in a Washington society column. No details were given, nor was there any mention of jazz.[9] But that was soon to change.

Later that year, the Washington Navy Yard Jazz Band played its first historic gig at the White House, as mentioned above. It performed again at the second and third Harding garden parties on May 25 and June 1. In each instance, newspaper accounts always mentioned the band and even provided interesting tidbits, but curiously, without any reference to jazz, save for the *New York Times* on June 2:

> When the Marine Band brought its concert to a close just at 7 p.m., President and Mrs. Harding returned to the White House where they joined the dancers in the East Room for the last number—not the jazz of the earlier hours—but the "Blue Danube," played by the Navy Yard Band, which the president was unable to resist.[10]

Except for the above, articles in either the *New York Times* or the Washington newspapers (*Post, Evening Star, Herald,* and *Tribune*) referred to the Navy Yard Band or Navy Band, and never the Navy Jazz Band or the Navy Yard Jazz Band.[11] Perhaps a word of caution is in order. No doubt, the band in question was a novel dance band with great appeal to the young that played "music quite different from that which the Marine Band was furnishing."[12] But was it a jazz band? Who were the musicians? What tunes did they play? No illuminating newspaper coverage to speak of. No recordings or set lists exist. There are photos, which show the instruments played, and based on the manner in which the bandsmen sometimes posed, it appears to be a 1920s hot jazz band. One can only speculate: vaudeville tunes, ragtime numbers, parlor songs probably, but there is no evidence the musicians played "hot" numbers inspired by the earliest jazz performances heard in dance halls and clubs, or on records.

Three tunes in the band's repertoire are known from newspaper accounts: "The Alcoholic Blues"—a novelty tune with serious anti-drinking lyrics—and two waltzes, the traditional "Blue Danube" by Strauss and "The End of the Perfect Day," a popular parlor song published in 1910 by Carrie Jacobs-Bond (the first American woman who made her living from composing) and a favorite of Mrs. Harding, who requested both the Navy and Marine bands play "A Perfect Day" at her garden parties.[13]

Mrs. Harding did more than just request her favorite waltz, as reported in the *Washington Evening Star:*

> The Navy Yard band played in the east room for the benefit of those who wished to dance, and Mrs. Harding's fondness for old-time melodies was traced in both the Marine and Navy bands, as she selected the greater part of each program.[14]

As far as we know, no jazz was played for dancing or in concert at the White House for the remainder of the Harding administration, which was cut short by the president's untimely death in 1923.

Moreover, an examination of the navy records at the National Archives and an examination of the public newspaper record at the Library of Congress provided no clues as to what the Yard Jazz Band played in 1921, or indeed throughout most of the 1920s. Complicating matters, the written record seldom distinguished between the full orchestra and the jazz band. That aside, it appears likely that the Yard Jazz Band played a State Fair in Richmond, Virginia, in October 1921, and concerts at Central High School, the Lincoln Memorial, and privately for President and Mrs. Harding in 1922.[15]

A most intriguing headline in the *Washington Post* in November 1923 declared, "Music World Here Waits for Jazz to Cut into Classics: Capital's Navy Band Is Arranging Concert." The Navy Band, the article reported, would play jazz at Memorial Continental Hall in December, but that was it.[16] Four years later, in September 1927, a newspaper announced a rehearsal concert at the Yard Sail Loft and "a few minutes with 'The United States Navy Jazz Band' right before intermission." No word on what they would play.[17]

One way to get at the tunes the Washington Navy Yard Jazz Band might have played at the White House is to uncover what the popular Boston Yard Jazz Band (based at Charleston, Massachusetts) performed at its public concerts during (and after) WWI, and then assume the Washington band followed suit. The Navy archival record adequately documents the Boston band during its Keith Vaudeville Theater circuit appearances during the 1918–1919 time frame. This band, under the direction of Ensign Alfred J. Moore, drew huge enthusiastic crowds at Keith Theaters up and down the East Coast (Boston, New York, Philadelphia, and Washington) and raised considerable sums for the war effort through the sale of war bonds.[18]

A separate research inquiry into the Boston Yard Jazz Band, as well as other navy bands active on the Vaudeville Theater Circuit, namely the Great Lakes Yard Jazz Band (initiated by John Phillip Sousa) and the Atlantic Fleet Jazz Band (directed by Nat Nazarro Jr.) could shed some light on the Washington band's repertoire, and possibly answer other questions.[19] Did the band play ensemble music only? Were there instrumental solos? On what instruments? Improvised or routinized? Of what duration?

The concern here with the authenticity of the 1921 band is not a matter of ideological purity, but a matter of historical accuracy. Jazz was not broadly understood in early 1921. Uncertainty existed as to what exactly jazz was. That's why it often appeared in quotes or was referred to as "so-called jazz." The word connoted a music that was novel and danceable to be sure. A group of musicians—a marching band, for example, normally confined to playing summertime gazebos in town squares—could play numbers at faster tempos, add ragtime tunes to their repertoire, don clown suits, and affect a circus style replete with instrumental animal sounds to get more gigs. This is not to imply that the nation's capital band came even close to this poorly drawn example. But until more specific information comes along—earwitness accounts would be helpful—the jazz-band-labeled band that played Mrs. Harding's garden parties should be assumed authentic, albeit with a note of caution.

This is not the case for the next jazz band to appear at the White House, for President Coolidge in 1924, as will be discussed next.

Finally, recall the last sentence in the opening quote: "And for the first time in the history of the White House garden parties, there was dancing in the east room." Sorry, dancing in the East Room first occurred during the administration of John Quincy Adams, on December 15, 1828. Dancers moved to the cotillion, a popular four-couple pattern dance accompanied by a small orchestra—three violins, two woodwinds—drawn from the Marine Band.[20] With all due respect to President Adams, whatever music the Washington Navy Yard Jazz Band played—and the young people danced to—in the Harding East Room, it just had to be livelier than the music performed at the Adams White House in 1828.

Ray Miller Jazz Band

On October 17, 1924, the Ray Miller Jazz Band accompanied vaudeville singer Al Jolson and a chorus of Broadway theatrical stars at a campaign rally for President Coolidge on the South Lawn of the White House. The Miller aggregation was a known, well-recorded top-flight dance band, and two of its members, Miff Mole and Frank Trumbauer, were at the time, widely influential jazz soloists.

So how did an authentic commercial jazz band end up at the White House in 1924? No such organization had appeared there before, and the idea for the event did not originate inside the residence either, but rather outside, by two ambitious individuals: a politician and a public relations expert.

How It All Came About

Rhinelander Waldo, the ex-police commissioner of New York City, had his eyes on becoming the governor of either New York State or the Philippine territories (where he had served four years while in the U.S. Army). For that, he needed help from people in high places, specifically from President Calvin Coolidge, if only he could get him reelected—a perceived dim prospect given silent Cal's "weaned on a pickle" image. To promote the president's cause and his own, Colonel Waldo, as he was often called, formed the Coolidge Non-Partisan League, necessary because the colonel was a Democrat, Coolidge a Republican. Waldo then solicited the help of famed publicist Edward L. Bernays, known today as the father of the public relations industry. [21]

After several unsuccessful publicity gambits, Bernays and Waldo decided to "go big," to transform the president's image from a serious-minded introvert into the sort of homespun man people wanted in the White House. As he revealed in his memoir, Bernays reasoned as follows:

> I racked my brain for some association that would reverse the impression of coldness. I decided that stage people symbolized warmth, extroversion and Bohemian camaraderie and if they breakfasted at the White House they would dissipate the impression. [22]

Bernays did not have to rack his brain too hard; he had only to copy a well-publicized precedent set by Albert Lasker four years earlier for Coolidge's predecessor, Warren Harding, during the latter's presidential campaign. [23] Every salient aspect of the campaign rally at Harding's home in Marion, Ohio, was copied with slight alteration for the Coolidge affair. This time, an Al Jolson–led Broadway contingent took an overnight sleeper train to the president's home in the White House, breakfasted, and then entertained the chief executive in his backyard for an hour, including a Jolson-penned campaign ditty sung by all, with the whole affair documented by print, still picture and film media. But this time, Jolson brought the jazz band.

On October 7, 1924, Waldo contacted C. Bascomb Slemp, secretary to the president, at the White House and asked if the president would be agreeable to receiving a delegation of actors led by Jolson on October 17. [24] A positive response was immediately forthcoming. Publicity benefits aside, Calvin and especially wife Grace would have been delighted to have the Great White Way descend en masse on 1600 Pennsylvania Avenue. The two of them regularly attended the theater and movies (screened for them in the mansion or on the presidential yacht) and enjoyed receiving actors at the White House. [25]

The music Coolidge brought to the presidential mansion—and there was ample—had a definite Eurocentric cast. Famous classical harpists, pianists (Rachmaninoff three times), violinists, string quartets, and chambers groups gave homage to the likes of Brahms, Beethoven, Schumann, Lizt, Chopin, and Debussy. Glamorous tenors and sopranos paid their respects to the operatic traditions. American music found its way into the mansion occasionally. Universities choirs (Missouri, Wisconsin, Furman, and Amherst), the Arion Singing Society, the Bethlehem Bach Choir, and the Vatican Choir all sent their choruses. [26]

What Coolidge thought when he signed off on the Miller Jazz Band is lost to history, but it can be assumed that a publicity-generating campaign rally on the South Lawn would be just fine—unlike, for example, a concert inside the White House.

ARRIVAL, HANDSHAKES, SAUSAGES, AND TABLE TALK[27]

After the curtains fell on Broadway the night of October 16, a troupe of some forty performers—twenty-seven actors and fifteen Miller bandsmen—boarded the midnight train to the nation's capital.[28] Just after daybreak some seven hours later, the train pulled into Washington's Union Station, where Cadillacs that Bernays had ordered waited to take the sleepy party to the White House. In his memoir, Bernays recounted what happened next:

> At the door of the White House President Coolidge and Mrs. Coolidge awaited us. "I have met you all across the footlights," Mrs. Coolidge said graciously, "but it's not the same as meeting you here. Let us go into breakfast."
>
> [Inside] the threshold I lined up a party for a handshaking ceremony with the president. Although I did not know most of their names . . . they had to whisper their names to me as they moved up the line toward the president, and then I relayed the information. I wondered how he would behave. To my surprise, he completely lived up to the mental picture of the country, including myself, had of him. He was practically inarticulate, and no movement of any kind agitated his deadpan face. He shook each hand perfunctorily, said "Good Morning" and then took the next hand extended to him . . . His face reflected no inner anything, in strong contrast to the warmth of Mrs. Coolidge.
>
> It was even more surprising to me, therefore, that after the last person on the line had shaken his hand, Coolidge turned to me and asked pleasantly, "Your name, please?"
>
> "Oh, Mr. President, that's not important," I said. "I'm the publicity man for the party."
>
> "Not unimportant either," the President replied, looking at me searchingly. "The publicity man—your name."
>
> Apparently, he was fully aware of my function and the political value of the performance he was participating in.
>
> President Coolidge, escorting the tall comedian Charlotte Greenwood, led us into the state dining room for a breakfast of hot, steaming coffee with cream, fruit, toast, hot griddle cakes, and

Deerfoot sausages. Mrs. Coolidge took the arm of Colonel Waldo and then spied Mr. Jolson. "Let me take your arm, too," remarked Mrs. Coolidge. "I want two partners for this occasion."[29]

Mr. Coolidge sat between Waldo and Charlotte Greenwood, the former being anxious to discuss phases of the Non-Partisan campaign work, the latter to inject life into the gathering. The president at first divided his attention equally, apparently trying to keep one side of his face serious and let the other stray off into a smile, but when the hilarity got underway, all attempts at seriousness were abandoned. Ms. Greenwood, star of *Linger Longer Letty*, was dieting at the time and looked at the wheat cakes in dismay. But the president urged her to try his favorite Vermont maple syrup. Charlotte promptly challenged him to run around the White House lawn with her for twenty minutes if she took the cake and syrup. Mrs. Coolidge's merry laughter could be heard across the table at that point.

Al Jolson, sitting next to Mrs. Coolidge, and Raymond Hitchcock, sitting on the same side, were the life of the occasion with their stories, jokes, and repartee and satire on political speeches. Hitchcock conducted a discussion of economics. The most memorable comments of the breakfast, however, came from the First Lady.

"Your dog must like me," Al told her. "He hasn't stopped licking my hands."

"Maybe he wouldn't do it," Mrs. Coolidge said, "if you used a napkin."

The breakfast lasted for more than an hour. As he got up to leave the table, Jolson remarked, "I ate everything but the sausages."

"Does that include the doilies?" Mrs. Coolidge asked.

"No, I have them in my pocket," Jolson said.

As they left the mansion, Jolson unwisely asked the First Lady if he would be able to find his coat. "Yes," said Mrs. Coolidge, "if I can get my doilies."

PHOTO OP AND SOUTH LAWN FRIVOLITIES

President and Mrs. Coolidge then led their guests onto the White House lawn by way of the western stairs where they paused and posed for still photographs while, as reported in *Billboard*, "movie camera men reeled off a thousand feet of film with the president surrounded by Broadway visitors."[30]

Media in tow, the entourage moved to a flat expanse of grass on the South Lawn, where the morning frivolities were about to begin, even though Ray Miller's Jazz Band had not yet made an appearance. The musicians presumably busied themselves with unpacking their instruments and warming up. The ceremony started off on a serious note. The designated emcee for the show, Al Jolson, assured the president of the support of the theatrical profession:

> We are all Republicans from now . . . Incidentally, I have been a Republican these twenty years. We members of the theatre are perhaps in more intimate touch with the people than any other profession. We came to assure you of our support and offer to work for you and the Republican Party. The theatrical profession is almost 100 percent for you. Those who are not, Mr. President, are those who are not working, and there are very few of us in that category.[31]

Switching gears, the emcee then warned that all jokes told must be dignified presidential jokes, but perhaps one or two must make the president laugh out loud. Hoping his joke would qualify, Jolson offered a story about two frogs and a turtle.[32] Mr. Coolidge participated in the laughter almost as heartily as the rest.

Next, Raymond Hitchcock made one of those impromptu speeches for which he became famous and had the audience laughing from start to finish. In his faux political address, he sought to show how much there is in a name, whether a germanium or a special kind of sauce, leading into a discussion of Raymond Hitchcock as a great name for the presidency—comparable only to such names as William Jennings Bryan, Oscar Underwood, Robert M. LaFollette, and Al Smith [all non-Republicans]. "Al Smith is a small-town name," said Mr. Hitchcock. "Just compare it for appeal to names like Raymond Hitchcock and Calvin Coolidge." One had to be there to appreciate the humor in his monologue.

At one point during the festivities, unclear when exactly, Jolson made Coolidge laugh by whispering in his ear. "If you don't laugh," he said. "I'll tell you a story that'll *really* make you laugh."

Gerald Griffin next sang "My Irish Rose" (with or without band accompaniment is not known, but probably not) followed by a Scotch joke by Hal Forde. This one made the president laugh out loud, almost complying with Jolson's request. He laughed all right, but not so heartily and long as the First Lady. "Don't tell the next one until Mrs. Coolidge is through laughing," the watchful Jolson warned his friend Forde.

With the band in place, and lead sheets distributed round the crowd, it was time for the campaign song penned by Jolson (no doubt with uncredited help from long-term friend and colleague Buddy DeSylva, on hand that morning ready to give voice.) The corps of New York actors, White House staff, actors from local theaters, and some members of the press, totaling more than a hundred, joined in a lusty chorus of "Keep Coolidge."

Mrs. Coolidge, who gave the appearance of having the time of her life, joined in the singing and at times her clear soprano tones could be heard above the other voices. She purposely held the last note, which was a high one, and Jolson turned and said so everyone could hear him, "Some note. That's so good, let's have it again." The song was sung half a dozen times. And it was sung well, even though it was the first time many of those present had seen the words. The press was silent on whether the Miller band accompanied the singing or even separately performed an instrumental number or two. They did, as will be discussed.

At the conclusion of the visit, and before he joined his Cabinet meeting, the president briefly thanked those who came to support and entertain him and told them the White House would be open to them for a return engagement at any time.

Above-the-fold headlines in the next day newspapers had to surpass what the event's initiators had hoped for—namely, the *New York World* headline: "Actors Lure Real Laugh to Coolidge Face: White House Breakfast Theatre of Fun-Making."

PRINT MEDIA ASLEEP AT THE WHITE HOUSE WHEEL

The written record of the event—periodicals, memoirs, biographies, and presidential archival materials—offers scant information on the band that accompanied Al Jolson that fine October day. Curious indeed, given the amount of detail we have on the handshaking ceremony, breakfast table talk, and South Lawn jokes.

The record is simply silent on how or why the Ray Miller Band was selected, and on what administration officials knew about the band in advance. Did the band members accompany Jolson on songs other than "Keep Coolidge"? Accompany performers other than Jolson? Play their own tunes? How about the band's performance? And who were its members? Fortunately some of these questions can be deduced from the visual record (photographs and newsreel footage) and other sources. But first: what about this Miller Jazz Band?

RAY MILLER

In the 1920s, Ray Miller was a well-known, highly respected bandleader whose orchestra made many recordings and radio broadcasts.[33] His first band, active in the 1917–1922 period, played in the style of white New Orleans bands that had migrated north (Original Dixieland Jazz Band, for example).

In 1923 Miller dropped the old style, and by the end of 1923, his band played like the newer, larger New York bands and were, according to musicologist Gunther Schuller, more spontaneous than most white bands of the era.[34] In the grand scheme of things, this was Miller's first unknowing step on the path that led to the White House. He took the second step that November when he signed an exclusive contract with Brunswick, a prestigious recording company with studios in both Chicago and New York. He began recording his orchestra at the latter studio immediately, waxing four sides in December 1923 and more than thirty over the course of the following year. Miller took the third unknowing step in the spring of 1924, when he urged two important soloists to join the band: saxophonist Frank "Tram" Trumbauer and trombonist Milfred "Miff" Mole. Fortified with these additions, the band played engagements at ballrooms in and around Manhattan.

THE JOLSON CONNECTION

Al Jolson signed an exclusive recording contract with Brunswick at about the same time Ray Miller did, and it took little time for the label to pair the two in the studio. October 2 and 15 were the dates chosen for their musical collaboration. It would make eminent sense that the singer would take his studio band to Washington to back him singing the campaign song he would compose for the occasion. Who knows? The song may have been rehearsed in the studio on October 15. Both Jolson and the Miller band were available and ready to train down to the nation's capital for a rendezvous with the president on October 17 (the date Waldo suggested to Slemp back on October 7).[35]

MILLER'S MUSICIANS

But what about the musicians—who were they? The band that recorded with Al Jolson in the Brunswick studios on October 15 only two days before the Coolidge event consisted of the following musicians: Charles Rocco and Roy Johnston (tps); Miff Mole and Andy Sindelar (tbs); Frank Trumbauer, Larry Abbott, Andy Sanella, and Billy Richards (reeds); Dan Yates (vn); Rube Bloom and Tommy Satterfield (ps); Frank DiPrima (bj); Louis Chassagne (tb); Ward Archer (dms); and Ray Miller (dir).

A photo of this Miller Band on the mansion grounds can be seen on the next page; the musicians are identified in the caption. Three were

The Ray Miller Orchestra accompanied Al Jolson on the South Lawn of the White House on October 17, 1924. President and Mrs. Coolidge stood next to Jolson; Miller had his back to the camera. Others visible: Dan Yates (*vn, head sandwiched between Jolson's and Miller's*); Tom Satterfield (*p, to the right of Miller's head*); Frank DiPrima (*bj*); Ward Archer (*dms*); Andy Sindelar and Miff Mole (*tbs*); Roy Johnston and Charles Rocco (*ts*); Frank Trumbauer (*partly visible*); Larry Abbott, Billy Richards, and Andy Sanella (*saxes*).

exemplary contributors to the music: pianist Rube Bloom, trombonist Miff Mole, and C-melody saxophonist Tram Trumbauer.[36]

Rube

During the 1920s, in addition to the many solos he recorded with the Miller Orchestra, Rube Bloom wrote many novelty piano tunes that are still well regarded today. Through the 1930s and beyond, he formed and played in bands that included the jazz lights of the day. But his lasting mark was as a songwriter. Working with prominent lyricists (Johnny Mercer, Ted Koehler, and Mitchell Parish), he etched several indelible entries in the Great American Songbook: "Day In-Day Out," "Fools Rush In (Where Angels Fear to Tread)," "Don't Worry 'Bout Me," "Give Me the Simple Life," and "Dear Hearts and Gentle People."[37]

Miff

The man Tommy Dorsey later called "the Babe Ruth of the trombone" came to prominence in the Original Memphis Five—the most frequently recorded band of the early jazz period (1918–1923). When Miff Mole joined Miller in the spring of 1924, no one on trombone could execute solo passages more cleanly, better in tune, with smoother slide work, and greater incisive attack in all registers. And Miller certainly gave him plenty of chances to shine, as the many recordings left behind certainly attest.

Following his gig with Miller, who moved to Chicago in 1925, Miff turned down numerous offers to stay around New York City. Miff's solos at this time (1927–1928) with various small bands show how far his concept had evolved. Some trombonists even thought he played valve trombone; no slide work, they insisted, could be *that* clean. Miff tended to play the beat, rather than play with it, in the manner of Louis Armstrong and other black soloists; his chief interests lie, rather, in matters of form and melodic organization. Inevitably such traits conferred a sense of tidiness upon his choruses—purposeful with forward motion—yet, even at their best, never quite escaping a sense of having been devised (which many in fact were), rather than rolling out of some inner consciousness (the purported essence of exciting jazz). Rhythmically, too, they evinced a certain constraint, even a stiffness of execution.

By the end of the 1920s, a slew of trombonists (Jack Teagarden, Jimmy Harrison, Joe Nanton, J. C. Higginbotham), many under the spell of Louis Armstrong, who had by then recorded his groundbreaking *Hot Fives and Sevens*, toppled the once lofty Mole. Though still widely admired, Miff's way was but one of several, and for many, not the one to emulate.[38]

Tram

Even before he joined Miller's outfit in the spring of 1924, Frank Trumbauer had acquired a following among musicians—black and white—on the basis of recordings with the Benson Orchestra in 1923 and the

Mound City Blue Blowers in 1924. Saxophonists widely imitated Tram's choruses on Benson's "I Never Miss the Sunshine," and the Blowers' "San." In common with his betwixt-and-between C-melody saxophone, Tram's playing style was similarly divided. On the one hand, he would roll off rehearsed, technically accomplished licks, and on the other, he would plasticize and smooth out a melodic line, lending it a grace and coherence with long held notes, gentle arcs of phrase, and a logic of development rare in hot music of the 1920s. Many of the best Trumbauer solos are minimally altered paraphrases of the parent melodies. Tram "routinized" many of his solos, as did most of the 1920s musicians. Still, his well-polished melodic excursions were several notches above the others.[39]

Trumbauer's time with Ray Miller (1924–1925) only enhanced his reputation as an all-rounder, blessed with near-virtuosic technique, equally skilled at reading and playing hot solos. His influence would only continue to grow after he left Miller to pair up with the legendary trumpeter Bix Beiderbecke, in both the Jean Goldkette and the Paul Whiteman orchestras and his own group. Tram's solo on the latter's "Singin' the Blues" tricked nearly every saxophonist, black and white. Swing tenor saxophonist Budd Johnson summed it up best:

> Of course, Frankie Trumbauer inspired a lot of cats, because he was the baddest cat back in those days, and everybody was trying to play his stuff. He was the boss of the alto like Coleman Hawkins was the boss of the tenor.

THE CAMERA DOES NOT LIE

While the print media was in the dark as far as the Miller band was concerned, the visual (still and motion picture) media had their lenses wide open and focused.[40] The surviving photos allow complete identification of all Miller's musicians save for pianists Tom Satterfield and Rube Bloom. Did they come along for the ride? Are they in the picture? Quite possibly.

Look carefully at the aforementioned photo (page 201). The candidates are the man at the end of the line holding the lead sheet (given where he is standing, he just has to be associated with the band), the man with glasses whose head is seen atop Miller's right shoulder, and the man whose head appears to rest on the bell of Andy Sindelar's trombone. Most who have seen these pictures agree that the man with the glasses, who would be standing between violinist Yates and tuba player Chassagne, is pianist and arranger Satterfield, who by the way went on to arrange for Paul Whiteman's Orchestra and then on to Hollywood to score films. A cautionary note, however: One source says the man wearing glasses is Jolson colleague Irving Caesar, the lyricist of "Swanee" and "Tea for Two."[41] No evidence exists that he made the trip to Washington. As for pianist Rube Bloom, some say it's the man nearest Sinclair's trombone, while others say it's the man at the end of line. Take your pick. In either case, it appears that the full fifteen-man entourage, including Miller, made the trek to DC.

Examination of the ninety-second-long Kinogram newsreel held by UCLA (University of California-Los Angeles) confirms that the Miller Band not only backed the singing of "Keep Coolidge," but also backed Jolson on another tune, as well as performing an instrumental-only number.[42] The three musical numbers on the Kinogram—"Keep Coolidge," Jolson's solo, and the band's feature—are so short (less than ten seconds each) that it is impossible to identify the song Jolson sang by himself and the tune the band played.

WHY NOT THE FIRST?

Why has the Miller Band not been given its props as the first jazz band to play the White House? Was it because print media coverage of the band at the time was almost nonexistent? It was "and Miller's band," and that was that. The print media concentrated on Coolidge and the Broadway delegation, and that's the way Waldo, Bernays, and Jolson wanted it. Their vested interests lay with themselves. Newsreel coverage served the same purpose and might have, as the instigators (and Coolidge) wanted, humanized the Vermont farmer in the minds of theatergoers, enough for some of them to vote in his favor three weeks after the White House event. Coolidge won, so who knows. With such little screen time and no sound on the Kinogram, the Miller Band probably didn't register.

As far as later coverage, the principals all had passed by the time the Paul Winter Sextet—the first jazz group to play a concert inside the White House—mounted the East Room riser for First Lady Jacqueline Kennedy in 1962, save one: Bernays, who lived to 101, but then the band was never of much interest to him. Waldo died three short years after the Coolidge event, and Jolson expired in 1950. Miller mysteriously disappeared in 1930, and both Tram and Miff faded from the scene early, aviation called the former and ill health plagued the latter, before they passed in 1956 and 1961, respectively. In effect, there was no one left to pump the 1924 event in press, radio, and TV interviews and in recording liner notes through the 1930s, '40s (except Jolson), and '50s, and no one around to make noise in 1962 when the press trumpeted the Paul Winter Sextet as a White House first.

Maybe it's none of the above; maybe the Miller Band is simply seen today as a dance band, not a jazz band worthy of the name, even from an early 1920s perspective. But how could that be? The Miller Band of 1924 had two of the most influential jazz players on their respective instruments of the time. True, their playing would remain frozen in a Jazz Age time capsule, never to absorb the newer developments, and would soon be eclipsed by a flock of players that had absorbed the sounds of Louis Armstrong, the wunderkind out of New Orleans by way of Chicago. Best to keep this in mind, though: As Brach was to Picasso, Tram was to Lester Young and Miff was to Tommy Dorsey. Do we value Brach any less because he chose to continue as he began, while Picasso expanded and elevated his cubism to mass acclaim? We shouldn't.

The Ray Miller Band of 1924 was indeed a jazz band worthy of the name. Any fair-minded music fan would come to this conclusion after listening to the *Ray Miller and His Brunswick Orchestra, 1924–1929*, CD (Timeless Historical). Perhaps the absence of follow-up by Coolidge and other presidents prior to Kennedy is the reason the Miller band is not credited as a White House first. All we know is that a year and three months after the Paul Winter Sextet performed in the East Room on November 19, 1962, jazz guitarist Charlie Byrd mounted the riser in said room, and thereafter followed a periodic, if not steady, stream of jazz artists to 1600 Pennsylvania Avenue.

The "Ray Miller Jazz Band" section in this appendix was previously published in Edward Allan Faine, *VJM's Jazz & Blues Mart*, Winter 2012. http://www.vjm.biz.

NOTES

1. "White House Gets First Taste of Jazz: 2000 Attend Party," *Chicago Daily Tribune*, May 19, 1921, 19.

2. While the founding dates for the Boston and Great Lakes Navy Yard Jazz Bands are not known exactly, early 1917 is likely for both based on their known activity in early 1918. Navy Bureau to Navy Yard Boston, memo, Great Lakes [presumably Navy Yard Jazz Band] played Washington Treasury Department and Baltimore Armory during Second Liberty Loan drive. Bureau does not want public to pay to hear Boston band at theaters, April 20, 1918, 24-19E4-2125-336, National Archives, Washington, DC. (See note 18 below for more on the Boston band.)

3. Navy Yard Commandant asked to supply a list of instruments needed for special orchestra known as a jazz band, memo, May 24, 1918, 24-19E4-2125, National Archives, Washington, DC; and first-known public performance in "Arrange Benefit Game," *Washington Post*, July 31, 1918, 8.

4. "20 Events Are Listed for Navy Yard Meet," *Washington Post*, August 4, 1918, 18; and "Navy Yard Field Day Will Be Big Event," *Washington Post*, August 7, 4; said to have gained a reputation in "Navy Yard Employees Ready for Big Games," *Washington Post*, August 10, 1918; appearance in "Zone 4 and 5 Tie in Navy Yard Meet," *Washington Post*, August 11, 1918, 18.

5. "Navy's Day for Loan: Dancing on the Streets," *Washington Post*, May 7, 1919, 1.

6. http://www.navyband.navy.mil/historic_moment_banter.shtml.

7. "Yeoman (F) and Marinettes Pass in Final Review as Band Plays Jazz," *Washington Post*, July 31, 1919, 8.; info on "Alcoholic Blues" at http://parlor songs.com/issues/2004-3 this month/feature.php.

8. Navy Yard Band (maybe jazz band) commence radio broadcasts at http://www.navyband.navy.mil/historic_moment_banter.shtml.

9. Sec. of Navy Admiral Washington orders "Jazz" orchestra of the Navy Yard Band to furnish music at a series of Congressional Club dances to be held on the following Fridays: January 14, January 28, February 11, February 25, memo, Sec. of Navy to Navy Yard Commandant, January 4, 1921, 24-19E4-2125-875, National Archives, Washington, DC; actual appearance noted in "Society," *Evening Star,* January 15 and 29, 1921.

10. *New York Times,* June 2, 1921.

11. NYJB either referred to as Navy Band or Navy Yard Band at White House fete in *New York Times, Washington Post, Washington Evening Star, Washington Herald,* and *Washington Tribune,* May 19 and 27, 1921, and June 2, 1921.

12. Jean Eliot, "Society," *Washington Times,* May 26, 1921, 10.

13. "Perfect Day" at http://en.wikipedia.org/wiki/A_Perfect_Day_(song).

14. Jean Eliot, "Society," *Washington Times,* May 18, 1921. Her "fondness for old-time melodies" in "Society," *Washington Evening Star,* May 26, 1921.

15. NYJB performed at Virginia State Fair, Central High School, Lincoln Memorial and Harding concert in Sec. of Navy files, 24-19E4-2125, National Archives, Washington, DC.

16. "Music World Here Waits for Jazz to Cut into Classics," *Washington Post,* November 18, 1923, 40.

17. NYJB sail loft concert in Elizabeth Ellicott Poe, "Among Musicians," *Washington Post,* September 25, 1927; and "Band Concerts Today," *Washington Post,* September 29, 1927.

18. Sec. of Navy authorized the Boston NYJB to play for one week each at Keith's Vaudeville Theater in Boston, New York, Philadelphia and Washington. Band raised $2 million and garnered praise of Boston Yard Commandant, memo, Senior Aide to Commandant, Boston Navy Yard, May 1, 1918, 24-19E4-3125-422, National Archives, Washington DC. After WWI, discharged members under the direction of Alfred J. Moore again toured theaters as the Boston NYJB in March 1919. Navy objected and Moore added "formerly" to the name, memos, Bureau of Navigation to Commandant, Third Naval District, March 11, 1919, and Aide for Information to Third Naval District, March 18, 1919, 24-19E4-3125, National Archives, Washington, DC. Capsule history of Boston band and its director Moore in "Jazzing from Navy to Vaudeville," *Baltimore Sun,* April 20, 1919, ENS2; and "Orpheum to Show Navy Jazz Band," *San Francisco Chronicle,* October 29, 1919, 6.

19. Great Lakes NYJB appearance at Grand Theater in Anderson, Indiana, on December 25, 1919, letter, H. Muller, Crystal Theater owner to Sec. of Navy,

December 20, 1919, 24-19E4-2125-752, National Archives, Washington, DC; Atlantic Fleet Jazz Band appearances in Denver and Los Angeles in February, 1920, memo, U.S. Navy Recruiting Station, Denver, Colorado, to Sec. of Navy, March 4, 1920, 24-19E4-2125, National Archives, Washington, DC; and Nat Nazarro Jr. in "Jazz Is the Ruling Power," *Los Angeles Times*, February 1, 1920.

20. Elise K. Kirk, *Music at the White House: A History of the American Spirit* (Urbana, IL: University of Illinois Press, 1986), 43.

21. Origins of the Non-Partisan League in Larry Tye, *Father of Spin: Edward L. Bernays and the Birth of Public Relations* (New York: Henry Holt & Co., 1998), 77–79; and Colonel Waldo's background information from Wikipedia.

22. Edward L. Bernays, *Biography of an Idea: Memoirs of a Public Relations Council* (New York: Simon & Schuster, 1965), 340.

23. Details on the first instance of entertainers campaigning for a presidential nominee in *Alan Schroeder, Celebrity-in-Chief: How Show Business Took Over the White House* (Boulder, CO: Westview, 2004), 115–16; John Morello, *Selling the President, 1920: Albert D. Lasker, Advertising, and the Election of Warren G. Harding* (Westport, CT: Praeger, 2001), 54–58; and Carl Sferrazza, *Florence Harding: The First Lady, the Jazz Age, and the Death of America's Most Scandalous President* (New York: William Morrow and Co., 1998), 219–20. Florence Harding's helpful role in the celebrity expedition to Ohio in Morello, *Lasker*, 60; and Sferrazza, *Florence Harding*, 219–20.

24. Waldo's initial contact with the White House on October 7 in memo to file, C. Bascomb Slemp, Coolidge Library, Library of Congress, Washington, DC; and Coolidge acceptance in Presidential Appointment Book for 1924 at the Coolidge Library, Library of Congress, Washington, DC.

25. Kirk, *Music*, 203–16; and *Isabel Ross, Grace Coolidge and Her Era: The Story of a President's Wife* (New York: Dodd, Mead & Co., 1962) 160–68.

26. Kirk, *Music*, 206–19.

27. White House happenings on October 17 (the celebrity arrival, breakfast, and South Lawn frivolities) have been compiled from various (and surprisingly similar) newspaper accounts and memoirs. Newspapers: "Theatrical Folk Coolidge Guests: Al Jolson Leads Actor Band in Pledge of Support at Breakfast Party," *Evening Star*, Washington, DC, October 18, 1924, 4; and "Actors Eat Cakes with the Coolidges: Thirty Enjoy Breakfast at the White House and Then Entertain Their Hosts, President Nearly Laughs, Guests Crack 'Dignified Jokes,' Sing Songs and Pledge Support to Coolidge," *New York Times*, October 18, 1924, 1; and "40 Stage Stars Eat Breakfast with Coolidges: President Receives Republican League, Led by

John Drew, Al Jolson, Raymond Hitchcock," *New York Herald Tribune*, October 18, 1924, 1; and "New York Actors Lure Real Laugh to Coolidge Face: President Joins Heartily in Merriment Induced by the Jokes of Stage Celebrities, White House Breakfast Theatre of Fun-Making, Only Serious Note Is Al Jolson's Assurance That His Thespian Guests Are for Him," *New York World*, October 18, 1924, 1; and "Jolson Makes President Laugh for the First Time in Public," *New York Review*, October 18, 1924, 1. Books: accounts in books cited above (starting with note 21) and below mirror those in the newspapers.

28. Bernays and/or the White House distributed the Broadway celebrity list to members of the press, who duly printed it verbatim in their periodicals: Al Jolson, John Drew, Ed Wynn, Charlotte Greenwood, Francine and Stella Larrimore, Justine Johnstone, Dolly Sisters, Brennan and Rogers, Mlle Herval, Lowell Sherman, McKay Morris, Alexander Leftwich, Buddy DeSilva, Lew Schriber, Gerald Griffin, Arnold Daly, Cleo Mayfield, Montague Love, William Griffin, Edward L. Bernays, Frank Cromit, Hal Forde, Leslie Chambers, Jed Prouty (twenty-seven total). The Miller Band without the pianists is thirteen; hence, forty total. But there could have been four more—the Dolly Sisters' French maid, the young English actor Ralph Reader, and Miller's two pianists—for "some forty."

29. Bernays verbatim description of the celebrity arrival in Washington, DC, and the handshaking ceremony at the White House in Bernays, *Idea*, 340–41.

30. October 18 byline, *Billboard*, October 23, 1924.

31. *New York Times*, October 18, 1924, 2.

32. *New York World*, October 18, 1924, 2.

33. Miller Band data in CD liner notes, *Ray Miller and His Brunswick Orchestra, 1924–1929* (Timeless Historical, CBC 1-066).

34. Miller Band more spontaneous than most white bands in Gunther Schuller, *The Swing Era* (Oxford: Oxford University Press, 1991), 515.

35. Jolson's Brunswick discography in Herbert G. Goldman, *Jolson: The Legend Comes to Life* (Oxford: Oxford University Press, 1988), 134, 383–85.

36. Miller Band musicians given in Phillip R. Evans and Larry F. Kiner, *Tram: The Frank Trumbauer Story* (Newark, NJ: Scarecrow Press, 1994), 314.

37. Info on Rube Bloom from Wikipedia.

38. Capsule bio on Miff largely condensed from Richard M. Sudhalter, *Lost Chords: White Musicians and Their Contribution to Jazz, 1915–1945* (Oxford: Oxford University Press, 1999), 101–29.

39. Bio on Tram largely condensed from ibid., 448–61.

40. Photos from http://www.loc.gov/pictures, 26313 (photo op) and 26338

(South Lawn). The latter is shown in this book on pages 29 and 201. Other extant photos in Evans and Kiner, *Tram*; Goldman, *Jolson*; CD liner notes to Ray Miller; and http://www.redhotjazz.com/millerinfo.html.

41. Man wearing glasses is Irving Caesar in Goldman, *Jolson* (photo caption), page 5 of sixteen-page photo insert.

42. Surviving Kinogram newsreel can be viewed at the UCLA Film & Television Archive, Los Angeles, CA.

Jazz Events at the Johnson White House

DATE	PERFORMER	EVENT/HONOREE
Mar 9, 1964	Charlie Byrd	Hill Families
Apr 14	Dave Brubeck Quartet	King Hussein/Jordan
Jun 10	Gerry Mulligan Quartet	Presidential Scholars
Oct 3	Stan Getz Quartet	College Leaders
Dec 17	George Barnes & Carl Kress Duo	White House Staff Party
Jan 12, 1965	Sarah Vaughan	Prime Minister/Japan
Jun 14	Duke Ellington Orchestra	Festival of the Arts
Jun 7, 1966	Stan Getz	Presidential Scholars
Oct 29	Stan Getz	King & Queen/Thailand
Jun 27, 1967	N. Texas State Lab Band/ Stan Getz/Duke Ellington	King & Queen/Thailand
Oct 12	Herbie Mann Sextet	Alexandria/Great Britain
Nov 1	Charlie Byrd	King & Queen/Nepal
Nov 14	Tony Bennett	Prime Minister/Japan
Mar 27, 1968	Duke Ellington Octet	President Tubman/Liberia
Nov 21	Duke Ellington (solo)	Arts Council
Dec 22	Skitch Henderson Combo/ Clark Terry & Toots Thielmans	Lady Bird's Birthday Party

Source: Elise K. Kirk, *Music at the White House* (Urbana, IL: University of Illinois Press, 1986); confirmed by the LBJ Presidential Library and a variety of other sources.

Ellington Orchestra at the LBJ Festival of the Arts

South Lawn Concert, June 14, 1965

Opening Remarks by Dancer Gene Kelly:

Historians tell us jazz began in New Orleans, and some historians tell us it began at a certain spot called Congo Square, a dusty lot down there. That may be so, I really don't know, but I know it's a long road from Congo Square to Carnegie Hall, and a longer musical way still. But jazz made it, riding on the well-tailored coattails of Duke Ellington some twenty-two years ago. He and the great artists of his ensemble took Lady Jazz out of her off-the-racks cotton dress and put her in a long velvet gown. Ladies and Gentlemen, if there had never been a Duke Ellington, jazz would have had to invent him. So it's with pride I present the Duke.

The Duke Ellington Orchestra:

"Take the 'A' Train"

[Applause follows.]

Duke Ellington Introduction:

Thank you very much, Ladies and Gentlemen. That's a warm welcome. Our first selection we would like to do is a result of our visit to the Far East a year and a half ago; we went to the Far East for the State Department on a cultural exchange program. And, of course, it was a tremendous inspiration to us all on being exposed to the beauty and enchantment of the Orient.

And so as a result, we wrote a suite of numbers. We would like to play some of them now. We would like to say this is being done also in gratitude for the great people of the State Department Foreign Service office, who guided us so magnificently through the tour. It is called "Impressions of the Far East":

The Duke Ellington Orchestra:
"Amad" feature for Lawrence Brown (tb)
"Agra" ballad feature for Harry Carney (bs)
"Bluebird of Delhi" feature for Jimmy Hamilton (cl)
[Applause follows.]

Duke Ellington Introduction:
Thank you. And now we would like to go from "Impressions of the Far East" to "Black, Brown and Beige," which of course was done originally in 1943, and hasn't really been done until this year in our concert appearances. This is our tone parallel to the history of the Negro in America.

Tonight, we should like to do a suggestion of the work song theme and the spiritual theme, and a development of the two into a sort of montage. "Black, Brown and Beige":

The Duke Ellington Orchestra:
Work theme
Spiritual "Come Sunday" theme feature for Ray Nance (v) and Johnny Hodges (as)
Work and spiritual theme montage for trumpet, Harry Carney (bs), and Lawrence Brown (tb)

Lady Bird Johnson Wrap-Up:

May I thank all the artists who have made this a rich, full, varied day for us all. It's been wonderful. And now I'd like to have you all go to the tents for a bit of refreshment. I expect some of you need a hot cup of coffee. Perhaps you'd like to view the art in the garden and the east corridor. Thank you all.

[Applause follows.]

Duke Ellington Encore Introduction:

I hate to impose on you like this, Ladies and Gentlemen, but we have a request for several of the things we have written and we'd like to play some of them for you that have become popular here.

The Duke Ellington Orchestra:

"Solitude"

"I've Got It Bad" feature for Johnny Hodges (as)

"Don't Get Around Much Anymore" feature for Duke (p)

"In the Mood"

"I'm Beginning to See the Light" (uptempo)

"Sophisticated Lady" feature for Harry Carney (bs)

"Caravan" (uptempo)

"The Opener" (uptempo feature for Paul Gonsalves (ts), Buster Cooper (tb), and Cat Anderson (tp)

"Things Ain't What They Used to Be"

Total time: 44:44 minutes. Sound recording available at the Library of Congress, Washington, DC.

—— ✳ ——

Worship Services
in the Nixon White House

DATE	SPEAKER	SOLOIST/CHOIR
Jan 26, 1969	Dr. Billy Graham	George B. Shea
Feb 2	Dr. Richard C. Halverson	James McDonald
Mar 16	Dr. Louis Evans	Washington National Cathedral Junior Boys Choir
Apr 27	Rev. Dr. Edward G. Latch	Richard Nicholson
May 4	Dr. R. H. Edwin Espy	Columbia Union College: Pro Musica
May 25	Terence Cardinal Cooke	Foundry Cathedral Choir
Jun 15	Dr. Norman Vincent Peale	Douglas Memorial Community Church
Jun 29	Dr. Louis Finkelstein	Christ Lutheran Church Choir
Jul 13	Rev. Paul H. A. Noren	Sanctuary Choir
Jul 20	Dr. Paul S. Smith	Colonel Frank Borman
Sep 21	Dr. Charles Malik	Madrigal Singers/Whitman H.S.
Sep 28	Rev. Allan R. Watson	Adult Church Choir Congregational Church
Nov 16	Rev. Harold Rawlings	NY Ave. Presbyterian Adult Choir
Dec 14		NY Ave. Presbyterian Adult Choir
Dec 21		Washington National Cathedral Junior Boys Choir

(continued)

DATE	SPEAKER	SOLOIST/CHOIR
Jan 11, 1970	Dr. Norman Vincent Peale	Vienna Choir Boys
Feb 1	Rev. Dr. M. L. Wilson	U. of Wisconsin Tudor Singers
Feb 8	Rev. Dr. Henry Russel	American U. Singers
Mar 15	Dr. Billy Graham	Bucknell U. Chorale
Apr 5	John Cardinal Krol	St. Paul's United Methodist Church
Apr 26	Rev. John A. Huffman Jr.	Laurentian Singers/St. Lawrence U.
May 10	Rev. Stephen P. Szilagyi	Calvin Theological Seminary Choir
Sep 13	Walter Judd/Wayne Hays	All Philadelphia Boys Choir
Oct 18	Bobby Richardson	Danish Boys Choir
Nov 22	Msgr. T. J. McCarthy	Hope College Choir
Jan 24, 1971	T. Eugene Coffin	Ethel Waters
Feb 7	Dr. Jacob A. O. Preus	Falls Church Presbyterian
Mar 7	Rabbi Joshua Haberman	Mrs. James Martin
Apr 18	Rev. Dr. Carl W. Haley	Texas A & M Singing Cadets
May 9	Rev. Dr. John C. Harper	Grafton Sr. High Concert Choir
Sep 12	Ben Haden	Norma Zimmer
Oct 10	Dr. D. Elton Trueblood	Wareham Chorale
Nov 14	A. B. Humberto Medireos	Gastonian Wesleyan Youth
Mar 19, 1972	Fred B. Rhodes	Campus Sing
Dec 17	John Cardinal Krol	Obernkirchen Children's Choir
Jan 21, 1973	A. Bernardin, Rabbi Maganin Rev. Dr. Billy Graham	Mormon Tabernacle Choir
Mar 11	Monsignor Kuhn	Takoma Park Baptist Choir
Apr 15	Rev. Dr. Edward V. Hill	Rochester Choir
Oct 14	William H. Hudnut III	New Wine Singers
Dec 16	Rev. Dr. Billy Graham	U.S. Army Chorus
Mar 17, 1974	Norman Vincent Peale	The Motet Singers

Source: Social Secretary Files, 5/1/74–5/31/74, Nixon Library, National Archives, College Park, MD.

Note: All services held on Sunday.

Nixon White House
Social Function Statistics

SOCIAL FUNCTION	1/1969–1/1972	2/1972–6/1974	TOTAL
Worship Services	32	12	46
Guests	9,452	3,360*	12,812*
White House Evenings	6	2	8
Guests	1,493	498*	1,991
State Dinners	45	18	63
Dinner Guests	4,172	1,674*	5,846*
After-Dinner Guests	5,193	2,070	7,263
Other Dinners	55	20	75
Guests	5,120	1,860*	6,980*
TOTAL GUESTS	25,430	9,462*	34,892*

Sources: The first three-year stats from memo, White House Entertainment Statistics, Lucy Winchester to Doug Hallett, March 3, 1972, Social Secretary Files, 3/1/72-3/31/72, Nixon Library, National Archives, College Park, MD; the last two-and-a-half-year event stats from the Social Entertainments Office Schedule of Events; number of guests proportionally extrapolated from first three-year stats. Total dinner figure above (138 [63 + 75]) is close to the 147 total given in the Sanford Fox exit interview at the Nixon virtual library at http://www.nixonlibrary.gov ("exit interviews"). Above does *not* include breakfasts, luncheons, teas, coffees, receptions, tours, or private dinner parties; when they are included, the total number of guests *quadruples*. According to Julie Eisenhower Nixon (*Pat Nixon: The Untold Story* [New York: Simon & Schuster, 1986], 283), in their first year in office, the Nixons entertained 45,313 people at 64 state and official dinners and 116 receptions, compared to the previous record of 28,000 in Johnson's final year in office.

*Estimates.

Sarnoff Talent List
May 1969

CLASSICAL INSTRUMENTALISTS	POPULAR INSTRUMENTALISTS	ACTORS
Van Cliburn*	Andre Previn	Lorne Green
Arthur Rubenstein	Peter Nero*	Charlton Heston*
Isaac Stern*	Al Hirt*	Robert Preston
Vladimir Horowitz	Henry Mancini*	Helen Hayes
Jack Benny w/violin	Roger Williams*	Frederick March
Andres Segovia	Ferranti & Teicher*	Henry Fonda
Carlos Montoya	Herb Alpert	John Wayne*
Jascha Heifetz	Erroll Garner	Cliff Robertson
Rudolf Serkin*	Louis Armstrong	Dina Merrill
Floyd Kramer	Peter Duchin*	Kathryn Hepburn
A. Fiedler/Boston Pops	Victor Borge	Rod Steiger
Philadelphia Orchestra	Richard Rogers	Claire Bloom
	Irving Berlin*	Richard Kiley
	Duke Ellington*	Hal Holbrook
	Chet Atkins	
	Count Basie	

CLASSICAL SINGERS	POPULAR SINGERS	
Roberta Peters (2)*	Perry Como	**Glen Campbell***
Robert Merrill	Aretha Franklin	**Tennessee Ernie Ford***
Eileen Farrell	Ella Fitzgerald	Gordon McRae
Leontyne Price	**Robert Goulet***	Carol Channing
Marian Anderson	Carol Lawrence	Florence Henderson
Richard Tucker*	**5th Dimension***	Howard Keel
Mary Costa*	Jose Feliciano	Kathryn Grayson
Rise Stevens	Shirley Jones	John Raitt
Patrice Munsel	Ed Ames	Steve Lawrence
Birgit Nilsson*	Diahann Carroll	Edie Gorme
Joan Sutherland	Mary Martin	Young Americans
Anna Moffo*	Nancy Wilson	Lana Cantrell
Beverly Sills*	Eddie Arnold	Jimmie Dean
	Dinah Shore	**Pearl Bailey (2)***
	Kate Smith	Barbara Streisand
	Jack Cassidy	Fess Parker
	Joel Grey	Barbara McNair
	Don Ho	**New Christy Minstrels***
	Nina Simone	Dionne Warwick
	Roy Rogers	John Gray
	Dale Evans	Rod McKuen

Source: List attached to memo, M. Carlson (Secretary to Mr. Sarnoff) to Rose Mary Woods, May 9, 1969, Special Files, EX SO3, 5/1/69–5/31/69, Nixon Library, National Archives, College Park, MD.

*Booked talent.

Ellington's Dinner Invitation List

PRIMARY LIST
(72 names, 44 accepted)

Arts Council member/singer Marian Anderson and spouse King Fisher*

Friend Bernard Flynn

Rev. and Mrs. John G. Gensel, Lutheran Church (Sacred Concert)

Comedian/actor Jackie Gleason*

Singer Mahalia Jackson and spouse Sigmund Galloway (*Black, Brown and Beige* album)

Nephew (sister Ruth's son) Stephen B. James

Rev. Bryant M. and Mrs. Kirkland, New York (Sacred Concert)

Honorable and Mrs. Lascelles*

Ellington Doctor Arthur C. and Mrs. Logan

Singer/actor Dean and Mrs. Martin*

Rev. Canon Hugh Montefiore (Sacred Concert, England)*

Actors Paul and Mrs. Newman (Joanne Woodward) (*Paris Blues* film)*

Producer (Stratford Theatre) Thomas & Mrs. Patterson (*Such Sweet Thunder* album)

Arts Council member/actor Sidney Poitier (*Paris Blues* film)*

Tribute concert coordinator/emcee Willis and Mrs. Conover

Film director Otto and Mrs. Preminger (*Anatomy of a Murder* film)

Actor Lee Remick (*Anatomy of a Murder* film)*

(*continued*)

PRIMARY LIST
(72 names, 44 accepted)

Rabbi and Mrs. Sanford Shapiro*

Singer/actor Frank Sinatra (Roulette Records)—no invite*

Actor James and Mrs. Stewart (*Anatomy of a Murder* film)*

TV host Ed and Mrs. Sullivan*

California friends, Robert and Mrs. Udkoff

Judge Thomas G. Weaver, New York

Rev. Harold H. Weicker, New York (Sacred Concert)

Conductor/arranger Tom Whaley (Ellington Orchestra)

Rev. John and Mrs. Yaryan, Ohio (Sacred Concert)

Rev. and Mrs. C. Julian Bartlett, San Francisco (Sacred Concert)

Composer/conductor Mr. and Mrs. Leonard Bernstein*

Singer/actor Diahann Carroll (*Paris Blues* film)*

Saxophonist Harry and Mrs. Carney (Ellington Orchestra)

Actor/singer/early collaborator Maurice Chevalier (France)—no reply*

Singer Rosemary Clooney*

Author/Ellington aide de camp Stanley and Mrs. Dance (Helen Oakley)

London friends Leslie and Mrs. Diamond

Rev. Horace B. W. Donegan, Bishop of New York (Sacred Concert)

Grandson Edward K. Ellington II

Granddaughter Gaye Ellington

Son Mercer and Mrs. Ellington (Ellington Orchestra)

Sister Ruth Ellington

Bandleader William "Count"* and Mrs. Basie

Bandleader/singer Cab and Mrs. Calloway

Bandleader/trumpeter Louis and Mrs. Armstrong (*Paris Blues* film)*

Bandleader/singer Billy and Mrs. Eckstine

Saxophonist Otto Hardwick (Ellington Orchestra)*

Banjoist Fred Guy (Ellington Orchestra)

Rev. Provost Williams Coventry Cathedral, England (Sacred Concert)*

Pianist David and Mrs. Brubeck

(*continued*)

BACKFILL LIST
(27 names, 10 accepted)

Duke's instructions: "Definite request for the after-dinner list. If any [dinner] availabilities, fill from this list":

Composer/conductor Arthur and Mrs. Fiedler (Boston Pops)*

Composer/lyricist Ira and Mrs. Gershwin*

Bandleader/clarinetist Benny and Mrs. Goodman

Bandleader/trumpeter Harry and Mrs. James*

Drama professor Mrs. Ethel Rich

Composer Richard and Mrs. Rodgers

Composer/conductor Leopold Stowkowski*

Composer/conductor Igor Stravinsky*

Composer Harold and Mrs Arlen

Composer Irving and Mrs. Berlin*

Singer/actor Bing and Mrs. Crosby*

Justice (New York Supreme Court) Edward D. and Mrs. Dudley

Actors Mr. and Mrs. Ossie Davis (Ruby Dee)*

Singer Leslie Uggams and spouse Graham Pratt*

Bandleader/trumpeter John B. "Dizzy" and Mrs. Gillespie

TRANSFERS FROM AFTER-DINNER LIST
(5 names, 5 accepted)

Singer Lou and Mrs. Rawls

Publisher John and Mrs. Johnson (*Ebony* and *Jet* magazines)

Rev. Norman J. O'Connor, California (Sacred Concert)

Source: "Duke Ellington Seventieth Birthday," White House Central Files, Staff Member Office Files: Sanford Fox, Box 5, Social Events Folder, April 29, 1969, Nixon Presidential Library, Yorba Linda, CA.

Note: Duke submitted 99 (72 + 27) dinner guest names to the White House, who extended formal invitations to all save one (Frank Sinatra); 54 accepted. To complete the planned dinner placements, the White House added 5 names from Duke's after-dinner list (see appendix 8). Duke, including himself, was thus responsible for three-quarters, or 60, of the 82 guests who attended the dinner in his honor.

*Invitees sent regrets, except where noted "no invite" or "no reply."

Ellington's After-Dinner Invitation List

ENTERTAINMENT ONLY
(35 names, 27 accepted)

Dr. Hans Wearheim

Thomas Detienne

Ellington Lawyer Benjamin Starr

Mr. and Mrs. Granville Woodson

Dancers Mrs. Geoffrey (Carmen de Lavallade) and Mr. Holder

Pianist/jazz impresario George and Mrs. Wein (Newport Jazz Festival)

Pianist Willie "the Lion" and Mrs. Smith

Pianist Marian McPartland

Mr. and Mrs. John Carter

Arthur Schultheiss

Pianist Teddy and Mrs. Wilson*

Pianist Mary Lou Williams*

Composer/conductor/writer Gunther Schuller (New England Conservatory of Music)

ASCAP President Stanley Adams*

Singer Lou and Mrs. Rawls—transferred to the dinner *

NAACP Director Roy Wilkins*

Urban League Chairman Whitney and Mrs. Young*

DownBeat jazz magazine editor Dan Morgenstern

Jazz columnist Leonard Feather

(continued)

ENTERTAINMENT ONLY
(35 names, 27 accepted)

AP feature editor Mary Campbell

Jazz critic/DJ Doug Ramsey (WDSU New Orleans)

Music critic Perdita Duncan (*New York Amsterdam News*)

Music critic emeritus Nora Holt (*New York Amsterdam News*)

Society editor Gerri Major (Johnson Publications, *Ebony*, *Jet*)*

Publisher John and Mrs. Johnson (*Ebony*, *Jet*)—transferred to the dinner*

Rev. Norman J. O'Connor, California—transferred to the dinner*

Source: "Entertainment following Duke Ellington Dinner," White House Central Files, Staff Member Office Files: Sanford Fox, Box 5, Social Events Folder, April 29, 1969, Nixon Presidential Library, Yorba Linda, CA.

Note: Overall, in sum, Duke submitted 135 names (including himself) to the White House for the dinner and after-dinner entertainment, 82, or 60 percent, accepted.

*Invitees who sent regrets, except where noted "transferred to the dinner."

Ellington Birthday Tribute Guest Lists

DINNER GUEST LIST (82)

Government Officials (13)

Vice President and Mrs. Spiro Agnew
Attorney General and Mrs. John Mitchell
Secretary of Labor and Mrs. George Schulz
Secretary of HEW and Mrs. Robert Finch
Director Office of EO and Mrs. Donald Rumsfeld
Director of USIA Frank Shakespeare
Asst. to the President and Mrs. Daniel P. Moynihan

Jurists (3)

Justice (New York Supreme Court) and Mrs. Edward Dudley
Judge Thomas G. Weaver

Art Institution Heads (8)

Secretary of the Smithsonian Institution and Mrs. S. Dillon Ripley
Director of the National Gallery of Art and Mrs. John Walker III
Producer (Stratford Shakespeare Theatre) Thomas and Mrs. Patterson
Chairman (Kennedy Center) Roger L. and Mrs. Stevens

Event Instigators (2)

Lawyer/clarinetist Leonard Garment
Lawyer/political consultant Charles McWhorter

(*continued*)

DINNER GUEST LIST (82)

Musicians (23)

Songwriter Harold and Mrs. Arlen
Bandleader Cab and Mrs. Calloway
Bandleader William Count Basie (Mrs. Basie only)
Pianist David and Mrs. Brubeck
Saxophonist Harry and Mrs. Carney
Singer Billy and Mrs. Eckstine
Bandleader and composer Edward Kennedy Ellington
Singer Mahalia Jackson with husband Mr. Sigmund Galloway
Bandleader/trumpeter John Birks "Dizzy" Gillespie
Bandleader/clarinetist Benny and Mrs. Goodman
Banjoist Fred Guy
Singer Lou and Mrs. Rawls
Composer Richard and Mrs. Rodgers
Conductor/arranger Tom Whaley

Duke Friends/Business Associates (16)

Program coordinator Willis and Mrs. Conover
Author/Ellington aide de camp Stanley and Mrs. Dance
London friends, Leslie and Mr. Diamond
Mr. Bernard Flynn
Publisher John and Mrs. Johnson (*Ebony*, *Jet* magazines)
Mrs. Ethel Rich
Doctor Arthur C. and Mrs. Logan (Ellington Doctor)
California friends Robert and Mrs. Udkoff
Film director Otto and Mrs. Preminger (*Anatomy of a Murder*)

Family (6)

Sister Ruth Ellington
Son Mercer and Mrs. Ellington
Nephew (sister Ruth's son) Stephen B. James
Granddaughter Gaye Ellington
Grandson Edward K. Ellington II

(*continued*)

DINNER GUEST LIST (82)

Duke-Invited Clergy (11)

Reverend and Mrs. C. Julian Bartlett, San Francisco
Reverend Horace B. W. Donegan, Bishop of New York
Reverend and Mrs. John G. Gensel, Lutheran Church
Reverend Bryant M. and Mrs. Kirkland, New York
Reverend Norman J. O'Connor, California
Reverend Harold H. Weicker, New York
Reverend John and Mrs. Yaryan, Ohio

Total dinner guests: 82 (plus President and Mrs. Nixon).

ENTERTAINMENT-ONLY GUEST LIST (133)

Government Officials (48)

Nixon special aide Robert J. and Mrs. Brown
Nixon aide Patrick Buchanan escorting Miss Jean Ann Toomey
Lawrence D. and Mrs. Buhl
HEW Asst. W. Russell G. and Mrs. Byers
Nixon aide Henry C. Cashen II (Chuck Colson aide)
Appointment Secretary Dwight and Mrs. Chapin
Domestic aide John and Mrs. Ehrlichman
Nixon aide Peter and Mrs. Flanagan
Chief of Staff H. R. Haldeman
Nixon aide Stephen and Mrs. Hess
Robert and Mrs. Hitt
Nixon aide William K. and Mrs. Howenstein
Assistant HUD Secretary Samuel and Mrs. Jackson
National Security Advisor Henry Kissinger
Press Secretary Herbert Klein
VP Agnew aide W. Ernest and Mrs. Minor
Nixon counsel Edward l. Morgan
Protocol Chief Emil and Mrs. Mosbacher

(continued)

ENTERTAINMENT-ONLY
GUEST LIST (133)

Government Officials (*cont.*)

House of Representatives restaurant maitre d' Ernest and Mrs. Petinaud
Nixon aide Raymond K. Price
Deputy, Office of EO Fred J. Russel
Speech Writer William and Mrs. Safire
Al Scott
Nixon secretary Shelly Ann Scarney (later Mrs. Patrick Buchanan)
NEA official Michael Straight
State Dept. Officer Timothy L. Towell (Bolivia)
Media Advisor Harry Trevalen
Under Sec. of Navy John W. and Mrs. Warner
Consultant Charles "Bud" and Mrs Wilkinson
Nixon personal secretary Rose Mary Woods
V. Backus Wood

Nixon Friends/Other (12)

Wife of Guyanese Ambassador Sarah Carter and escort Samuel Insanally
Publisher John H. and Mrs. Murphy, III (*Afro-American* newspaper)
Daughter Trisha Nixon
Crime and Law Enforcement Advisor Mr. and Mrs. Pollner
Lt. Colonel John and Mrs. Silvera
William Stover
Brother of Rose Honorable and Mrs. Joseph L. Woods

Jazz Writer/Critics (9)

Whitney and Mrs. Balliett (*New Yorker*)
Perdita Duncan (*New York Amsterdam News*)
Leonard Feather (Syndicated)
Phyl Garland (*Ebony*)
Nora Holt (*New York Amsterdam News*)
Dan Morgenstern (*DownBeat* editor)
Douglas Ramsey (WDSU New Orleans)
Hollie I. West (*Washington Post*)

(*continued*)

ENTERTAINMENT-ONLY
GUEST LIST (133)

Musicians (33)

All-star drummer Louis Bellson

All-star trumpeter Bill and Mrs. Berry

All-star alto saxophonist Paul Desmond

All-star trombonist Urbie Green

All-star guitarist Jim and Mrs. Hall

All-star singer Mary Mayo and spouse Albert Ham

All-star pianist Earl Hines

All-star bassist Milt and Mrs. Hinton

All-star trombonist J. J. and Mrs. Johnson

All-star pianist Hank and Mrs. Jones

Pianist Marian McPartland

Conductor Howard and Mrs. Mitchell (Washington Symphony)

All-star baritone saxophonist Gerry and Mrs. Mulligan (Sandy Dennis)

Conductor Gunther and Mrs. Schuller (New England Conservatory of
Music)

Pianist Willie "the Lion" and Mrs. Smith

All-star Billy and Mrs. Taylor

All-star trumpeter Clark and Mrs. Terry

Pianist, impresario George and Mrs. Wein (Newport Jazz Festival)

All-Star singer Joe and Mrs. Williams

Duke Friends/Business Associates (13)

John and Mrs. Carter

Thomas Detienne

Dancers Geoffrey and Mrs. Holder (Carmen de Lavallade)

Ellington publicist Joe Morgen

Arthur Schultheiss

Benjamin Starr

William Stover

Educator Dr. Harold Taylor, Sarah Lawrence College

Dr. Hans Wehrheim

Mr. and Mrs. Granville Woodson

(continued)

ENTERTAINMENT-ONLY
GUEST LIST (133)

Press: Columnists/Reporters/Photographers (18)
  Mary Campbell (feature reporter), AP*
  Eleni (single name only), *Washington Evening Star*
  George Clinton Cabell (photographer), *Baltimore Afro-American*
  Harvey Georges (photographer), UPI
  Nina S. Hyde, *Washington Daily News*
  Margaret A. Kilgore (reporter), UPI
  Irv and Mrs. Kupcinet, *Chicago Sun Times**
  Amy Lee, *Christian Science Monitor**
  Wally McNemes (photographer), *Newsweek*
  Myra McPherson, *Washington Post*
  Nan Robertson, *New York Times*
  Isabel Shelton, *Washington Evening Star*
  Bob and Mrs. Sylvester, *New York Daily News**
  Monetto Sleet Jr. and Maurice Sorrell (photographers), *Jet* magazine
  Earl Wilson, *New York Post**

Total after-dinner entertainment-only guests: 133

Sources: Dinner guest list as published in the *Washington Post*, April 30, 1969; confirmed by "Duke Ellington Seventieth Birthday," White House Central Files, Staff member Office Files, Sanford Fox, Box 5, Social Events Folder, April 29, 1969, Nixon Presidential Library, Yorba Linda, CA; after-dinner guest list in "Unconfirmed After-Dinner Guest List," President Richard Nixon's Daily Record for April 29, 1969, appendix F, 6–8; and in "Entertainment Following Duke Ellington Dinner," in the Sanford Fox Collection, Box 5, Social Events Folder, April 29, 1969, Nixon Presidential Library at Yorba Linda, CA.

Note: Excluding the press, Nixon selected half the entertainment-only guests (60), Ellington the other half (55), the latter including members of the all-star band. Estimated unidentified working press (15) plus military (marine, navy) musicians (6) is 21 total. The total number of East Room attendees at the Ellington tribute jam session on April 29, 1969, is estimated to be 236 (82 dinner guests + 133 after-dinner entertainment only guests + 21 estimated working press and military musicians).

*Invited guests. Other press listed are known members of the working press.

———————————— ✳ ————————————

Duke Ellington Interview
April 29, 1969

O N THE AFTERNOON OF APRIL 29, 1969, Harold Boxer of the Voice of America (VOA) recorded a nine-minute interview with Duke Ellington. The surviving tape held at the Library of Congress, Washington, DC, includes Mr. Ellington's answers, but not Mr. Boxer's questions. The subsequent VOA broadcast dates for the interview are not known.

Reluctance to Discuss Early Career

A lot of people have been [making noise about] the biographical stuff in the early part of my career and I think nothing has been said about the day I was born ... I was born in Newport in July of 1956. And I don't see any reason for talking any further [back] than that ... because for this particular purpose, that was the beginning of the jazz festivals and I think that was the major concern [of your question, and] as far as I am concerned, this is the part of my biography which is the most interesting from your point of view and in the interest of the International Jazz Festival.

Jazz: Yesterday and Today

Jazz is a funny thing. Today jazz is not the same thing as it was when it first started, back when the old Dixieland boys down on Rampart Street used to do their business—that was something for the people who chose to listen to ... well, they sort of looked down on it. They gave it all sorts of bad marks of identification . . . like it's the equivalent to saying that jazz was born—I'm sure you've read this many times, so this is not new and it's not my idea—but it's just something that I've heard, and I've heard it over and over again that jazz was sort of born in a house of ill-repute. So, I mean, that's what it was when it came out of New Orleans.

In addition, there was a lot of jazz on the East Coast that didn't come out of any houses, or anything else. It was just music that came about as a result of musicians who were thoroughly schooled in music who played with musicians who were not schooled, but had ability, and they played very well and right here in Washington, DC. I think one of the great examples of it . . . they had people like Louis Brown, who is still around, a pianist, and Doc Perry who had passed away—two of the greatest piano players I think in the whole world—and then there were people around who didn't read music, like Lester Dishman, Clarence Bowser . . . these are great people, great exponents of what was known as jazz in those days.

Now this was one thing, but the thing that came out of New Orleans was something else. And now I think the Eastern jazz has more or less taken over, and has dominated the entire field because the music today is much more academic. I mean, an example, for instance . . . a conservatory graduates a class every year . . . but I am sure you can safely say that one-fourth of them go into the symphonic world, and one-fourth of them go into radio, television, and the movies to play and write, and one-fourth of them go into what is known as jazz, and there is the other fourth that go into teaching. These people are all engaged in writing music, and there is absolutely no difference in one's writing than the other. They are all writing from the same perspective, no matter what label you put over it. So you see jazz isn't the same today as it was then. Today, jazz is performed by very highly skilled musicians.

Jazz: A Schooled Music Now

As I say, it's highly academic now. It draws on many extractions . . . some of the great masters' works, they drew on folk themes, but their finished product wasn't folk music. It was much too involved musically. Jazz as it is today has absorbed so many people. It started out, I would say, with a foundation of Negro music . . . but in the schooling, as a musician, the Negro goes to school today, he learns the techniques of the European people, and applied to the bottom of it, a little bit of the folk music of the Negro seeps through—but on top of it, or the supporting or framework of it, it is all very well prepared in a very musical manner.

Duke on Improvisation and American Music

Spontaneity has its limitations because, say, for instance, a guy is going to ad-lib. If he doesn't anticipate what he is going to play, he doesn't play anything. Spontaneity is a limited word—it doesn't mean anything; it may appear that he is playing off the top of his head. But he has to anticipate, no matter if it's three days before or two bars ahead. This is equal to arranging, orchestration, whatever you call it. Jazz is probably, I might say, not even a good word for the music of today. The music today—played by overall well-schooled musicians—is American music.

American music is the most imitated music in the world under the label of jazz. More time and money is spent listening to the music and trying to play it. You go to Europe and you hear the guys playing identically the same things that are played in America. I've always insisted on American music for years, but seems that jazz is a more comfortable word for people to operate under.

Duke on Improvisation and Composition

Discipline is fine. I mean, you can get these guys to come out here and drill them like little soldiers, and be punctual, right on the minute, and go out and blow. But I don't know how well they are going to play. And the major interest here now is not discipline or spontaneity. It only has to do with—as in any kind of music—how it sounds. Music is an aural art. It only has to do with the ear. If it isn't agreeable to the ear, it isn't musical . . . or it isn't music.

I think I am an up-and-coming musician struggling for a new note just like everybody else. You start dreaming and an idea comes and then you go and put it down, or you go try it on an instrument, and if you like it, or if it works out, or if it offers an opportunity for development or something like that; it's good. Sometimes it's just that, and it's good as it is when you got it. And sometimes there's no room for it to go anywhere else . . . and you leave it there. Sometimes you write them and hear them and tear them up. You thought it was going to be something, but it wasn't.

Duke on American Music

The reason I keep saying American music and referring to this so-called jazz music—which covers so many different characters of sound—is that this music parallels the times of the people in America all the way from the beginning. It's moved along. It comes along as the world has become more mechanical, the music has employed more devices of precision, and the velocity is there—velocity, I would say, is parallel to a word like swing or lilt, which of course is related to the electronic thing in radio, the waves they bounce around the world—this is swing. They bounce. They vamp. It parallels. It goes go. And so forth. And so here we are today in the space age—probably you are on the threshold of an era in music where all categories will be eliminated and will be boiled down to what I've been claiming for a long time: the only thing that is important in music is that it sounds good.

Source: Transcribed by the author from the *Duke Ellington Interview, 1969-04-29,* audiotape, VOA Music Library Collection, call number RAA 51070, Library of Congress, Washington, DC.

U.S. Newspaper Coverage of the Ellington Tribute

STATE	NEWSPAPER	COVERAGE		
		Photo	Front	Service
AL	Birmingham News	Yes	No	AP
AK	Juneau Alaska Empire	No Coverage		
AZ	Arizona Republic	No	No	C
AR	Arkansas Democrat	Yes	No	AP
CA	Los Angeles Times	Yes	No	—
CA	Sacramento Union	Yes	No	—
CA	San Francisco Chronicle	Yes	No	NYT
CO	Denver Post	Yes	No	—
CT	**Hartford Courant***	No	No	—
DC	Evening Star	Yes	Yes	C
DC	Daily News	Yes	No	SH
DC	Washington Post	Yes	Yes	C
DC	**Washington Afro-American***	Yes	Yes	C
DE	Evening Journal	Yes	Yes	AP
FL	Miami Herald	Yes	No	UPI
GA	Atlanta Journal	No	No	UPI
GA	Atlanta Constitution	No Coverage		
ID	Idaho Daily Statesman	No Coverage		
IL	**Chicago Defender***	Yes	No	C
IL	Chicago Sun-Times	No	No	C

(continued)

STATE	NEWSPAPER	COVERAGE		
		Photo	Front	Service
IL	Chicago Sun-Times	Yes	No	UPI
IL	Chicago Tribune	Yes	Yes	AP
IN	Indianapolis Star	No	No	NYT
IA	Davenport Time-Democrat	Yes	No	AP
KS	Wichita Eagle	No	Yes	AP
KY	Louisville Courier-Journal	No	Yes	WP
LA	New Orleans Times Picayune	No Coverage		
ME	Augusta Daily Kennebec Journal	No	No	AP
MD	**Baltimore Afro-American***	No	No	C
MD	Baltimore Evening Sun	No Coverage		
MA	Boston Herald	Yes	Yes	AP
MA	Christian Science Monitor	No	No	C
MA	Boston Globe	No	No	WP
MI	Detroit Free Press	Yes	Yes	—
MI	Detroit News	Yes	Yes	—
MN	Minneapolis Morning Tribune	Yes	No	NYT
MS	Jackson Clarion-Ledger	No Coverage		
MO	Kansas City Times-Star	Yes	No	AP
MO	St. Louis Globe Democrat	No	Yes	AP
MO	St. Louis Post Dispatch	Yes	No	AP
MT	Butte Montana Standard	No Coverage		
NE	Lincoln Evening Journal	Yes	No	UPI
NV	Las Vegas Sun	Yes	No	—
NH	Concord Daily Monitor	Yes	No	—
NJ	Newark Evening News	No	No	AP
NM	Albuquerque Journal	No Coverage		
NY	Buffalo Evening News	Yes	No	AP
NY	**New York Amsterdam News***	No	No	C
NY	New York Post	No	No	C
NY	New York Times	Yes	Yes	C
NY	Wall Street Journal	No Coverage		

(continued)

STATE	NEWSPAPER	COVERAGE		
		Photo	Front	Service
NC	Charlotte Observer	No Coverage		
OH	Cleveland Plain Dealer	No	No	NYT
OH	Cleveland Press	Yes	No	SH
OH	Columbus Evening Dispatch	Yes	No	AP
OK	Daily Oklahoman	No	No	AP
OR	Portland Oregon Daily Journal	Yes	No	UPI
PA	**Pittsburgh Courier***	No	No	C
PA	Pittsburgh Press	Yes	No	SH
PA	Philadelphia Inquirer	Yes	No	WP
RI	Providence Journal	Yes	Yes	NYT
SC	Charleston News & Courier	No Coverage		
SD	Pierre Capital Journal	No	Yes	AP
TN	Memphis Commercial Appeal	No Coverage		
TN	Nashville Banner	No	No	AP
TN	Nashville Tennessean	No Coverage		
TX	Austin American	Yes	No	AP
TX	Dallas morning News	No Coverage		
TX	San Antonio Express	No Coverage		
UT	Salt Lake Tribune	No	No	NYT
VT	Burlington Free Press	Yes	No	AP
VA	Alexandria Gazette	No Coverage		
VA	**Norfolk Journal and Guide***	No	No	UPI
VA	Richmond Times Dispatch	No	No	AP
WA	Seattle Daily Times	Yes	No	AP
WV	Wheeling Intelligencer	No	No	AP
WI	Madison Wisconsin State Journal	Yes	No	AP
WI	Milwaukee Journal	No	No	AP
WY	Cheyenne Wyoming State Tribune	No	No	UPI

Source: Newspaper and Current Periodical Reading Room, Library of Congress, Washington, DC.

*African American newspapers.

Jazz Events at the Nixon White House

DATE	PERFORMER	EVENT/HONOREE
Apr 29, 1969	Jazz All-Stars	Duke Ellington 70th Birthday
Jun 30	Henry Mancini (solo piano)	Apollo 10 Astronauts
Oct 21	Modern Jazz Quartet	Shah Pahlevi/Iran
Dec 3	Al Hirt & 5th Dimension	Governors Dinner
Feb 24, 1970	Peggy Lee (jazz singer)	President Pompodou/France
Mar 19	Nicole Williamson/ World's Greatest Jazz Band	Evening at the White House
Apr 4	Bobby Short Piano Trio/ Young Saints Musical Review	Duke & Duchess/Windsor
Apr 10	Pearl Bailey	Chancellor Brandt/Germany
Dec 19	David Frost/Billy Taylor	Christmas Evening at the White House
Jun 15, 1972	Pete Fountain	President Echeverria/Mexico
Apr 17, 1973	Frank Sinatra	Prime Minister Andreotti/Italy
Oct 9	Billy Taylor Trio	President Houphouet-Boigney/ Ivory Coast
Mar 7, 1974	Pearl Bailey	Governors Dinner

Source: Social Entertainment Office, Schedule of Events for the Nixon Administration, President's Personal Files, White House Social Files, 1964–1974, Box 136, Nixon Library, National Archives, College Park, MD.

APPENDIX 13

❋

All Nixon Events
1969–1974

DATE	PERFORMER	EVENT/HONOREE
	1969	
Jan 30	Film: *Debrief: Apollo 8*	Apollo 9 Astronauts
Mar 15	The Brother's Four	Gridiron Wives (Pat)
Mar 24	Robert Goulet	Prime Minister Trudeau/Canada
Apr 10	Valley Forge Military Academy Band & Glee Club	Ray Bliss Dinner
Apr 23	Mildred Miller (soprano)	Chief Justice Warren
Apr 29	Jazz All-Stars	Duke Ellington 70th Birthday
May 6	Zara Nelsova (cellist)/ Grant Johansen (pianist)	Prime Minister Gorton/ Australia
May 10	The Turtles/The Temptations	Masque Ball (Trisha)
May 15	Peter Nero Piano Trio	Foreign Service
May 22	DC Youth Chorale	Senate Ladies Lunch
Jun 11	Film: *Summer in the Parks*	Reception (Pat Nixon)
Jun 12	Jack Lowe & Arthur Whittemore (piano duo)	President Carlos Lleras Restrepo/Colombia
Jun 30	Book: *The Inaugural Story*	Reception (Pat Nixon)
Jun 30	Henry Mancini (solo piano)	Apollo 10 Astronauts
Jul 8	Eugene List (pianist)	Haile Selassie I/Ethiopia
Jul 15	Marine Band	Apollo 10 Dinner

(*continued*)

DATE	PERFORMER	EVENT/HONOREE
	1969 (*cont.*)	
Aug 7	Kyung-Wa Chung (violinist)	Chancellor Keisinger/Germany
Aug 13	Army Chorus and Band	Apollo 11 Astronauts
Aug 21	The Romeros-Guitarists (St. Francis Hotel California)	President Park/South Korea
Sep 25	Leonard Bernstein (piano)/ Isaac Stern (violin)	Prime Minister Golda Meir/ Israel
Oct 21	Modern Jazz Quartet	Shah Pahlevi/Iran
Oct 22	Marine Corps Parade	White House Families
Nov 19	American Ballet Theatre *Fancy Free*	Prime Minister Sato/Japan
Dec 1	Ranch House Seven (youth)	Boys Club of America
Dec 3	Al Hirt & 5th Dimension	Governors Dinner
Dec 14	Bob Hope Christmas Show	Reception
Dec 17	U. of Maryland Madrigals	Press Families
	1970	
Jan 14	Film: *Civilization*	White House Staff
Jan 17	Cole Porter Musical Revue	Fed Chairman Martin
Jan 27	Roberta Peters (Opera)	Prime Minister Wilson/Britain
Jan 29	Red Skelton (comic)	Evening at the White House
Feb 3	Film: *Topaz*	Press Ladies
Feb 17	Army Chorus	General Hershey
Feb 19	Rudolf Serkin (pianist)	Andrew Wyeth Dinner
Feb 22	Cast of *1776*	Evening at the White House
Mar 14	*The Fantasticks*	Gridiron Wives (Pat)
Mar 19	Nicole Williamson/ World's Greatest Jazz Band	Evening at the White House
Mar 23	Army Chorus	African Diplomats
Apr 4	Bobby Short Piano Trio/ Young Saints Musical Review	Duke & Duchess/Windsor

(continued)

DATE	PERFORMER	EVENT/HONOREE
	1970 *(cont.)*	
Apr 10	Pearl Bailey	Chancellor Brandt/Germany
Apr 14	Ferrante & Teicher Pianists (canceled due to Apollo 13)	Prime Minister Baunsgaard/Denmark
Apr 17	Johnny Cash	Evening at the White House
Apr 22	Army Chorus	Press Award Dinner
May 22	DC Youth Chorale	Senate Ladies (Pat)
May 26	Jerome Hines (basso)	President Suharto/Indonesia
May 28	DC Youth Symphony	Elementary Kids
June 2	Vicki Carr (singer)	President Caldera/Mexico
Jul 17	Marine Orch/The Guess Who/ Kirby Puckett & The Union Gap	Dinner Dance, Prince Charles & Princess Anne
Jul 23	Camerata Singers	President Kekkonen/Finland
Jul 29	The Harkness Ballet	Summer in the Parks
Aug 4	Andre Watts (pianist)	President Mobuto/Congo
Sep 3	Marine Orchestra/Mex Band Hotel Del Coronada (CA)	President Diaz Ordaz/Mexico
Sep 7	Army Torchlight Tatoo	Labor Day Dinner
Sep 22	Johnny Mann Singers	Mrs. Marcos/Phillipines (lunch)
Oct 24	James McCracken & Sandra Warfield (opera)	U.N. 25-Year Dinner
Oct 26	Anna Moffo (soprano)	President Ceausescu/Romania
Nov 19	Navy Sea Chanters	Roy Ash Dinner
Nov 25	Book: *Living White House*	Coffee (Pat Nixon)
Nov 26	The Spurrlows (youth group)	Thanksgiving Dinner
Dec 16	Mormon Tabernacle Choir	National Christmas Tree
Dec 17	Garrick Ohlsson (pianist)	Prime Minister Heath/Britain
Dec 18	David Frost/Billy Taylor/ Army Chorus	Christmas Evening at the White House
Dec 22	Sesame Street Players	Christmas Kids Party

(*continued*)

DATE	PERFORMER	EVENT/HONOREE
	1971	
Jan 26	Sergio Mendes & Brazil '66	Prince Juan Carlos/Spain
Feb 2	Beverly Sills (opera singer)	Evening at the White House
Feb 17	Military Entertainment	Military Reception
Feb 18	Anna Marie Alberghetti	Prime Minister Columbo/Italy
Mar 1	Army Chorus/Strolling Strings	Apollo 14 Astronauts
Mar 16	Shannon Castle Entertainers	Evening at the White House
Apr 5	Roger Williams (pianist)	Senate Ladies (Pat)
May 7	Glen Campbell (singer)	Salute to Agriculture
Jun 3	Philly & Poland Boys Choirs	80th Congress Club
Jun 15	Army Chorus	Chancellor Brandt/Germany
Jun 29	Sing Out South	Postmaster Blount
Oct 28	Kate Smith & Gail Robinson (singers)	President Tito/Yugoslavia
Nov 2	Richard Tucker (opera)	PM McMahon/Australia
Nov 4	New York City Ballet/Edward Villella/Pat McBride	Prime Minister Indira Ghandi/India
Dec 7	Itzhak Perleman (violinist)/Rita Reichman (pianist)	President Medici/Brazil
	1972	
Jan 28	Ray Conniff Singers	*Readers Digest* at 50
Feb 6	Army Chorus	King Hussein/Jordan
Mar 21	Ethel Merman & Dorothy Kirsten	Prime Minister Bayulken/Turkey
Mar 28	Army Chorus	King Hussein/Jordan
Apr 15	Birgitt Nilsson (opera)	Latino Ambassadors
Apr 25	Army Chorus	Congressional Retirees
Jun 15	Pete Fountain	President Luis Echeverría Alvarez/Mexico
Oct 31	Emmett Kelly Jr.	Halloween Party

(continued)

DATE	PERFORMER	EVENT/HONOREE
		1972 *(cont.)*
Dec 16	New Zoo Revue	Diplomat Kids Party
Dec 16	Fred Waring Pennsylvanians	Cabinet Christmas Dinner
		1973
Feb 6	Mike Curb Congregation	King Hussein/Jordan
Feb 28	Army Chorus	Governors Dinner
Mar 1	Van Cliburn (pianist)	Prime Minister Golda Meir/Israel
Mar 3	Sammy Davis Jr.	Evening at the White House
Mar 6	Army Chorus	Contributors Dinner
Mar 7	Navy Sea Chanters	Contributors Dinner
Mar 17	Merle Haggard/Osborne Brothers	Pat Nixon's Birthday/Evening at the White House
Apr 10	Mary Costa (opera)	Prime Minister Lee/Singapore
Apr 12	Nurserymen (pop folk)	Reception (Pat Nixon)
Apr 17	Frank Sinatra	Prime Minister Giulio Andreotti/Italy
May 1	The Carpenters	Chancellor Brandt/Germany
May 15	Ginatta La Blanca	Haile Selassie I/Ethiopia
May 24	Bob Hope Show	Vietnam POW Dinner
Jun 5	Johnny Mathis	President Tolbert/Liberia
Jun 18	Johnny Mann Singers	Secretary Breshnev/USSR
Jul 24	Tony Martin (singer)	Shah Pahlevi/Iran
Jul 31	Roberta Peters (opera)	Prime Minister Tanaka/Japan
Sep 18	Richard & Francis Hadden (piano duo)	Prime Minister Bhutto/Pakistan
Oct 9	Billy Taylor Trio	President Houphouet-Boigney/Ivory Coast
Oct 15	Roger Williams (pianist)	Secretary of State W. Rogers
Dec 4	Opera Society of Washington	President Ceausescu/Romania

(*continued*)

DATE	PERFORMER	EVENT/HONOREE
	1974	
Feb 11	Army Chorus	Oil Ministers Dinner
Feb 28	Film: *The Sting*	Congress Supporters
Mar 1	Film: *Friendly Persuasion*	Congress Supporters
Mar 7	Pearl Bailey	Governors Dinner
Mar 26	Naval Academy Glee Club	Melvin Laird Dinner
Apr 4	Army Chorus	Chowder March Club
Apr 5	Nurserymen (pop folk)	Reception (Pat Nixon)
Apr 17	Army Chorus	OAS Foreign Ministers

Source: Social Entertainment Office, Schedule of Events for the Nixon Administration, President's Personal Files, White House Social Files, 1964–1974, Box 136, Nixon Library, National Archives, College Park, MD.

Government-Sponsored Jazz Ambassador Tours

Artists Who Also Played the White House

ARTIST	DATES	DESTINATION
	Dwight D. Eisenhower	
Dizzy Gillespie Band	03/27/56–05/21/56	Middle East
Dizzy Gillespie Band	07/25/56–08/21/56	Southeast Asia
Benny Goodman	12/06/56–01/17/57	Far East
Dave Brubeck Quartet	03/06/58–03/18/58	Eastern Europe
Dave Brubeck Quartet	03/21/58–05/09/58	Middle East/Far East
Herbie Mann Group	12/31/59–04/05/60	Africa
	John F. Kennedy	
Charlie Byrd Trio	03/12/61–06/04/61	Southeast Asia
Paul Winter Sextet	02/06/62–07/13/62	Southeast Asia
Benny Goodman	05/28/62–06/30/62	Eastern Europe
Benny Goodman	06/30/62–07/08/62	Soviet Union
Duke Ellington Band	08/28/63–11/22/63	Middle East/Asia
	Lyndon B. Johnson	
Duke Ellington Band	03/31/66–04/09/66	Africa
Earl Hines Group	07/07/66–08/17/66	Soviet Union

(*continued*)

ARTIST	DATES	DESTINATION
	Lyndon B. Johnson (*cont.*)	
Stan Getz	10/22/66–11/03/66	Thailand
Charlie Byrd Trio	03/31/68–05/25/68	Middle East/Far East
	Richard M. Nixon	
Charlie Byrd Trio	06/29/69–08/23/69	Africa
Giants of Jazz (Dizzy)	00/00/70–00/00/70	Eastern Europe
Duke Ellington	01/31/70–02/01/70	Rangoon
Modern Jazz Quartet	04/00/70–05/00/70	Middle East/Asia
Brubeck/Mulligan/Hines	10/11/70–10/00/70	Europe
Lionel Hampton	04/00/71–04/00/71	Eastern Europe
Count Basie	04/00/71–04/00/71	Asia
Brubeck/Mulligan/Hines	12/22/71–12/27/71	Eastern Europe
Duke Ellington	09/10/71–10/03/71	Soviet Union
Lionel Hampton	10/29/71–11/04/71	Eastern Europe
Sarah Vaughan	10/29/71–11/04/71	Eastern Europe
Duke Ellington	10/29/71–11/10/71	Europe/Eastern Europe
Duke Ellington	11/16/71–12/10/71	Southeast Asia
Duke Ellington	01/20/72–01/26/72	Far East
Dizzy/Eckstine/Getz/Tyner	11/02/73–02/06/73	Eastern Europe
Duke Ellington	10/27/73–11/25/73	Europe/Africa
Dizzy Gillespie	12/05/73–12/08/73	Kenya
Pearl Bailey Trio	00/00/74–00/00/74	Middle East
	Gerald R. Ford	
Ellington/Dizzy/Coleman	10/23/74–11/16/74	Eastern Europe
Sarah Vaughan Trio	00/00/75–00/00/75	Eastern Europe
Charlie Byrd Trio	00/00/75–00/00/75	Far East
Charlie Byrd Trio	01/00/76–02/00/76	Asia

(continued)

ARTIST	DATES	DESTINATION
	Jimmy Carter	
McCoy Tyner	00/00/76–00/00/76	Eastern Europe
Clark Terry	01/23/78–02/26/78	Middle East
	Ronald Reagan	
Billy Taylor	01/25/82–03/07/82	Middle East
Billy Taylor	00/00/86–00/00/86	Eastern Europe
Dave Brubeck	08/03/87–08/25/87	Soviet Union

JAZZ AMBASSADOR	WHITE HOUSE
Pearl Bailey	Nixon, Ford, Carter
Louis Bellson	Nixon, Ford, Carter
Dave Brubeck	LBJ, Nixon, Reagan
Charlie Byrd	LBJ, Ford
Ornette Coleman	Carter
Billy Eckstine	Nixon, Carter
Duke Ellington	LBJ, Nixon
Stan Getz	LBJ, Carter, Reagan
Dizzy Gillespie	Nixon, Carter, Reagan
Benny Goodman	Reagan
Lionel Hampton	Carter, Reagan
Milt Hinton	Nixon, Ford, Carter
Earl Hines	Nixon, Ford, Carter
Herbie Mann	LBJ
Modern Jazz Quartet	Nixon
Gerry Mulligan	LBJ, Nixon, Carter
Billy Taylor	Nixon, Ford, Carter, Reagan
Clark Terry	LBJ, Nixon
McCoy Tyner	Carter
Sarah Vaughan	LBJ, Ford, Carter, Reagan
Paul Winter	JFK

Sources: University of Arkansas Libraries, Special Collections, Fayetteville, AR; Elise K. Kirk, *Musical Highlights from the White House* (Malabar, FL: Kreiger Publishing, 1992); and confirmed by the JFK, LBJ, Nixon, Ford, Carter, and Reagan presidential libraries.

❋

Notes

Prologue: The Year Everything Changed for Jazz

1. Rob Kirkpatrick, *1969: The Year Everything Changed* (New York: Skyhorse Publishing, 2009), xvi.

2. Some say Jimmy Carter was the first president to honor jazz at his first White House jazz concert on the South Lawn in August 1978 because it embraced, in the players selected to perform, everything from ragtime through 1960s avant-garde. But by the time of the South Lawn concert, five U.S. presidents (Kennedy through Carter) had presented a combined total of forty-two White House jazz events that encompassed a broad sweep of the music from ragtime to Dixieland to swing to modern. Further, since 1969, the federal government via the NEA had been honoring jazz in its own homeland with its continuing financial support.

3. Two precedents bear mention: the Washington Navy Yard Jazz Band, whose music is little known, played for President Harding in 1921; and the Ray Miller Jazz Band played at a campaign rally on the South Lawn for President Coolidge in 1924 (see appendix 1). No other jazz bands appeared at the mansion until 1962 for President Kennedy.

4. Al Hirt's New Orleans band played for President Nixon on December 3, 1969, and Gunther Schuller's New England Ragtime Ensemble played for President Ford on September 25, 1964.

5. Jazz funding and projects sponsored found in *NEA Jazz Masters, 1982–2010* (National Endowment for the Arts, Office of Public Affairs, 2010) 1–2.

6. During the five years of Nixon's presidency (1969–1974), the annual appropriation for the NEA increased from $9 million to $80 million. In 2012, the appropriation was only $150 million!

7. *2008 Survey of Public Participation in the Arts* (National Endowment for the Arts, 2009).

8. *Jazz: The Smithsonian Anthology*, SFW CD 40820 (Smithsonian Folkways Recordings, 2010).

9. Paul Lopes, *The Rise of the Jazz Art World* (Cambridge: Cambridge University Press, 2002), 236.

10. Ibid., 237.

11. Ibid., 238.

12. Data on foundations based on the author's research of materials held at the Foundation Center, Washington, DC.

13. Phyl Garland, "Jazz at the White House," *Ebony*, September 1980, 60.

Chapter 1: America's Premier Composer

1. After Duke, six jazz stars received this award: Pearl Bailey, Count Basie, Eubie Blake, Ella Fitzgerald, Mabel Mercer, and Frank Sinatra. In addition, only two other composers—Irving Berlin and Aaron Copland—have been so honored.

2. Gary Giddins, *Visions of Jazz: The First Century* (Oxford: Oxford University Press, 1998), 103, 106.

3. Ibid., 104.

4. John Edward Hasse, *Beyond Category: The Life and Genius of Duke Ellington* (New York: Simon & Schuster, 1993), 309.

5. Whitney Balliett, *Collected Works: A Journal of Jazz, 1954–2001* (New York: St. Martin's Griffin, 2000), 807.

6. Ibid., 808.

7. Harvey G. Cohen, *Duke Ellington's America* (Chicago: The University of Chicago Press, 2001), 66, 70, 93, 96, 101, 174, 182, 194, 207, 252, 272, 280, 284, 288, 304, 330, 340, 390, 402.

8. Ibid., 112.

Chapter 2: A Long Road to the White House

1. For an overview of jazz origins and evolution, consult Geoffrey C. Ward and Ken Burns, *Jazz: A History of America's Music* (New York: Alfred A. Knopf, 2005).

2. President Roosevelt and ragtime in Elise K. Kirk, *Music at the White House: A History of the American Spirit* (Urbana, IL: U. of Illinois Press, 1986), 183; Harding and the Navy Yard Band in ibid., 204–5; and the jazz band rally

for Coolidge in ibid., 203. See appendix 1 for more information on these two White House events. For an overview of White House entertainment, consult the definitive Kirk, *Music,* available in the used-book market. A more readily available but slightly abridged version: Elise K. Kirk, *Musical Highlights from the White House* (Malabar, FL: Krieger Publishing, 1992).

3. Ibid., 221–52.

4. Lem Graves Jr., "24 Film Stars at Washington Birthday Ball: Hollywood Personalities Appear At Lincoln Dance and Howard Theater Party," *New Journal and Guide*, February 7, 1942.

5. Cohen, *America*, 42–64.

6. Hasse, *Beyond Category*, 151, 181.

7. Kirk, *Music*, 121.

8. Ralph J. Gleason, *Celebrating the Duke and Louis, Bessie, Billie, Bird, Carmen, Miles, Dizzy, and Other Heroes* (Boston-Toronto: Atlantic Little Brown, 1975), 165.

9. Duke Ellington, *Music Is My Mistress* (Garden City, NY: Doubleday & Co., 1973), 432.

10. Ibid., 431.

11. White House letter, President Dwight D. Eisenhower to Mr. Duke Ellington, March 12, 1955, courtesy of the Dwight D. Eisenhower Library, Abilene, Kansas.

12. Ralph J. Gleason liner notes, *Jazz Premier: The Paul Winter Sextet,* Jazz Collectibles, COL-CD 6671 SONY A-50657.

13. Cohen, *America,* 421–23.

14. Pierre Salinger, *Pierre Salinger: With Kennedy* (Garden City, NY: Doubleday & Co., 1966), 310.

15. USIA Bombay concert documentary *Film Journal 4 Duke Ellington Selections* available for viewing at the National Archives in College Park, MD.

16. Cohen, *America*, 498–99.

17. Ken Vail, *Duke's Diary, Part Two: The Life of Duke Ellington, 1950–1974* (Lanham, MD: Scarecrow Press, 2002); "Honored at 'Pan Alley,'" *Washington Post*, May 23, 1964.

18. Liz Carpenter, *Ruffles and Flourishes* (Garden City, NY: Doubleday & Co., 1969), 205.

19. Ibid., 200; Donald L. Maggin, *Stan Getz: A Life in Jazz* (New York: William Morrow, 1996), 236.

20. Ellington, *Mistress*, 430.

21. Roxanne Battle, "Jeff Casteleman: Bass Player and Lone Survivor," MinnPost, http://www.minnpost.com, March 27, 2008.

22. Claudia T. Johnson, *Lady Bird Johnson: A White House Diary* (New York: Holt, Rinehart and Winston, 1970), 739.

23. "Disenchanted: Will Brooke Bolt GOP?" *Los Angeles Sentinel*, March 26, 1970.

Chapter 3: Prelude to a Tribute

1. Frank Getlein, "The Man Who's Made the Most Solid Contribution to the Arts of Any President since F.D.R.," *New York Times Magazine*, February 14, 1971.

2. Herbert Klein, *Making It Perfectly Clear* (Garden City, NY: Doubleday & Co., 1980), 418.

3. David Lester, *The Lonely Lady of San Clemente* (New York: Crowell 1978), 3; Julie Nixon Eisenhower, *Pat Nixon: The Untold Story* (New York: Simon & Schuster, 1986), 276, 320.

4. Richard M. Nixon, *RN: The Memoirs of Richard Nixon* (New York: Grosset & Dunlap, 1978), 14, 23.

5. Mark Feeney, *Nixon at the Movies* (Chicago: University of Chicago Press, 2004), 281.

6. Ibid., 14, 85, 204, 286.

7. Ibid., 89, 231.

8. Betty Beale, *Power at Play: A Memoir of Parties, Politicians, and the Presidents in My Bedroom* (Washington, DC: Regnery Publishing, 1993), 117.

9. Feeney, *Movies*, 231.

10. Sheila Baab Weidenfeld, *First Lady's Lady* (New York: Putnam, 1979), 38.

11. Memo, Constance Stuart to Rose Mary Woods, March 29, 1972, White House Central Files, Staff Member Office Files, Lucy Winchester, Nixon Library, National Archives, College Park, MD.

12. Frank Getlein, "The Man Who's Made the Most Solid Contribution to the Arts of Any President since F.D.R," *New York Times Magazine*, February 14, 1971.

13. Memo, H. R. Haldeman to Mr. Garment, November 20, 1969, Leonard Garment Collection, Manuscript Division, Library of Congress, Washington, DC. Also see Nixon memo to Bob Haldeman, January 26, 1970, at http://www.nixonlibrary.gov/virtuallibrary/documents/jan10.php.

14. Myra MacPherson, "Honor at 70," *Washington Post*, April 30, 1969.

15. J. B. West with Mary Lynn Kotz, *Upstairs at the White House: My Life with the First Ladies* (New York: Warner Books, 1973) 362–64.

16. Sally Placksin, *American Women in Jazz: 1900 to the Present* (New York: Wideview Books, 1982) 24–28.

17. Charles Stuart, *Never Trust a Local: Inside the Nixon White House* (New York: Algora Publishing, 2005), 61–62, 107.

18. Memo, Nixon to Rose Woods, February 17, 1969, Special Files, EX SO3, February 17, 1960–March 18, 1969, Nixon Library, National Archives, College Park, MD.

19. "More About Sarnoff, Part Two," PBS American Experience television program *Big Dream Small Screen*, WGBH, http://www.pbs.org/wgbh/amex/technology/bigdream/masarnoff2.html.

20. Robert Sarnoff's Cold War patriotism and "mass appeal" television views from the Museum of Broadcast Communications Archives (http://www.museum.tv).

21. Vera Glaspar and Malvins Stephenson, "Watchdogs at the White House," *Washington Evening Star,* December 21, 1969.

22. Don Fulsom, *Nixon's Darkest Secrets: The Inside Story of America's Most Troubled President* (New York: St. Martin's Press, 2012), 123.

23. Memo, Nixon to H. R. Haldeman, July 9, 1969, Special Files, SO3, July 1, 1969–July 17, 1969, Nixon Library, National Archives, College Park, MD.

24. Memo, Dwight L. Chapin to H. R. Haldeman, Schedule Planning, December 29, 1969, Special Files, EX SO3, December 1, 1969–December 13, 1969, Nixon Library, National Archives, College Park, MD.

25. Memo, H. R. Haldeman to R. Woods, March 23, 1970, Special Files, SO3, July 1, 1969–July 17, 1969, Nixon Library, National Archives, College Park, MD.

26. Memo, Pat Buchanan to the President, July 14, 1969, Special Files, EX SO3, September 5, 1969–September 30, 1969, Nixon Library, National Archives, College Park, MD.

27. Memo, H. R. Haldeman to Mr. Klein, September 19, 1969, Special Files, EX SO3, July 18, 1969–August 7, 1969, Nixon Library, National Archives, College Park, MD.

28. Memo, Henry A. Kissinger to Hugh Sloan, Vietnam Entertainers, Special Files, SO3, November 1, 1969–November 30, 1969, Nixon Library, National Archives, College Park, MD.

29. Memo, Report on May 15 Meeting, May 13, 1971, Special Files, Nixon Library, National Archives, College Park, MD.

30. Memo, Lucy Winchester to Alexander Butterfield and Davis Parker, Entertainers' Homecoming, February 10, 1972, in White House Central Files, Staff Member Office Files, Lucy Winchester, Nixon Library, National Archives, College Park, MD.

31. Memo, H. R. Haldeman to Steve Bull, January 22, 1973, Special Files, EX SO3. Nixon Library, National Archives, College Park, MD.

32. Note, Penny Adams to Gwen, April 5, 1970, White House Central Files, Staff Member Office Files, Lucy Winchester, Nixon Library, National Archives, College Park, MD.

33. Note, Maria Downs to Lucy Winchester, 1974, White House Central Files, Staff Member Office Files, Lucy Winchester, Nixon Library, National Archives, College Park, MD.

34. Memo, Dwight L. Chapin to Henry Cashen, Mike Curb Congregation, June 21, 1971, White House Central Files, Staff Member Office Files, Lucy Winchester, Nixon Library, National Archives, College Park, MD.

35. Memo, Stephen Bull to Lucy Winchester, October 27, 1971, White House Central Files, Staff Member Office Files, Lucy Winchester, Nixon Library, National Archives, College Park, MD.

36. Marlene Cimons, "Slow Down in Swinging Washington," *Los Angeles Times*, May 3, 1970.

37. Ronald Kessler, *Inside the White House* (New York: Pocket Books, 1996), 154.

38. Mercer Ellington with Stanley Dance, *Duke Ellington in Person: An Intimate Memoir* (Boston: Houghton Mifflin Co., 1978), 186.

39. Hollie I. West, "Duke at 70: Honor from the President," *Washington Post*, April 24, 1969.

40. Cohen, *America*, 514–17.

41. The nine big bands that played Nixon's inaugural were selected for their popularity with the public and style of music—a balance between big jazz band and businessman's bounce. Joining the Ellington Orchestra was the Lionel Hampton jazz band, the Meyer Davis and Lester Lanin society dance bands, the Les Brown and Doc Severinsen TV show bands, the Sammy Kaye and Guy Lombardo old line dance bands, and the World's Greatest Jazz Band, a swing/dixie outfit.

42. For more on the Voice, see Terence M. Ripmaster, *Willis Conover: Broadcasting Jazz to the World* (Lincoln, NE: iUniverse, 2007); and Alan J. Heil Jr., *Voice of America: A History* (New York: Columbia University Press, 2003).

43. Memo, Charles McWhorter to H. R. Haldeman, February 13, 1969, White House Special Files, EX SO3, March 28, 1969–April 30, 1969, Nixon Library, National Archives, College Park, MD.

44. Memo, Dwight L. Chapin to John Ehrlichman, February 14, 1969, White House Special Files, EX SO3, March 28, 1969–April 30, 1969, Nixon Library, National Archives, College Park, MD.

45. Letter, Willis Conover to Social Secretary Lucy Winchester, February 20, 1969, White House Special Files, EX SO3, March 28, 1969–April 30, 1969, Nixon Library, National Archives, College Park, MD.

46. H. R. Haldeman, *Haldeman Diaries: Inside the Nixon White House* (New York: NY Pocket Books, 1996), 31.

47. Letter, Willis Conover to Social Secretary Lucy Winchester, February 20, 1969, White House Special Files, EX SO3, March 28, 1969–April 30, 1969, Nixon Library, National Archives, College Park, MD.

48. Letter, Willis Conover to Leonard Garment, March 26, 1969, White House Special Files, EX SO3, March 28, 1969–April 30, 1969, Nixon Library, National Archives, College Park, MD.

49. Letter, Willis Conover to band members, McWhorter, Garment, Winchester, April 19, 1969, White House Special Files, EX SO3, March 28, 1969–April 30, 1969, Nixon Library, National Archives, College Park, MD.

50. Ethel L. Payne, "Nixon's Party for Duke: An Evening to Remember," *Chicago Daily Defender*, May 1, 1969.

Chapter 4: The Jazz All-Stars

1. *NEA Jazz Masters, 1982–2010*, 77; piano style quote in Balliett, *Collected Works*, 837.

2. *NEA Jazz Masters*, 55.

3. Ibid., 70

4. Ibid., 21.

5. Doug Ramsey, *Take Five: The Public and Private Lives of Paul Desmond* (Seattle: Parkside Publications, 2005).

6. Leonard Feather, *The Pleasures of Jazz* (New York: Horizon Press, 1976), 148; Balliett, *Collected Works*, 378.

7. From http://www.urbiegreen.com and http://www.trombones.com.

8. *NEA Jazz Masters*, 75.

9. From obituary posted on http://www.depanorama.net/dems.

10. *NEA Jazz Masters*, 107; the trumpet style quote from Gary Giddins, *Weather Bird: Jazz at the Dawn of Its Second Century* (Oxford: Oxford University Press, 2004), 252.

11. *NEA Jazz Masters*, 28.

12. Balliett, *Collected Works*, 213; Gene Rizzo, *The Fifty Greatest Piano Players of All Time* (Milwaukeee, WI: Hal Leonard Corporation), 156.

13. *NEA Jazz Masters*, 105.

14. Info on Mayo in http://www.spaceagepop.com/mayo.htm; and in Dorothy Hunt Smith, "Mary Mayo's Musical Career Swings with Pop," *Christian Science Monitor*, October 7, 1969.

15. *NEA Jazz Masters*, 116.

16. Hasse, *Beyond Category*, 240.

17. Duke's press conference remarks distributed by AP to numerous newspapers; for example, "Nixon Plays 'Happy Birthday' to Duke," *Milwaukee Sentinel*, April 29, 1969, 8, part 1; supplemented by Duke Ellington Press Conference 1969-04-29 audio tape, VOA Music Library Collection, call number RAA 51071, Library of Congress, Washington, DC.

18. Newsmakers, *Los Angeles Times*, April 28, 1969.

Chapter 5: The Banquet

1. Description of the banquet and ceremony compiled from accounts given in newspapers (*Washington Post, Washington Star, New York Times, Los Angeles Times*, various others, April 30, 1969); in magazines (*Newsweek, Time, Ebony*, and *Jet*); in Doug Ramsey liner notes, *1969 All-Star White House Tribute to Duke Ellington*, Blue Note Records CD, 2002; and in books: Hasse, *Beyond Category*, 373–75; Balliett, *Collected Works*, 304–8; Dan Morgenstern, *Living with Jazz* (New York: Pantheon Books, 2004), 502–5; Leonard Feather, *From Satchmo to Miles* (New York: Stein and Day, 1974), 55–57; Stanley Dance, *The World of Duke Ellington* (New York: Charles Scribner & Sons, 1970), 285–89; Ellington, *Music*, 426–28; Leonard Garment, *Crazy Rhythm* (New York: Times Books, 1997), 175–79; Ramsey, *Take 5*, 252–55; Don George, *Sweet Man: The Real Duke Ellington* (New York: G. P. Putnam's Sons, 1981), 183–85; and Derek Jewell, *Duke: A Portrait of Duke Ellington* (New York: W. W. Norton & Co., 1977), 26, 189–91.

2. Cohen, *America*, 355, 510.

3. Cohen, *America*, 332.

4. Poppy Cannon White, "'Coke with Sugar' in Side Thoughts on a Ball," *New York Amsterdam News*, May 17, 1969.

5. Ellington, *Music*, 426.

6. Haldeman, *Diaries*, 54.

7. Ethel L. Payne, "So This Is Washington," *Chicago Daily Defender*, May 10, 1969.

8. Haldeman, *Diaries*, 54; and Ellington, *Music*, 427.

9. Dinner seating arrangement in White House Central Files, Staff Member Office Files, Sanford Fox, Box 9, Seating Chart, Nixon Presidential Library, Yorba Linda, CA.

10. Table setting in Lillian Wiggins, "President Hosts Party for Duke," *Afro-American*, May 1969.

11. Dizzy Gillespie and Al Fraser, *To Be or Not to Bop* (Garden City, NY: Doubleday & Co., 1979), 495; and in Feather, *Pleasures*, 138.

12. Ellington, *Music*, 428.

13. Poppy Cannon White, "You Too Can Dine as Pat and Dick Do," *Hartford Courier*, May 26, 1969.

14. Nixon's banquet speech at American Presidency Project, http://www.presidency.ucsb.edu/ws/index.php?pid=2025.

15. Robert E. Johnson, "History-Making Honor for Black American Draws Plaudits," *Jet*, May 1969, 30.

Chapter 6: The Ceremony

1. Balliett, *Collected Works*, 304–6.

2. Irving Kupcinet with Paul Neimark, *Kup: A Man, an Era, a City* (Chicago: Bonus Books, 1988), 258.

3. Balliett, *Collected Works*, 305–6; medal ceremony speeches by Nixon and Duke transcribed by the author from *Duke Ellington at the White House*, 1969 Highlights, USIA Motion Picture, ARC 53501, Nixon Library, National Archives, College Park, MD.

Chapter 7: The Concert

1. Willis Conover concert remarks from Ellington Evening broadcasts on May 28, 29, and 30, 1969, from Willis Conover, *Music USA*, CD 306.MUSA.5299B, CD 306.MUSA.5300B, and 306.MUSA.5301B MPD, National Archives, College Park, MD.

2. Dance, *World of Duke*, 33.

3. Ellington, *Music*, 162.

4. In *The Jazz Standards: A Guide to the Repertoire* (Oxford: Oxford University, 2012), author Ted Gioia delineates and discusses more than 250 standards. Top honors go to Ellington and associates (son Mercer, Billy Strayhorn, and Juan Tizol) with nineteen entries and to runner-up composers George Gershwin and Richard Rodgers, with fifteen and eleven, respectively.

5. Dance, *World of Duke*, 175–79.

6. Mercer Ellington with Dance, *Duke in Person*, 94.

7. Balliett, *Collected Works*, 306.

8. Morgenstern, *Living*, 103.

9. Giddins, *Visions*, 243.

10. "Chelsea" links to composer Ravel in liner notes by Leonard Feather, *Ella Fitzgerald Sings the Duke Ellington Songbook*, Verve 3-CD set, 1988, 28.

11. Ramsey, *Take 5*, 254.

12. Philip Furia and Michael Lasser, *America's Songs: The Stories behind the Songs of Broadway, Hollywood, and Tin Pan Alley* (New York: Routledge, 2006), 265.

13. Hasse, *Beyond Category*, 313.

14. Don George, *Sweet Man*, 188.

15. Alec Wilder and James T. Maher, *American Popular Song: The Great Innovators, 1900–1950* (Oxford: Oxford University Press, 1972), 415.

16. Hollie I. West, "Serenaded by All-Star Jazz Musicians," *Washington Post*, April 30, 1969.

17. Morgenstern, *Living*, 504.

18. Ramsey liner notes, *White House Tribute* CD.

19. Furia and Lasser, *America's Songs*, 113.

20. Giddins, *Visions*, 112.

21. Hasse, *Beyond Category*, 189.

22. Ellington, *Music*, 106.

23. Furia and Lasser, *America's Songs*, 202.

24. Balliett, *Collected Works*, 306; Morgenstern, *Living*, 504; Hollie I. West, "Serenaded."

25. Giddins, *Vision*, 344.

26. Burns, *Jazz*, 444.

27. Gene Lees, *Oscar Peterson: The Will to Swing* (New York: Cooper Square Press, 1988), 245.

28. Morgenstern, *Living*, 504.

29. Dance, *World of Duke*, 287; Balliett, *Collected Works*, 306; Ramsey liner notes, *White House Tribute* CD.

30. Ramsey, *Take 5*, 256.

31. Ellington, *Music*, 88.

32. Furia and Lasser, *America's Songs*, 174.

33. Ellington, *Music*, 88.

34. Ken Bloom, *The American Songbook: The Singers, the Songwriters, and the Songs*, (New York: Black Dog & Levanthal Publishers, 2005), 217.

35. "Very lovely and delightful" in Wilder, *Popular Song*, 414; "yearning and haunting" in Hasse, *Beyond Category*, 191.

36. Wilder, *Popular Song*, 414.

37. Hasse, *Beyond Category*, 229.

38. Hollie I. West, "Serenaded."

39. Ramsey liner notes, *White House Tribute* CD.

40. "Ingenious" in Balliett, *Collected Works*, 306; "highly original" in Morgenstern, *Living*, 504; and "zesty" in Ramsey, *Take 5*, 256.

41. Earl Wilson, "It Happened Last Night," *New York Post*, April 30, 1969, 74.

42. Hasse, *Beyond Category*, 129.

43. Mercer Ellington with Dance, *Duke in Person*, 50.

44. Ella's "Harlem" can be heard on *Ella Fitzgerald Sings the Duke Ellington Songbook*, 3-CD set, Verve 1988.

45. Giddins, *Visions*, 245.

46. Ellington, *Music,* 419.

47. Ibid., 154.

48. Ramsey, *Take 5*, 254.

49. Gene Lees, *Oscar Peterson*, 247.

50. Hollie I. West, "Serenaded"; Dance, *The World of*, 288; Feather, *From Satchmo to Miles*, 56; Ramsey liner notes, *White House Tribute* CD.

51. Garment, *Crazy*, 171.

52. Giddins, *Visions*, 245.

53. Hasse, *Beyond Category*, 228.

54. Ellington, *Music*, 78–79.

55. Barney Bigard, *With Louis and the Duke: The Autobiography of a Jazz Clarinetist* (Oxford: Oxford University Press, 1986), 64.

56. Giddins, *Visions*, 105.

57. Dance, *Duke in Person*, 23.

58. Ellington, *Music*, 80.

59. Janna Tull Steed, *Duke Ellington: A Spiritual Biography* (New York: The Crossroad Publishing Co., 1999).

60. Dance, *The World of*, 260.

61. Giddins, *Visions*, 22.

62. Hasse, *Beyond Category*, 263; Steed, *Spiritual Biography*, 26, 90; Balliett, *Collected Works*, 718.

63. Giddins, *Visions*, 250.

64. Leslie Gourse, *Every Day: The Story of Joe Williams* (London: Quartet Books, 1985), 32, 143.

65. Feather, *From Satchmo*, 56.

66. Morgenstern, *Living*, 504.

67. Earl Wilson, "It Happened Last Night," 74.

68. "The Duke and His Friends," *San Francisco Chronicle*, May 2, 1969.

69. Duke's intro to "Heritage" from *Duke Ellington: A Concert of Sacred Music from Grace Cathedral, 1965*, STATUS CD DST1015.

70. Ramsey liner notes, *White House Tribute* CD.

71. Gleason, *Celebrating the Duke*, 264.

72. Hasse, *Beyond Category*, 315.

73. Balliett, *Collected Works*, 161.

Chapter 8: The Jam Session

1. Description of the after party compiled from accounts given in newspapers (*Washington Post, Washington Star, New York Times, Los Angeles Times*, and others, April 30, 1969); in magazines (*Newsweek, Time, Ebony*, and *Jet*); in Ramsey liner notes, *White House Tribute* CD; and in books (Hasse, *Beyond Category*, 373–75; Balliett, *Collected Works*, 304–8; Morgenstern, *Living*, 502–5; Feather, *Satchmo to Miles*, 55–57; Dance, *The World of*, 285–89; Ellington, *Music*, 426–28; Garment, *Crazy Rhythm*, 175–79; Ramsey, *Take 5*, 252–55; George, *Sweet Man*, 183–85; and Jewell, *A Portrait of*, 189–91.).

2. Johnson, "History-Making," 46.

3. Earl Wilson, "It Happened Last Night," 7.

4. Eleni, "Duke Was King for a Night, Says He: It Was Lovely," *Evening Star*, April 30, 1969, C-1.

5. Balliett, *Collected Works*, 307.

6. Garment, *Crazy Rhythm*, 171.

7. Payne, "So This Is Washington," May 10, 1969, 9.

8. Leonard Feather, "Ellington Tribute a Victory for Jazz," *Los Angeles Times*, May 11, 1969.

9. Willie "the Lion" Smith with George Hoefer, *Music on My Mind: The Memoirs of an American Pianist* (New York: Da Capo Paperback, 1973), 34, 190.

10. "The Duke and His Friends," *San Francisco Chronicle*, May 2, 1969.

11. The Lion's comment on melody in Nina S. Hyde, "Duke Was King for the Night," *Washington Daily News*, April 30, 1969.

12. Paul de Barros, *Shall We Play That One Together?: The Life and Art of Jazz Piano Legend Marian McPartland* (New York: St. Martin's Press, 2012), 249–50.

13. "Jean A. Smith Married to Rev. Harold H. Weicker," *New York Times*, March 22, 1970.

14. Payne, "So This Is Washington," May 10, 1969, 9.

15. Lionel Hampton with James Haskins, *Hamp* (New York: Warner Books, 1989), 96–97, 120, 132, 154.

16. Nan Robertson, "Duke Ellington, 70, Honored at White House," *New York Times*, April 30, 1969, 40.

17. John Fass Morton, *Backstory in Blue: Ellington at Newport '56* (New Brunswick, NJ: Rutgers University Press, 2008), chaps. 13 and 14.

18. "President Hosts Party for Duke," Lillian Wiggins, *Afro-American*, May 1969.

19. Johnson, "History-Making," 32.

20. Duke, sister Ruth, Johnson, Jones, Terry, Calloway, Williams, Bellson, Taylor, Hines, Eckstine, and Abell in Johnson, "History-Making," 24–50; Whaley and unnamed Californian in Robertson, "Duke Ellington, 70"; Preminger and Kupcinet in Kupcinet with Neimark, *Kup*, 259; Mulligan in MacPherson, "Honor at 70"; Rawls in Hollie I. West, "Serenaded"; veteran observer in Morgenstern, *Living*, 504; unnamed butler and musicians in Eleni, "Duke Was King"; Nancy Balliett from personal communication with the author, February 13, 2012.

Chapter 9: An Affair to Remember

1. Feather, *Satchmo to Miles*, 57.
2. Musicians everywhere honored, letter, Doug Ramsey to Richard Nixon, May 13, 1969, White House Special Files, EX SO3, May 1, 1969–May 10, 1969, Nixon Library, National Archives, College Park, MD.
3. Phyl Garland, "Duke Ellington: He Took the 'A' Train to the White House," *Ebony*, July 1969, 69.
4. Kirk, *Music*, 322.
5. Nixon letter to Duke in USIA files, RG 306, Entry A1 1061, Records relative to USIA programs, Box 6, National Archives, College Park, MD.
6. Marie Smith, "Governors 'Rock' in East Room," *Washington Post*, December 4, 1969.
7. Nixon: "Ellington night will never be topped," June 4, 1971, telecon transcript at http://nixontapeaudio.org/005-154.mp3.
8. Nixon, *Memoirs*, 540.
9. Thomas Meehan, "Washington Society Isn't Exactly Swinging," *New York Times*, March 8, 1970.
10. Marlene Cimons, "Slow Down in Swinging Washington," *Los Angeles Times*, May 3 1970.
11. Casals on radio in Richard F. Shepard, "Broadcasts Set for Casals Tape, White House Concert to Be Heard on Radio Next Week," *New York Times*, November 18, 1961.
12. Pablo Casals (cello), Alexander Schneider (vn), Mieczyslaw Horszowski (p), *A Concert at the White House*, KL 5796, Columbia LP 3/1962.
13. Ramsey, *Take 5*, 254–56.
14. Nixon lambasts JFK, LBJ events in Chris Matthews, *Kennedy & Nixon: The Rivalry That Shaped Postwar America* (New York: Free Press 2011), 313.
15. Cohen, *America*, 505.
16. Ethel L. Payne, "So This Is Washington," *Chicago Daily Defender*, May 3, 1969.

17. Ethel L. Payne, "Story behind Ellington's White House Fete," *Chicago Daily Defender*, May 5, 1969.

18. Diggs Datrooth, "National Hotline," *New Pittsburgh Courier*, May 24, 1969.

19. "Duke and His Friend Dick," *Baltimore Afro-American*, May 17, 1969.

20. "Icing on the Cake," ibid.

21. Description of the NBC and ABC broadcasts transcribed by the author from the "Ellington Honors" news clips (April 30, 1969) available at the Vanderbilt Television News Archive online at the Library of Congress, Washington, DC. http://tvnews.vanderbilt.edu.

22. Description of the "Presidential 'Do' for the Duke" article including specific text from USIA *Photo Bulletin*, July 1969, issues of the USIA *Photo Bulletin*, compiled 1964–1973, 306-PB, Still Pictures Records Section, Specific Media Archives Services Division, National Archives, College Park, MD.

23. JFK filmed three events featuring entertainers in performance in the East Room all without sound—Pablo Casals concert (November 13, 1961), Paul Winter Jazz Sextet (Nov. 19, 1962), and Brigadoon (March 27, 1963)—as well as a children's dance troupe/orchestra outside with sound (May 5, 1963). LBJ filmed two performances both with sound in the East Room as part of *The President* series (an account of his monthly activities), featuring *Hello, Dolly!* with Carol Channing in one (January 17, 1967) and the Alvin Ailey Dance Theater in the other (November 21, 1968). This information obtained from the respective presidential libraries.

24. Matthews, *Kennedy & Nixon*, 276.

25. Author and film producer Sidney J. Stiber, personal communication with author, December 14, 2011.

26. Temporal statistics and description of *Duke* transcribed by the author from a copy in author's possession, which is identical to that held by the Library of Congress, Washington, DC, National Archives, College Park, MD, and the Nixon Library at Yorba Linda, CA.

27. Footage from which the *Duke* film was cut (some ninety minutes long and silent) can be seen on the video tape Duke Ellington 3067535 at the MPD, National Archives, College Park, MD.

28. For a critical examination of U.S. propaganda and Africa, see Melinda M. Schwenk-Borrell, *Selling Democracy: The U.S. Information Agency's Portrayal of American Race Relations, 1953–1976*, Doctoral Dissertation, University of Pennsylvania, 2004.

29. Positive response to *Duke* film at Moscow FilmFest in memo, Mr. Loomis from Eugene Rosenfeld, USIA Director's Subject Files, Speech Files 1958–71 Entry A1 20 306-230-48-16-03, Box 6,7 National Archives, College Park, MD.

30. *Duke* Film Review Memorandum, All IMV Officers from O. Rudolph Aggray, September 8, 1969, Textual material included with *Duke Ellington at the White House*, National Archives, College Park, MD.

31. Initial distribution statistics in USIA Circular *Duke Ellington at the White House* Film, October 10, 1969, Textual material included with *Duke Ellington at the White House*, National Archives, College Park, MD.

32. Memo, USIA/IMV Washington from USIS Blantyre, October 23, 1969, reclassified November 17, 2011, USIA Office of the Assistant Director for Africa, Records Relating to the Distribution of Motion Pictures for African Posts, compiled 1969–1970, P 99, National Archives, College Park, MD.

33. Memo, *Duke Ellington at the White House*, USIA/IMV Washington from USIS Bamko, October 27, 1969, reclassified November 17, 2011, USIA Office of the Assistant Director for Africa, Records Relating to the Distribution of Motion Pictures for African Posts, compiled 1969–1970, P 99, National Archives, College Park, MD.

34. Memo, *Duke Ellington at the White House*, USIA/IMV Washington from USIS Dar es Salaam, November 4, 1969, reclassified November 17, 2011, USIA Office of the Assistant Director for Africa, Records Relating to the Distribution of Motion Pictures for African Posts, compiled 1969–1970, P 99, National Archives, College Park, MD.

35. *Duke Ellington at the White House* film approved for CINE/festivals in memo, Committee from Wilbert H. Pearson, Chairman, November 7, 1969, Files of the Interdepartmental Committee on Visual/Auditory Materials for Distribution Abroad 1950–1982, P-28 306-230-47-42-2, Box 3, National Archives, College Park, MD.

36. Clay Evans, "USIA under Attack; Scratch Duke for Cartoon," *New York Amsterdam News*, December 27, 1969.

37. Halloran, "Silent Majority," January 29, 1970.

38. Portugal digs real *Duke* in memo, Frank Shakespeare to Bruce Herschensohn, April 24, 1970, USIA Motion Picture and Television (IMV) 1970, A1 42- 360-230-46-3, Box 14, National Archives, College Park, MD.

39. *Duke* film enjoys substantial TV exposure in Statement of the Director before the Zablocki Committee, U.S. House of Representatives, April 30, 1970, USIA, Director Frank Shakespeare's Speeches 1963–73, A1-19 306-230-46-03, National Archives, College Park, MD.

40. Ben Gross, TV Week, *New York Sunday News*, April 5–11, 1970.

41. *Duke* film wins Golden Eagle in memo, Committee from Wilbert H. Pearson, Chairman, November 7, 1969, Files of the Interdepartmental Committee on Visual/Auditory Materials for Distribution Abroad 1950–1982, P-28 306-230-47-42-2, Box 3, National Archives, College Park, MD.

42. Stats on Czechoslovakia film in memo, Mr. Loomis from Eugene Rosenfeld, USIA Director's Subject Files, Speech Files 1958–71, Entry A1 20 306-230-48-16-03, Box 6,7 National Archives, College Park, MD.

43. Halloran, "Silent Majority," January 29, 1970.

44. USIA submitted forty-five films to forty-nine festivals in memo, William H. Pearson from Mr. Russell, 1970, Files of the Interdepartmental Committee on Visual/Auditory Materials for Distribution Abroad 1950–1982, P-28 306-230-47-42-2, Box 3, National Archives, College Park, MD.

45. Former USIA IMV director Bruce Herschensohn, personal communication with author, January 17, 2012.

46. Author and producer Sidney J. Stiber, personal communication with author, December 14, 2011.

47. Johnson White House jazz stars broadcast on the VOA from Willis Conover, *Music USA* Recording Schedule, 1965–1977, UNT Digital Library, http://digital.library.unt.edu.

48. Conover remarks transcribed by the author from *Music USA*, April 29, 1969, CD 306.MUSA.5234B, MPD, National Archives, College Park, MD.

49. Ellington evening broadcasts on May 28, 29, and 30, 1969, from *Music USA*, CD 306.MUSA.5299B, 306.MUSA.5300B, and 306.MUSA.5301B, MPD, National Archives, College Park, MD.

50. Ellington evening repeat broadcasts on July 3, 4, and 5, 1969, from Willis Conover, *Music USA* Recording Schedule, 1965–1977, UNT Digital Library, http://digital.library.unt.edu.

51. "Pat" played on *Music USA* December 6, program 5455B, Individual Program List, 1969–1970, UNT Digital Library, http://digital.library.unt.edu.

52. White House performances of the MJQ and Al Hirt/Fifth Dimension broadcast on December 5, 1969, and January 17, 1970, respectively, from Willis Conover, *Music USA* Recording Schedule, 1965–1977, UNT Digital Library, http://digital.library.unt.edu.

53. Ellington evening "two-segment" broadcasts on July 31 and August 1, September 29 and 30, and October 9 and 16, 1970; and on October 15 and 22, 1971; and on August 15 and 16, 1972, from *Music USA*, CD 306. MUSA.5692B, 306.MUSA.5693B, National Archives, College Park, MD; and subsequent dates—5752B, 5753B; 5762A, 5769A; 6133A, 6140A; and 6438A, 6439A—from Willis Conover, *Music USA* Recording Schedule, 1965–1977, UNT Digital Library, http://digital.library.unt.edu.

54. Duke White House tribute rebroadcast on April 23, 24, 25, and 26, 1974, from *Music USA*, CD 306.MUSA.7054A, 306.MUSA.7055A, 306. MUSA.7056A, and 306.MUSA.7057A, MPD, National Archives, College Park, MD.

55. *Music USA*, CD 306.MUSA.7060A, MPD, National Archives, College Park, MD.

56. Hours of Ellingtonia per year calculated by the author from Willis Conover, *Music USA* Recording Schedule, 1965–1977; and Individual Recording List for each year 1969 through 1974, UNT Digital Library, http://digital.library.unt.edu.

57. Cohen, *America*, 542.

58. Ibid., 541.

59. Stratemann, *Day by Day*, 1992.

60. Ripmaster, *Conover*, 142.

61. See Edward Allan Faine, *Al Hirt at the White House, 1969,* at http://jazz.tulane.edu/archivist/ja_online_index, 2010.

62. Cohen, *America*, chapter 15.

63. Cohen, *America*, 538.

64. *DownBeat*, April 25, 1974.

65. Cohen, *America*, 575.

66. Ripmaster, *Conover*, 2007.

67. McWhorter info from "Paid Notice: Deaths Mcwhorter, Charles K.," *New York Times.*

68. Garment info from http://www.wikipedia.org/wiki/Leonard_Garment; and http://www.nea.gov/news/news05/medals/Garment.html.

69. Kirk, *Music*; and various presidential library communiqués.

❋

Selected Bibliography

This bibliography is not a complete record of all the work I consulted. It indicates the substance and range of sources upon which I based my writing, and I intend it to serve as a convenience for those interested in pursuing the study of Duke Ellington, jazz, and the White House.

I. GENERAL

Ambrose, Stephan *A. Nixon: The Triumph of a Politician, 1962–1972*. New York: Simon & Schuster, 1989. A broad political overview.

Balliett, Whitney. *Collected Works: A Journal of Jazz, 1954–2001*. New York: St. Martin's Griffin, 2002. A critical jazz review.

Beale, Betty. *Power at Play: A Memoir of Parties, Politicians, and the Presidents in My Bedroom*. Washington, DC: Regnery Gateway, 1993. A view of the Nixon administration and others through the eyes of the society editor of the *Washington Star*.

Cull, Nicholas J. *The Cold War and the United States Information Agency: American Propaganda and Public Diplomacy, 1945–1989*. Cambridge: Cambridge University Press, 2010. A broad tour-de-force overview of the USIA.

Feeney, Mark. *Nixon at the Movies: A Book about Belief*. Chicago: The University of Chicago Press, 2004. A different but related look at Nixon's taste in popular culture.

Fulson, Don. *Nixon's Darkest Secrets: The Inside Story of America's Most Troubled President*. New York: St. Martin's Press, 2012. A view of a conflicted president.

Furia, Phillip, and Michael Lasser. *America's Songs: The Stories behind the Songs of Broadway, Hollywood, and Tin Pan Alley*. New York: Routledge, 2006. Inside information on songs in the Great American Songbook.

Giddins, Gary. *Visions of Jazz: The First Century*. Oxford: Oxford University Press, 1998. A critical jazz review.

———. *Weather Bird: Jazz at the Dawn of Its Second Century*. Oxford: Oxford University Press, 2004. A critical jazz review.

Giddins, Gary, and Scott DeVeaux. *Jazz*. New York: W. W. Norton & Co., 2009. A critical jazz review.

Kirk, Elise K. *Music at the White House: A History of the American Spirit*. Urbana, IL: University of Illinois Press, 1986. The definitive work on White House entertainment, available through the used-book market.

Kirk, Elise K. *Musical Highlights from the White House*. Malabar, FL: Krieger Publishing, 1992. A more readily available but slightly abridged version of *Music at the White House*.

Kirkpatrick, Rob. *1969: The Year That Changed Everything*. New York: Skyhorse Publishing, 2009. An overview of that pivotal year.

Lopes, Paul. *The Rise of the Jazz Art World*. Cambridge: Cambridge University Press, 2000. A different angle on jazz history.

Lusane, Clarence. *The Black History of the White House*. San Francisco: City Lights Books, 2011. A look at the presidency and race.

Matthews, Chris. *Kennedy & Nixon: The Rivalry That Shaped Postwar America*. New York: Free Press, 2011. An account of Nixon's obsession with the Kennedys and vice versa.

Nixon, Richard M. *RN: The Memoirs of Richard Nixon*. New York: Grosset & Dunlop, 1978. A broad political overview.

O'Reilly, Kenneth. *Nixon's Piano: Presidents and Racial Politics from Washington to Clinton*. New York: Free Press, 1995. A detailed study of the presidency and race, and Nixon's southern strategy.

Schroeder, Alan. *Celebrity-in-Chief: How Show Business Took Over the White House*. Boulder, CO: Westview Press, 2004. An insightful account of the symbiotic relationship between entertainers and presidents.

Schwenk-Borrell, Melinda M. *Selling Democracy: The U.S. Information Agency's Portrayal of American Race Relations, 1953–1976*. Doctoral Dissertation. Philadelphia: University of Pennsylvania, 2004. A specific analysis of U.S. propaganda and Africa.

Von Eschen, Penny M. *Satchmo Blows Up the World: Jazz Ambassadors Play the Cold War*. Cambridge, MA: Harvard University Press, 2004. A look into the intertwining of jazz, the White House, and global politics.

Ward, Geoffrey C., and Ken Burns. *Jazz: A History of America's Music*. New York: Alfred A. Knopf, 2005. An overview of jazz origins and evolution.

2. DUKE ELLINGTON

Cohen, Harvey G. *Duke Ellington's America.* Chicago: U. of Chicago Press, 2010.

Dance, Stanley. *The World of Duke Ellington.* New York: Charles Scribner & Sons, 1970.

Ellington, Duke. *Duke Ellington: Music Is My Mistress.* Garden City, NY: Doubleday & Co., 1973.

Ellington, Mercer, with Stanley Dance. *Duke Ellington in Person: An Intimate Memoir.* Boston: Houghton Mifflin, 1971.

George, Dan. *The Real Duke Ellington.* New York: G. P. Putman's Sons, 1971.

Hasse, John Edward. *Beyond Category: The Life and Genius of Duke Ellington.* New York: Simon & Schuster, 1993.

Howland, John. *Ellington Uptown: Duke Ellington, James P. Johnson, and the Birth of Concert Jazz.* Ann Arbor: The University of Michigan Press, 2009.

Jewell, Derek. *Duke: A Portrait of Duke Ellington.* New York: W. W. Norton & Co., 1970.

Morton, John Fass. *Backstory in Blue: Ellington at Newport '56.* New Brunswick, NJ: Rutgers University Press, 2008.

Schiff, David. *The Ellington Century.* Berkeley, CA: University of California Press, 2012.

Steed, Janna Tull. *Duke Ellington: A Spiritual Biography.* New York: Crossroad Publishing, 1999.

Stratemann, Klaus. *Duke Ellington, Day by Day and Film by Film.* Copenhagen: JazzMedia, 1992.

Vail, Ken. *Duke's Diary: Part Two: The Life of Duke Ellington, 1950–1974.* Lanham, MD: Scarecrow Press, 2002.

3. OTHER

de Barros, Paul. *Shall We Play That One Together?: The Life and Art of Jazz Piano Legend Marian McPartland.* New York: St. Martin's Press, 2012.

Feather, Leonard. *The Pleasures of Jazz: Leading Performers on Their Lives, Their Music, Their Contemporaries.* New York: Horizon Press, 1976.

Hajdu, David. *Lush Life: A Biography of Billy Strayhorn.* New York: North Point Press, 1996.

Morgenstern, Dan. *Living with Jazz.* New York: Pantheon Books, 2004.

Ramsey, Doug. *Take Five: The Public and Private Lives of Paul Desmond.* Seattle: Parkside Publications, 2005.

❋

Suggested Recordings

This list of Duke Ellington recordings provides a broad sampling of the maestro's vast body of work.

Afro-Bossa. Collectibles Records Corp. CO1-CD-6730. Originally released in 1963. Instrumentalists identified: Ellington, Billy Strayhorn (p); William Cat Anderson, Cootie Williams, Ray Nance (tp); Lawrence Brown, Buster Cooper (tb); Jimmy Hamilton (cl); Johnny Hodges (as); Paul Gonsalves (ts); Harry Carney (bs); Sam Woodyard (d); Roy Burrowes (perc).

The Afro-Eurasian Eclipse. Original Jazz Classic OJC-645-2. Originally released in 1971. Ellington (p); Cootie Williams, Money Johnson, Mercer Ellington, Eddie Preston (tp); Booty Wood, Malcolm Taylor, Chuck Coonors (tb); Russell Procope, Norris Turney (as); Paul Gonsalvez, Harold Ashby (ts); Harry Carney(bs), Joe Benjamin (b); Rufus Jones (d).

And His Mother Called Him Bill. RCA 74321851512. Originally released in 1967. Duke Ellington Orchestra tribute to Billy Strayhorn with superb Johnny Hodges solos.

Black, Brown and Beige. Columbia 65566 CD, 1999. Originally recorded in 1958. Ellington (p); William Cat Anderson, Harold "Shorty" Baker, Clark Terry (tp); Ray Nance (tp, vn); Quentin Jackson, John Sanders, Britt Woodman (tb); Jimmy Hamilton (cl); Bill Graham (as); Russell Procope (cl, as); Paul Gonsalvez (ts); Harry Carney (bs); Jimmy Woode (b); Sam Woodyard (d); Mahalia Jackson (v). Quintessential version of Ellington hymn "Come Sunday."

Duke Ellington and John Coltraine. Impulse! 87042. Originally released in 1963. Ellington collaboration with modernist Coltrane producing a gorgeous rendition of "In a Sentimental Mood" with Aaron Bell or Jimmy Woode (b), and Sam Woodyard or Elvin Jones (d).

The Far East Suite. Bluebird 82876-55614-2. Originally released in 1966. Ellington
   (p); William Cat Anderson, Cootie Williams, Mercer Ellington, Herbie Jones
   (t); Lawrence Brown, Buster Cooper, Chuck Connors (tb); Jimmy Hamilton,
   Johnny Hodges, Russell Procope, Paul Gonsalvez, Harry Carney (reeds); John
   Lamb (b); Rufus Jones (d).

Latin American Suite. Original Jazz Classics OJC-469-2. Originally released in
   1968. Ellington (p); Lawrence Brown, Buster Cooper (tb); Johnny Hodges
   (as); Paul Gonsalves (ts); Harry Carney (bs); only instrumentalists identified.

Live at Newport, 1956 (Complete). Columbia S12918-2 CD, 1999. Originally recorded in 1956. Ellington band with famed Paul Gonsalves twenty-seven-chorus tenor solo on "Diminuendo and Crescendo in Blue."

Never No Lament: The Blanton-Webster Band, 1940–1942. Bluebird 82876-50857-2
   CD, 2003. Early versions of ten of the twenty-eight songs performed at the
   White House 1969 tribute.

New Orleans Suite. Atlantic 81227-3670-2. Originally released in 1970. Ellington (p);
   Wild Bill Davis (org); Cootie Williams, Cat Anderson, Money Johnson, Mer-
   cer Ellington, Al Rubin, Fred Stone (tp); Booty Wood, Julian Preister, Dave
   Taylor, Chuck Connors (tb); Russell Procope, Johnny Hodges, Norris Turney
   (as) Paul Gonsalvez, Harold Ashby (ts); Harry Carney (bs); Joe Benjamin (b);
   Rufus Jones (d).

1969 All-Star White House Tribute to Duke Ellington. Blue Note 7243 35249 2 0 CD,
   2002. Originally recorded in 1969. Bill Berry, Clark Terry (tp); Urbie Green,
   J. J. Johnson (tb); Paul Desmond (as), Gerry Mulligan (bs); Jim Hall (g); Milt
   Hinton (b); Louis Bellson (d), Dave Brubeck, Duke Ellington, Earl Hines,
   Hank Jones, Billy Taylor (p); Mary Mayo, Joe Williams (v).

Piano in the Foreground. Columbia 87042 CD, 2004. Originally released in 1960.
   Ellington in a rare standard trio setting with Aaron Bell or Jimmy Woode (b),
   and Sam Woodyard (d).

Permissions

Grateful acknowledgment is made to the following publishers and authors for permission to reprint the material from their books:

From *America's Songs: The Stories Behind the Songs of Broadway, Hollywood, and Tin Pan Alley* by Philip Furia and Michael Lasser. Copyright © 2006 by Routledge, a division of Taylor & Francis Group. Reprinted by permission of Routledge.

Excerpts from *Collected Works: A Journal of Jazz, 1954–2000* by Whitney Balliett. Copyright © 2000 by Whitney Balliett. Published by St. Martin's Press. Reprinted by permission of Nancy Balliett.

Excerpts from *Duke Ellington's America* by Harvey G. Cohen. Copyright © 2010 by the University of Chicago. Reprinted by permission of the University of Chicago Press.

Excerpts from *Duke Ellington in Person: An Intimate Memoir* by Mercer Ellington and Stanley Dance. Copyright © 1978 by Mercer Ellington and Stanley Dance. Reprinted by permission of Houghton Mifflin Harcourt Publishing Company. All rights reserved.

From *Music Is My Mistress* by Duke Ellington. Copyright © 1973 by Duke Ellington Inc. Reprinted by permission of Doubleday, a division of Random House Inc.

Excerpts from *NEA Jazz Masters, 1982–2010* by the National Endowment for the Arts, Office of Public Affairs. Copyright © 2010. Reprinted by permission of the National Endowment for the Arts.

From *Visions of Jazz: The First Century* by Gary Giddins. Copyright © 1998 by Gary Giddins. Reprinted by permission of Oxford University Press.

Photography Credits

Associated Press: 31 (bottom), A-26 (top), A-27, A-28 (center)

Harvey Georges: 84, A-10 (top), A-11 (top and bottom), A-16 (bottom), A-22 (bottom), A-23 (bottom)

Marty Lederhandler: A-28 (top)

Columbia University, Eileen Barroso: A-28 (bottom)

Corbis Stock Photography, Bettmann: 29 (bottom), 30 (top and bottom), A-6 (bottom), A-9

Edward Allan Faine (author): 11 (graph)

LBJ Presidential Library, Austin, TX, Robert Knudsen: 2, 18, 32 (top), 33

John F. Kennedy Presidential Library, Boston, MA: 31 (top), 57

Library of Congress, Washington, DC: 29 (top), 201

National Archives, Still Picture Division, College Park, MD
Ollie Atkins: 34, 58, 70, 85 (top and bottom), 86, 92, 134, A-1, A-2, A-3, A-4, A-5, A-6 (top), A-8 (top and bottom), A-10 (bottom), A-12 (top and bottom), A-13 (top and bottom), A-14 (top and bottom), A-15 (top and bottom), A-17, A-16 (top), A-18 (top), A-19, A-20 (top and bottom), A-21 (top and bottom), A-22 (top), A-23 (top left and right), A-24, A-25 (all)

USIA *Photo Bulletin*: 148, A-7

USIA *World* (newspaper): 12, 32 (bottom), A-18 (bottom), A-26 (bottom)

Navy Historical Foundation, Washington, DC: 28

Richard Nixon Presidential Library, Yorba Lynda, CA: 80

Sidney J. Stiber, producer of *Duke Ellington at the White House* film: 83 (all)

Index

Throughout this index, the following abbreviations are used: DE (Duke Ellington), MOF (Medal of Freedom), and RN (Richard Nixon). Page numbers in italics refer to pages containing photographs. Material in the appendices has not been indexed.

About the Author

EDWARD ALLAN FAINE, a lifelong jazz fan, is the author of eleven children's books, notably *Bebop Babies*, and several articles on jazz (see below). Mr. Faine lives in Takoma Park, Maryland, with squirrels in his attic.

"A Thousand Worthy Angels: A Critique of the Teleseries Jazz." *Potomac Review*, Spring/Summer 2002.

"Al Hirt at the White House 1969." *The Jazz Archivist* XXIII (2010). http://jazz.tulane.edu/archivist/ja_online_index.

"The First Jazz Band at the White House." *VJM's Jazz & Blues Mart*, Winter 2012. http://www.vjm.biz.

Ellington at the White House 1969

Typeset by Sandra Jonas, Your Book Partners, Boulder, Colorado
Index by Teri Jurgens Lefever, Nimble Index, Loveland, Colorado
Photo processing by Photo Response of Gaithersburg, Maryland, and
    U-Photo of Beltsville, Maryland
Printed and bound by Rockville Printing & Graphics, Rockville,
    Maryland

Composed in Adobe Caslon Pro
Printed on Cougar 70# Offset Vellum Natural
Photo insert printed on Chorus Art 80# Dull Text
Cover printed on 10-point C1S